Praise for *Working Well*

I loved this insightful and refreshingly honest book. *Working Well* is a solid guide to nurturing a healthy life. I highly recommend the tools Stephanie provides for increasing productivity and reducing work and life stress. If you manage your internal self well, health and happiness will flow in abundance.

—Dr. John Izzo, bestselling author of *The Purpose Revolution*

Workplace stress is something I see patients, colleagues, and friends struggling with on an almost daily basis. Stephanie Berryman's experiences as an HR professional and coach come through in this excellent resource full of practical advice and tools. This book was a pleasure to read, and I strongly recommend it.

—Dr. Christina Campbell, family physician

Working Well is a great book for any leader in any business or industry. Stephanie does an amazing job outlining the effects of stress on leaders. I felt like she climbed inside my head and knew what I was feeling and dealing with. I have already started to employ the ideas outlined in the book and working through the simple questions and techniques has helped me balance my home and work life.

I will be buying this book for my team and sharing her approach to handling stress and improving productivity. This was a great read!

—Stephen Hillier, president, MPIS-Integrated Solutions, Worley

Working Well provides excellent tools, advice, and suggested actions that can move new or experienced managers towards becoming respected, confident, and empathetic leaders. The twelve cornerstone strategies, vital for success with leading people, have a consistent message throughout: to be better at managing others, you must get better at managing yourself first. *Working Well* is the textbook for improving our performance, reducing our stress, and building quality relationships with our workplace partners. I highly recommend you read this book today.

—John McKearney, MA, ECFO, MIFireE, fire chief / general manager (Ret.), Vancouver Fire Rescue Services

This is not just a leadership book for work, it's a blueprint for a life well lived. The twelve gifts that Stephanie Berryman offers allow you to bring out the best in yourself and others. Berryman embraces stress as real part of our lives and then provides us with the keys to positively transform how we live.

The book is as much a story as it is reference guide and a life hack that you will keep on your desk at work or at home. It does not attempt to change the reader rather it helps us discover and unlock our unique and powerful gifts allowing us to make the most of our lives. The real-life scenarios peppered throughout the book bring the strategies to life and allow you to see yourself in the learning.

Stephanie shares her compelling, challenging journey that underpins the valuable lessons and tools in the book. Most importantly the book encourages and teaches us how to care of ourselves so we can bring out the best in others. You have just made a great investment for yourself and others. . . . Enjoy the journey!

—Colin Moore, director, Food Services

If you are looking for relevant, impactful advice on how to be more successful in your career and how to manage stress and increase productivity, *Working Well* is a wonderful place to start. Stephanie Berryman . . . excels at describing the most relevant and pressing issues that leaders and working individuals are facing today. Her warm, influential, and authentic approach makes you feel as if you are actually sitting in front of a top-notch leadership coach who is facilitating your own transformation while mentoring you through her twelve resounding strategies. Her questions at the end of each chapter are powerful and compel one to take her advice into action immediately. This actionable, strategic book is one that I highly recommend as a great practical guide when seeking to gain your power back and enjoy your career and life.

—Angela Grosvenor, peak performance results coach, Robbins Research Intl.

Ms. Berryman has given us a real gem with this book. Her strategies for stress and productivity are practical and straightforward, well-researched and well-rounded, on top of being effective. She presents the ideas of her twelve strategies so clearly and accessibly that they really do seem as simple as the subtitle suggests. . . . The investment of buying and reading this book will pay itself off in spades—I recommend it wholeheartedly!

—Scott Erickson, MEd, CCC, therapist, performance consultant, and speaker

WORKING WELL

WORKING WELL

TWELVE SIMPLE STRATEGIES TO MANAGE STRESS AND INCREASE PRODUCTIVITY

STEPHANIE BERRYMAN

Published by Manage to Engage, Vancouver, BC, Canada
http://www.managetoengage.com

Edited and designed by Girl Friday Productions
www.girlfridayproductions.com
Cover design: Paul Barrett

ISBN (paperback): 978-1-9991708-0-6
ISBN (ebook): 978-1-9991708-1-3

*5% of all profits from the sale of this book will be donated
to the Canadian Mental Health Association.*

This book is dedicated to the close friends I have made at work.

*Lauri Thompson and Gerhard Maynard, you are
friends who have become family, godparents to my
children, and a godsend to Andrew and me.*

Your friendship has made both my work and my life richer.

Contents

Invitation

Welcome to *Working Well*. I'm really excited to share all of my tips, tools, and practical strategies to help you reduce your work-related stress and get more work done. If you're interested in hearing more from me, please join me at: https://www.managetoengage.com/join-us/. You'll receive my *Working Well* companion video for free. You'll also get monthly articles about workplace challenges and solutions, stress management, life-work balance, and leadership. You can find out more about the *Working Well* online course, free resources and community here at https://www.managetoengage.com/working-well/.

Introduction

Stress, My Story, and How to Use This Book

I'm so glad you've picked up this book. Congratulations for taking action to manage your stress. This book will help you to:

- Identify how your stress impacts you and the people around you.
- Change your response to the stressors you experience.
- Learn tools that will reduce your feelings of anxiety and overwhelm when faced with all the challenges of living in today's world.
- Learn specific strategies and exercises that you can adopt right away to increase your productivity and reduce your stress.

But I want to be clear. All these amazing strategies you're about to learn will not make your stress go away. To manage your stress does not mean you will eliminate it. When we reduce our stress, it's because we've changed our relationship with stress. We respond to challenges from a place of ease and we're no longer as impacted by our stressors as we once were.

Too often we think we shouldn't be stressed out, and this belief causes us even more stress. It's normal to have stress in our lives. Life is not meant to be perfect; it's meant to be real, and that includes stress and challenges. Stress is a natural part of living in a world with traffic, deadlines, work, money, bills, relationships, and family. And if we have all those things in our lives, we're lucky (except for the traffic part—it would be awesome to get rid of that!).

Stress is part of life and when we can accept that, we can relax and use tools and strategies to help us manage and reduce our stress. I've shared these twelve simple strategies with thousands of people to help them successfully reduce the inevitable stress associated with work. Every strategy I share is based on research coupled with lived experience. The stories that you'll read about my clients have been modified to protect their confidentiality and are shared with their permission. I'm grateful for their willingness to trust me with their challenges as well as allowing me to share their stories.

If you're feeling stressed out at work, you're not alone. Stress is incredibly prevalent in the workplace today, and it's increasing all the time. A recent report found that "80% of workers feel stress on the job, nearly half say they need help in learning how to manage stress and 42% say their coworkers need such help,"[1] and another source states that "stress is estimated to cost American businesses up to $300 billion a year."[2]

Stress is a serious problem—for us and our employers. And you and I are the only ones who are going to solve this problem. As much as we would like our workplaces to hire more staff, fire all the difficult people, and give us more time off and better pay, that's not likely to happen.

When we stop expecting life to be stress-free and find healthy ways to respond to our stressors, that in itself can reduce our anxiety. Many of the strategies I share are related to our response to stress because changing our response reduces the impact of stress on us. And we have to adapt our response to our stressors because getting highly stressed out is literally killing us.

In a 2014 study cited in the *Washington Post,* "researchers found that [people] who perceived their everyday hassles as very stressful had a similar mortality risk as people who consistently reported more highly stressful events. . . . How a person perceived their stress and then reacted to it emotionally was associated with increased risk for heart disease and death."[3]

If we want to live long, healthy, fulfilling lives, we need to change our stress response. And we can conquer that hardwired response with awareness and practice. When you learn and use the twelve strategies, you'll have all the tools you need to respond to stressors and challenges calmly.

We all know that stress has impacts on our physical and mental health, but we often spend a little too much time floating along on the river of denial. Here's a wake-up call from a national study on the reasons for many doctor's visits:

> Emotional stress is a major contributing factor to the six leading causes of death in the United States: cancer, coronary heart disease, accidental injuries, respiratory disorders, cirrhosis of the liver and suicide. . . . The Centre for Disease Control and Prevention of the United States estimates that stress account[s for] about 75% of all doctor's visits. This involves an extremely wide span of physical complaints including, but not limited to headache, back pain, heart problems, upset stomach, stomach ulcer, sleep problems, tiredness and accidents.[4]

Stress takes a serious toll on our mind as well. There's a clear correlation between stress and mental health problems. A 2018 survey, conducted by Morneau Shepell in partnership with *The Globe and Mail,* found that "workplace stress was a top cause of mental health problems or illnesses." According to the same survey, "Mental health issues were also a main reason for missing work with 78 percent of respondents missing work due to mental health concerns—with 34 percent of those missing work for two months or more. . . . On the productivity side, 68 percent of employees reported that they could only maintain their optimal performance for less than 70 percent of their workday."[5]

Too much stress is really bad for us. It can destroy our lives or even end them. Stress has been called the "Health Epidemic of the 21st Century"[6] by the World Health Organization for good reason.

Stress isn't a result of what happens to us, but a result of *how we respond to it.* This is great news—because our response is one of the only things in this world that we can control. While we have no power over what other people do or events that happen, we have complete control over how we respond to difficult experiences.

Stressful things happen. All the time. Every day. I experience many stressors on a daily basis, and I know you do too. Sometimes I choose to be stressed out by the littlest things, and other times I choose to face my stress like a Buddhist monk. I let it float by me; I know that it's a temporary situation that will pass. How we respond to our stressors is one of the most powerful choices we have. If we can choose a different response, we'll reduce our stress.

We also need to find ways to decrease our overall stress levels. When we are already highly stressed out, the smallest thing can send us over the edge. Even something good can make you feel more stressed if it requires more of you. It's great that your son got into the elite hockey league, but how on earth are you going to fit that in with everything else? It's fantastic that you just got a promotion, but it's daunting to figure out how you're going to manage that with all of the other demands in your life.

The more our standard operating mode can be calm and relaxed, the more able we are to handle the inevitable stressors that arise in our lives. What's your natural operating mode? Are you overwhelmed most of the time, or are you relatively calm day-to-day and you only get stressed out by particular events?

When we are stressed out all the time, we can actually get addicted to feeling stressed. As Dr. Gabor Maté says in his book *When the Body Says No: The Cost of Hidden Stress*:

> For those habituated to high levels of internal stress since early childhood, it is the absence of stress that creates unease, evoking boredom and a sense of

meaninglessness. People may become addicted to their
own stress hormones, adrenaline and cortisol.[7]

We get used to all that adrenaline and cortisol coursing through our systems, and when it's not there, we crave it. This is bad news for us because it means when things do calm down, we'll create more stress in our lives.

Dr. Maté describes me to a T. I grew up with lots of stress (you can read more about that in my book *Nine Strategies for Dealing with the Difficult Stuff*), so in the past, if there wasn't enough stress in my life, I'd create some. I might take on more work than was reasonable, worry about things beyond my control, or spend too much time focusing on my stressors rather than on what was working well in my life. Or I'd turn something really good (I ate chocolate every day last week and still lost weight) into something really bad (I must have cancer). I'm breaking my addiction to stress, and, these days, I need a lot less adrenaline and cortisol in my life, but sometimes I still do create stress for myself. Being aware that I have a tendency to create stress for myself has helped me make the necessary changes to start living a calmer, happier life.

I'll give you all the tools you need to create a mindset that will leave you feeling calmer and steadier on a day-to-day basis as well as ways to take a more relaxed approach to your stressors. Challenges will arise, stressors will knock on our door and invite themselves into our lives for long or short periods; that's life. But when we can still live an enjoyable and fulfilling life in spite of those challenges and stressors, then we've managed our stress and we're *Working Well*.

MY STORY

In 2003, as I was fast approaching thirty, I concluded one of the most stressful experiences of my life: teacher's college. I had gone confidently into my program; I'd been working with youth for almost ten years leading youth programs and guiding wilderness trips—and I loved teenagers. By the time I finished my program I had a tic in my left eye, I'd gained ten pounds, I had bronchitis and I hadn't slept properly in months. I knew for sure that I never wanted to be a high school teacher.

I graduated with a degree in English, a degree in Education, $35,000 in student loans, and zero chance of becoming a teacher—thanks to the combination of my dread and a terrible job market.

Luckily, I found a job at a wonderful not-for-profit organization, the Canadian Mental Health Association, managing their education department. If you've ever worked at a not-for-profit, you know that it's high-paced, low-resourced, meaningful work that consumes every part of you. It was my first job managing staff—twelve staff (because that's an easy start).

Due to the mandate of the program, half of my staff lived with mental illness. Two of them were in their thirties and had never been able to work before. I learned an immense amount, not just from managing staff who lived with severe and persistent mental illness, but from my staff themselves. The ability to work, which I had always taken for granted, was an incredible privilege for them. Going to work was something that my staff fought hard to be able to do. I learned so much from them about resilience, the strength of the human spirit, and the importance of taking care of ourselves, especially in times of stress. It was an inspiring job among inspiring people. It was also a draining job with endless demands.

I worked until eight or nine almost every night, frequently putting in ten- to twelve-hour days, working through my lunch break, and often going into work on weekends. I felt passionate about my work and all that I was accomplishing. I designed a powerful two-day course called Mental Illness First Aid that was co-taught by a mental health professional and a person who lived with mental illness. The course was designed to reduce stigma, explain the symptoms and realities of living with mental illness, and provide participants with strategies to respond to coworkers, clients, friends, or family who might be experiencing mental health challenges. I spent three high-pressure months designing the course; I trained staff in how to deliver it, then promoted and sold the course; I did interviews on the radio, on TV, and with newspapers; I spoke at conferences; I met with managers and directors, ministry officials, and CEOs.

Soon the course I'd created was reducing stigma and effecting real changes in how people with mental illness were viewed in the workplace and beyond, a result that felt even more meaningful to me because I have a brother who lives with bipolar disorder. I was engaged and committed and inspired by my work. I was also very stressed out and overwhelmed.

Three months into my all-consuming new job and two months after my thirtieth birthday, my uncle called me from the retirement town where my mother lived in Mexico. The call came at just past six on a February evening, when the sky was turning from dusk to dark. I was in my tiny office, looking out the window to the view of another office building where I could see other people just like me, working late. My neck and shoulders were tight, and my eyes were sore when the ringing of my cell phone pulled me from my trance.

I opened up my little flip phone, and my whole life changed. My uncle told me that something was very wrong with my mother. He was packing up her life and sending her to live in Vancouver so I could look after her.

"She's your problem now," he said gruffly and hung up the phone. Three days later, when my mother arrived from Mexico, it was apparent that something was indeed very wrong. A lifelong world traveler, she had forgotten to collect her luggage before coming through customs. My normally impeccably groomed mother was wearing a stained blouse, and her hair was unkempt.

After two agonizing and heartbreaking months of tests, we got the diagnosis: Alzheimer's. I became my mother's sole caregiver. I was the only person she knew in Vancouver.

I was working a high-stress job with a high-stress personal life. Many of you have been or may be in this situation. It's incredibly challenging and heartbreaking. I have so much empathy for you if that's your current reality. My experience taught me that we can learn and grow from these incredibly stressful experiences if we can open ourselves up to the heartbreak, the growth and the wisdom that comes from living through these challenges.

Learning to manage stress, both at work and at home, became central to my survival. Stress bleeds back and forth from our personal life to our work life; how could it not? We are the same person at work as we are at home. If we have a dying mother at home, that situation impacts us at work. If we've spent our workday dealing with difficult people, anxious about work and falling behind on our deadlines, we usually come home stressed. During those high-stress years, I had huge demands in every aspect of my life. I was single, deeply in debt, caring for my mother, and dealing with multiple workplace pressures.

As part of my job, I delivered presentations on how to manage workplace stress. As I walked out of those presentations, I felt frustrated with myself because I wasn't using any of the strategies that I taught. I knew what the research said, I just wasn't living it.

Exercise? I had no time to exercise. Meditate? Nice in theory but it just wasn't my kind of thing. Get more sleep? Impossible when I spent each night tossing and turning for hours, my anxious mind unable to find calm.

Then I had a lightning bolt of insight. If I went down, the program that I'd worked so hard to build would go down. If I went down, my mother would go down. If I went down, my staff, whose jobs meant so much to them, went down.

I knew what going down looked like. I'd heard story after story from my workshop participants about the cause and effect of unmanaged stress. Some of my staff and volunteers had been full-time professionals who had experienced extreme stress that led to a mental health breakdown.

So I started living what I was teaching. I had to. My mental and physical health, as well as the people I loved and cared for, were counting on it. I began biking to work because that was an easy way to implement exercise into my day. I scheduled one night a week when a friend looked after my mother and I turned off the phone, had a bath, wrote in my journal, and ate take-out sushi. I started going to bed earlier. I woke up fifteen minutes early to stretch and attempted to meditate (and failed miserably).

These lifestyle strategies helped immensely, but what had the biggest impact on my ability to manage and reduce my stress was changing my mindset and my response to the stressors in my life.

I gained perspective during those years. I didn't work nights and weekends anymore. Even though I was struggling to pay off my student loans, I asked my manager to reduce my hours to four days a week so I could spend more time with my mother.

I knew what mattered most, and it wasn't the work I was so passionate about. It was the mother I was losing.

During the devastating time of losing my mother piece by piece, one of my younger brothers passed away. Less than three years later, my mother died. It was an incredibly heartbreaking and difficult time, and, through all of it, I had workplace stress to manage as well.

The strategies that I'll be sharing with you helped me come through those challenging times and become both stronger and more compassionate. In losing my mother and brother, my heart was broken, but I'm proud to say that it was broken open. If you're interested in that story, you can read more about it in my book *Nine Strategies for Dealing with the Difficult Stuff*.

MY WORK

When I was in my midthirties, I decided to pursue a master's degree in leadership while working full-time as an internal leadership development consultant at a large organization. I've spent a lot of time studying what makes us good leaders and how we can be most productive and engaged at work.

For the past eight years, I've run my own business as a leadership development consultant and coach juggling multiple clients, projects, and deadlines. I've worked with countless leaders to help them deal with their unique workplace stressors and enjoy more meaningful and productive work lives.

What makes this book different than other workplace stress management books is that my focus is not just on workplace stress but on how our work and personal lives fit together. Stress in any part of our lives impacts every aspect of our lives, and when we look at the big picture of our lives, it often helps us put our work stress in perspective.

I want to help you find the life-work balance that is optimal for you. That's not a typo . . . I write it that way deliberately, to remind us that life should come first. Obviously, I've had some experiences that have led me to have very strong feelings about living a life that we enjoy and spending time with the people we love most.

Over the course of the next few hundred pages, I'll share a lot of ideas about how to manage workplace stress while looking through the lens of your entire life. I promise to give you some very straightforward and practical strategies to reduce your stress both at home and at work.

I've been fortunate enough to be a consultant and coach to CEOs, fire chiefs, middle managers, and frontline and emerging leaders who work in municipalities, universities, not-for-profit organizations, and corporations. I've also taught leadership courses in the private and public sectors, including large government and post-secondary institutions, municipalities, property development firms, engineering and trucking firms, and smaller organizations. I've worked with a lot of stressed out people. No matter what job people have, they have stress. *I* still have stress. Stress doesn't go away. That's why it's so important that we learn to manage it effectively, so we can live good, fulfilling lives no matter what external stressors we might be experiencing.

A few of the common stressors I come across, whether I'm working with a high-level CEO or a frontline supervisor, include:

- Interpersonal challenges
- Heavy workload
- Discomfort with conflict
- Lack of role clarity
- Managing up and across
- Managing staff
- Dealing with difficult people and situations
- Dealing with a highly stressful personal situation (personal or family illness, divorce, financial struggles, etc.)
- Inability to set boundaries between work and life

Do any of those sound familiar? Most of us are dealing with a number of those stressors at any given time, and that doesn't even include the many opportunities for stress management that our personal lives present us with.

Even with all of these stressors, we are incredibly privileged to be able to work, grow, learn, and contribute our unique gifts to the world.

I feel so grateful for my work. I love what I do. But loving my work doesn't eradicate all the associated stress.

I'm in the trenches right along with you, getting sucked into feeling stressed and using the strategies I teach to pull me back to center. I wrote this book for both of us. Learning to manage our stress is a life-long lesson, at least in my case.

My goal isn't to help you eliminate all your stress because the right level of stress can be really healthy and motivating. Instead, my aim is to give you all the tools and strategies you need to be *Working Well.* We all have ways of coping with our stress; the problem is that many of our strategies are inherently unhealthy, so they will ultimately just cause us more stress.

When I am feeling particularly stressed out, I eat a lot of chocolate (and not much else). I stay up too late worrying about work and wake up way too early (hello, 4:00 a.m.). And I try to work even though I'm exhausted. Many of my clients and students have shared some of their "super fun" coping strategies with me. Here are a few of the more common ones:

- Drinking too much (in varying degrees from a few too many drinks at dinner to outright passing out)
- Sleeping only three to four hours a night
- Working fifteen-hour days
- Closing their office door and not talking to anyone at work for days
- Ceasing to exercise or eat well and starting to eat only junk food
- Calling in sick and binge-watching Netflix

How about you? What are your fabulous, unhealthy coping strategies? I know they're easy go-to quick fixes, but, ultimately, they land us in far more stress than using healthy stress-reduction tools.

There are many excellent strategies in this book, and I don't use them all of the time. I don't expect you to either. Sometimes when I'm stressed, I sit down and meditate, or I call a friend and we go for a walk. Other times, I eat a lot of chocolate and stay up too late, trying to get work done.

We are all doing our best. We are imperfect and flawed, and each one of us is trying to figure out how to manage our stress the best way we can. That's all we can hope for ourselves: to do the best we can.

HOW TO USE THIS BOOK

This book has two goals: to help you reduce your stress and to help you enhance your productivity.

When we are truly productive, we make the best use of our time and energy, getting our most important work done, feeling satisfied and accomplished, and our energy isn't depleted. True productivity means that at the end of the workday, we still have plenty of energy and attention left to enjoy our personal lives.

I've structured this book to help you focus first on reducing your stress and then on increasing your productivity. That's because our first priority should be to reduce our stress. When we reduce our stress, we naturally increase our productivity. And when we increase our productivity, we reduce our stress. My initial focus is on ways to reduce and manage your stress because if we're highly productive but still really stressed out, we're not *Working Well*. I truly believe that if you're *Working Well*, you're working from a place of ease and flow rather than from pressure and stress.

This book is full of ideas, questions, exercises, and strategies. If you're like me, you're going to want to read the whole book all at once without stopping to do one exercise or answer one question; that's just how some of us work. We want to get all the information and get the big picture before we move towards action. But if you're like me, after you've read the book, you'll get too busy to go back and actually answer the questions or implement the strategies. I feel your pain. It's why I've got a stack of books on my bedside table—sometimes it's easier to read one book after another without actually taking action.

To help you take action, I've scattered questions throughout each chapter and placed questions and action items at the end of each chapter. I did this because I learned in teacher's college that if you just sit passively and read the strategies, you're less likely to act on them. If I ask you questions and get you thinking about actions you can take, you're more likely to actually do something. That said, you don't have to do anything that I suggest. Focus on what resonates with you—don't bother doing the activities that feel like they'd be too much work. Skip over the questions you don't feel are relevant. Give yourself permission to take from the book only what will work for you. If possible, force yourself to slow down, answer a few questions, try a few of the suggestions and strategies, and see how they work.

Please check out the companion video I created for the book. It will guide you through experiences of some of the strategies I share in the book. You can get it for free when you join the *Working Well* community here: https://www.managetoengage.com/join-us/.

I've also got some free videos on my website that further explain the key elements of the twelve strategies. You can find them here: https://www.managetoengage.com/online-courses/.

Even if you take just one or two concepts and give them a try, that's probably more helpful than buying another stress management book.

After you've implemented some strategies that work and you're feeling less stressed, maybe you'll want to come back and try a few more.

For those of you who are far more diligent and detail oriented than I am, I've done my best to provide options and exercises for you to make lists, collect data, and take the steps that will help you systematically manage your stress. You may want to designate a notebook (or a digital document) for answering the questions and keeping track of the data you collect.

There's a resource list at the end of the book with many of the articles, books and TED Talks that I reference throughout the book. You can also download the resource page on my website as I update it regularly: https://www.managetoengage.com/working-well/. Feel free to send me some of your favorite resources to add to the list.

WORKING WELL

Working Well means we stay physically and mentally healthy while we work. We take care of ourselves because we recognize that everything—the quality of our relationships, our work, our ideas, our focus, our very lives—rests on our health. When we are *Working Well*, we are nourished by our work. We come home at the end of the day filled with a sense of accomplishment and plenty of energy and attention for the people we love and the activities we enjoy.

I'm grateful for all of the life experiences I've had, not only because losing my mother and brother has taught me the importance of the people we love, but because I've learned a lot about how to manage stress. I've experienced grief that I thought would break me, and I've found strength I didn't know I had. I've gained a healthy perspective on my priorities and on my stressors.

I'm confident that if you use any of these strategies for your work and personal life, you'll reduce your stress and increase your productivity. But that's the key. You have to *use* the strategies.

I wrote this book because I really want to see people reduce their stress and live happier and more fulfilling lives. I'm giving you all the tools I know to build a life of *Working Well*: a life where you can manage the multiple stressors you deal with every day and feel highly productive, fulfilled, and engaged. I'm not promising you a perfect, stress-free life, but if you use these strategies, you'll have a different perspective on your stress and plenty of tools to manage whatever challenges come your way. I'm excited to share what I've learned with you and to give you all the tools you need to live a highly productive life of *Working Well*. I hope you enjoy the book and find it valuable. Feel free to send me your comments and questions at: stephanie@managetoengage.com.

Chapter One

Take Personal Responsibility

"In the long run, we shape our lives, and we shape ourselves. The process never ends until we die. And the choices we make are ultimately our own responsibility."

—Eleanor Roosevelt

Taking personal responsibility is the foundation of reducing our stress. When we practice true personal responsibility, our entire outlook on life changes. And our results change too: when we focus on taking personal responsibility, we achieve far more. We no longer put energy into complaining and feeling stressed out about what we can't control; instead, we focus on what we can control: ourselves. Our focus shifts from what is external to what is internal: our thoughts, actions, and behaviors.

When we take responsibility for ourselves, we become accountable not just for the work that we do, but for the decisions we make, the way we treat others, the way we spend our time, and the way we prioritize our lives. Every aspect of our lives reflects the choices we've made and how we've responded to our life experiences.

We aren't responsible for everything that happens in our lives, but we are responsible for how we respond to it.

When we stop blaming external circumstances and recognize our power to make different choices, we have achieved true personal responsibility. It's a simple concept but very challenging to live.

TAKING OUR POWER BACK

One of our biggest sources of stress is that we give our power away to people and situations that are beyond our control. We think that external events and individuals make us feel a certain way rather than recognizing that we choose to feel that way. When my mom first got sick, all I could focus on was how upset I was. But choosing to be upset and distraught didn't help me. It just increased my stress. So, I made different choices. I moved to action: I looked at what I could control, and I focused on that. I asked friends for help, and I reached out to the Alzheimer's society. I started to take better care of myself so I was more capable of managing my stress. I focused on what I was grateful for. Yes, I was still heartbroken, but I made different choices about how to respond to that heartbreak. I shifted my internal world to be better able to respond to my external stressors.

When we blame external circumstances or other people for our stress, we give our power away.

We point to something outside of us and say, *That's the cause of my stress and I can do nothing about it.* Almost all of us do this as a natural first reaction to a stressor. How many times have you pointed at your coworkers or your boss or your kids or your workload and thought, *You're making me so stressed out*? When I catch myself thinking those totally natural, but utterly useless thoughts, I switch my focus back to myself and think about healthy ways I can respond to my stressors. Then I'm taking personal responsibility.

Many of us can also blame ourselves for the situation we are in or the stressors we have. When I get super stressed out, the first thing I do is get mad at myself—why did I take on so much work, why am I not managing my time better? The next thing I do is blame my husband or my kids (but only in my mind because some wise part of me knows it's not really their fault). My train of thought flies along like this: *How could he be on this business trip when I have two sick kids and a huge deadline looming? Why are the kids having meltdowns every seven minutes; it's their fault I don't get any writing done!*

How about you, who is your first blame victim?

How does blaming others help you deal with the situation?

It feels good to be righteous and infuriated for about five seconds; then it just feels pointless because it doesn't resolve the situation. When we're blaming something outside of ourselves, we aren't taking personal responsibility.

If we can slow down enough to notice that we're playing the blame game and it's getting us nowhere, then we can make a different choice. When I'm in my wise place, I take a deep breath and realize that all I have to do is feel what I'm feeling. Usually talking to a friend about how anxious or overwhelmed I'm feeling is enough to calm me down. After I've done that, I can look at what I've done to create the situation, seek solutions to resolve the situation, and then take action.

When we concentrate on taking personal responsibility, we're able to create true change in our lives. Instead of blaming others, we focus on ourselves and how we can respond differently to our challenges and stressors.

And we have to focus on ourselves because we are the only ones we can change. Trying to change someone else only causes us more stress.

I'm sure we've all lived this; I've certainly tried and failed to change many people in my life. If my boss would just give me more feedback, if my husband would just bring home more chocolate, if my kids would just magically clean up after themselves, then I would be happier. Do you know how much stress I've caused myself (and others) trying to change other people? Way too much. How about you? How much stress have you created by attempting the impossible?

I've finally got the message loud and clear: the only person I can change is myself and when I focus on that, I'm way more calm. When I focus on myself, I've got power in the situation because I can take action rather than trying to change something outside of myself.

If you are like many of my clients, you have numerous sources of stress that are completely beyond your control. You might have difficult coworkers, impossible clients, an evil boss, or completely unrealistic workloads. In addition to those, you might have financial pressures or aging parents or challenging children. If you're really unlucky, you'll have all of those stressors happening at once. If I could give you a magic wand to make them all go away, I would. Since that's not possible, I suggest you focus on the only magic you have: transforming how you respond to your stressors. That's how you'll reduce your stress.

Let's look at how a client of mine transitioned to taking personal responsibility by shifting his focus from his stressors to his response.

GEORGE'S JOURNEY FROM PANIC TO PEACE

George Haynes was unusually flustered when he called me: "I need a coaching session in the next two days if at all possible. Please tell me you can fit me in."

George was a student from one of my leadership programs—I'd spent two years working with his company, so I knew him well. He was a high-level executive in his late forties who was both confident and competent.

When we spoke, everything became clear. A new CEO had taken over the company two months earlier, and, based on his behavior, George was quite sure that this new guy was out to fire him. George had a hunch to his posture I'd never seen before and dark circles beneath his brown eyes.

The CEO was micromanaging George, taking work away from him, dealing directly with his staff, and cutting him out of the loop. George was angry about this behavior, but he was also beginning to doubt himself. He'd always felt competent in his role, and he was good at making decisions and building rapport with his staff. Now that he was being micromanaged and losing connection with his staff, he was losing confidence.

When we first spoke, George was really worked up. He was having trouble sleeping, working late every night, and very tense. He knew his stress was damaging his relationship with his wife and kids as he was distracted, less patient, and snapped easily, but he couldn't get it under control.

He spent the first fifteen minutes of our conversation citing specific and deeply upsetting examples of how his new CEO was treating him. Every time I tried to steer the conversation back to George, he turned it back to his CEO.

His response to the situation was completely natural.

The problem is that when we give too much of our energy to what's stressing us out, we are focused on the problem, not the solution.

Finally, I said to George, "I know you're really upset about the CEO, but there's nothing you can do to change his behavior. Can we please focus on what you can do to manage the situation?"

"What I can do? I can't do a damn thing. I've thought about talking to him, but I'm so frustrated I'm sure I'd blow a gasket. I can't stand this guy."

We've all felt this way, but it's a dangerous trap to get into because we're giving all our power away. We're allowing a person or a situation to make us feel upset or when we can choose a different response.

George and I talked more, and he realized that there were actions that he could take. He had power in the situation, he just wasn't using it.

"I know I should ask him why he's micromanaging me, and I should call him out when he talks to my staff directly without including me."

"Okay, so why haven't you done that so far?"

"Because I might get really angry. And I'm afraid if I push him at all, he'll fire me."

Now we had something to work with! We talked through George's anger and his fear; then I asked a question: "What will happen if you don't talk to your boss and give him this feedback?"

"Oh man, it'll just get worse. He'll keep walking all over me. I'll spend every minute of the day in a rage. Plus, I'll get even more stressed and keep losing sleep, and things will get even worse at home."

Well, that was pretty good incentive to take action. We identified some specific small steps that George could take. One of the first places we focused was on George getting a better handle on his stress so that when he did engage with his manager, he would be calm and collected. He committed to leaving work on time and meditating before bed because working late and not sleeping were killing his ability to manage any kind of stress.

Next, I asked George, "What are you doing that is contributing to the situation?"

"Nothing. I'm not getting angry; I'm just taking it all. I'm putting up with all this guy's crap."

"So that's how you're contributing to the situation then," I said.

"What?" His eyes widened. "I just told you I'm not doing anything. He's the one with the problem."

"You have a problem too. You're 'putting up with all his crap.' You're not giving your new manager feedback or helping him to understand his impact on you."

"Oh, I see what you mean." He nodded.

"You've also made up a story that he wants to fire you. That may be true, but another possibility is that he's in over his head, desperate to prove himself in his new role, totally overwhelmed, and defaulting to micromanaging."

George shook his head. "Seems unlikely."

"I'd just like you to be open to the possibility that the story you've made up isn't the truth, that there might be something else altogether going on."

"Sure, if you say so," he said in a tone that said he'd never believe that. He stared at his notebook, but he'd stopped taking notes.

"George, this is important. If you keep treating this guy like he's your enemy and he's out to get you, he's going to pick up on that hostility, and it'll be hard to make your relationship work."

George's head snapped up and his brown eyes were bright. "You're right. That's another thing I'm responsible for, how I'm treating him, if only in my mind. I can't even say out loud all the terrible thoughts I've had about this guy."

"So, what can you do the next time you start ranting about him, even if it's just in your mind?" I asked.

"I can remind myself that I don't know his story. He might not be trying to piss me off. He might just not know how we work here."

"Great. I just think if you can relax about him, your relationship dynamics might start to shift. Now, what can you do to deal with some of his more frustrating behavior?"

"The next time he micromanages me or talks to my staff without me in the loop, I'm going to give him some feedback."

George knew a feedback model from my leadership courses—you'll learn it in Chapter Three: "Have Difficult Conversations." We role-played the conversation, and George found the words that felt authentic to him and felt confident that he could deliver them in a calm and curious tone. This is what he came up with after a few attempts:

> Bill, I've noticed that you're giving me lots of specific directions on handling this project. I'm not sure if you realize that I've been the project lead for over a year. Is there a specific way you'd like me to handle it, or are you just making sure I know what I'm doing?

We talked about the importance of tone and delivery, and George acknowledged how important it was for him to let go of his hostility and approach the conversation with openness and curiosity.

George left our meeting feeling like he'd taken his power back by identifying what he'd been doing to contribute to the situation and how he could respond to his boss differently.

GEORGE'S RESULTS

When I met with George two weeks later, I was curious to hear how it had gone. Had he managed to focus on what he could control and reduce his stress by putting less energy into his manager, getting more sleep, and leaving work at a reasonable hour? Did he have the courage to have the conversation and give his manager feedback? Was he able to maintain a curious tone, or had the frustration and hostility built up too much?

When he walked into the room, George looked like the man I'd known for the past few years. His shoulders were no longer hunched, but relaxed, his eyes were clear and bright and the dark circles beneath them had faded.

"I've been sleeping! I feel like a different person."

I refrained from telling him he looked like one too. "And how's it going with the CEO?"

"I admit that the first time he micromanaged me after we met, I didn't say anything. I was just too nervous about how he'd react. That night I couldn't sleep, and I was all caught up in frustration and fear again. I felt like I was working myself back into the knot we'd just untangled."

I nodded. "It's pretty normal to have to psych ourselves up for a tough conversation."

"You got that right." He nodded. "But I knew that the only thing I could do in this situation was to tell him how he was impacting me and that the sooner I did it, the better. I'd be less frustrated and hostile, and, hopefully, it would change things. So, a few days later he was giving me instructions on how to do something I'd done a thousand times before, and I said almost verbatim what we'd practiced. I was really calm, and I was genuinely curious. I said, 'I'm not sure if you realize it, but I've been doing this task for nearly five years. I'm happy to adjust my approach if you want it done the way you've just described, but this is why I do it this way.' Then I explained why I handled it the way I do."

"And . . . how did he respond?"

"I think he was a bit surprised as I'd never reacted to his micro-managing before, but he listened, and then he said, 'I understand why you'd do it that way—it makes sense to me, but I still think you should add in this step. How does that sound?' To be honest, I was a bit annoyed about the step he wanted added in because I don't think it's necessary, but I was thrilled that he was asking me, not telling me. More than that, it was liberating to finally speak up. I wanted to dance out of his office, I felt so good."

Over the next few months, George still had challenges to work out with his manager, they had more conversations and disagreements, and occasionally George fell into the trap of focusing on his frustration with his manager rather than focusing on himself and his response to his manager. But overall, things improved dramatically after he took his power back by taking personal responsibility.

George took control of what he could influence, and that made the difference. Even though their relationship was still challenging, George felt his manager had new respect for him because he'd started to speak up for himself.

YOUR POWER

Is there someone at work that you give your power away to?

How could you change the way that you respond to that person?

How can you focus on yourself so that you have power to change the situation?

As we've established, you can't change another person.

When you find yourself putting a lot of thought and energy into thinking about someone else and their actions and behavior, catch yourself and stop. It's wasted energy. Start thinking about yourself and what you can do to take care of yourself while dealing with this difficult person.

That's where your power lies. Consider different ways that you can respond to the challenges you're having. That's useful energy. That'll get you somewhere.

I've developed the following questions to use with my clients. I encourage you to start using them for yourself when you are in a stressful situation. They will help you take personal responsibility and focus on how you can resolve the situation rather than staying stuck and stressed out.

PERSONAL RESPONSIBILITY QUESTIONS

1. **Why is this so upsetting for me?** This question helps you identify what you're feeling and why.
2. **How did I contribute to this?** This question helps you identify how your behaviors might have contributed to the stressful situation and begin to change them.
3. **What can I learn from this situation?** When you focus on learning from the situation, you can concentrate on growth rather than stressing out.
4. **What can I do about this situation?** This question helps you focus on specific solutions and strategies.
5. **What can I do differently next time?** This step helps you identify the specific behavior that you need to alter to get different results in the future.

The next time you feel really frustrated by a person or situation, take a few minutes to ask yourself these questions. By exploring the answers, you start to shift your mindset. Answering these questions will help you stop giving your power away and take true personal responsibility.

COMMIT TO YOURSELF

Taking personal responsibility means that we become accountable to ourselves. We recognize that taking care of ourselves and meeting our own personal commitments is crucial to our well-being (yes, I am going to exercise three times a week, really, I am!). When we look at our lives, we can see that our reality reflects the choices we have made and how we have or have not committed to ourselves.

I've wanted to write books since I was in my teens, but, for a long time, I chose to watch television, go out dancing, hang out with friends, and do pretty much everything but write. When I turned forty, I felt incredibly happy with my life—I had a wonderful relationship with my husband, two happy, healthy kids, and a flourishing and fulfilling business. I had great friends and I'd traveled a lot. I'd committed to myself and taken action to build a life that I loved. My only disappointment was that I hadn't published a book. On my fortieth birthday, I committed to myself and my writing in a way that I wasn't able to before. If you're reading this book, it means I followed through.

What are the ways you want to commit to yourself more?

How can you take small steps to build your commitment to yourself into your life?

Over the last few years, I've taken both large and small steps to build more writing into my life. I've scheduled writing time in my calendar and stuck to it. I've hired writing coaches and joined writing programs. Those actions have made a world of difference because I've invested in my goals financially and emotionally. I've gotten tools and feedback that have helped me grow as a writer, and I've had deadlines.

But before I could do all those things and truly commit to my writing, I had to give myself permission. Permission to pursue my passions, to risk being seen as self-indulgent, to work on something that wasn't about earning money or looking after our family but was just about me wanting to share what I know and to grow as a writer. It's been challenging, and I still have moments of guilt, but I'm pushing through those feelings to do what I've given myself permission to do: to write.

What do you need to give yourself permission to do?

It might sound ridiculous for me to say, "give yourself permission," but give it a try. For me, it was a game changer. I don't know about you, but often I don't make time to take care of myself or focus on my goals because I prioritize other people's needs before my own.

- Is it a challenge for you to put your own needs first?
- How often do you give up what's important to you in order to take care of other people?
- How much would you reduce your stress if you committed to meeting your own needs?

We have to start prioritizing our own needs if we want to have fulfilling careers and personal lives.

Just think of one small action you can take to commit to yourself and start doing it. It can be as simple as going to bed without cleaning up the kitchen because using that time to have a bath or read a book will help you reduce your stress more. Maybe you need to push back on other people's priorities at work to ensure that you're meeting your own. You know what you need to do. The key is to take action.

Last year, I told my husband that I wanted to spend a bit more time writing and a bit less time consulting and asked him how he felt about the financial impact of that. His answer shocked me to no end.

He said, "I'm totally fine with it, but you realize this is the third time in the last two years that we have had this conversation?"

What a wake-up call that was for me.

I've clearly tried before and failed to prioritize my writing. Putting myself and my needs first is hard. Really hard. I grew up with a younger brother with a disability and a mother with serious health challenges.

I've always felt that my needs had to come last. Prioritizing my needs has been one of the great lessons of my forties. I'm still learning it.

I'm learning to say no to clients and friends and to my husband and kids so I can say yes to myself. It's awkward and unsettling and feels very wrong, but I'm doing it anyway. And guess what? Our relationships aren't suffering. If anything, they are improving, because I'm taking better care of myself.

If you're in the same boat as I am, and poking yourself in the eye with a fork feels like a preferable option to saying no, here are a few tips on how to put yourself first and just say no:

- Identify what your top three to five priorities are and filter all requests through those priorities.
- Have a visible Post-it note with your top priorities on it in your work space to remind you to say no to requests that don't align with them.
- Schedule time in your calendar for working on your priorities and don't give that time up for anyone.
- Don't respond immediately to a request, but let the person know you'll get back to them within a few days. This strategy gives you time to think through whether the request aligns for you and, if necessary, to prepare your "no" response.
- Outline for people what you're working on and where your priorities are, which might prevent some requests from coming in.
- Ask yourself, "What will I be saying no to if I say yes to this request? What is more important to me?"

And for those of you who just can't find the words, I've been using these phrases lately:

- "I'd love to help, but I'm really maxed out right now."
- "Thanks so much for thinking of me to help with this, but I'm going to have to pass."
- "No, I can't help you out right now. Do you think (insert name of best friend/worst enemy here) might be able to?"

- "I'm working on having a better life-work balance, so I'm going to have to say no."
- "Not in this lifetime." This one's usually reserved for inane requests from my children, but I'd love to try it out at work one day.

So many of us have been raised to put others first and while that's a lovely idea, I'm not raising my kids that way. I'm raising them to balance their needs with the needs of others, so they don't get lost in taking care of everyone but themselves.

I'm working hard to get better at committing to myself and saying no to requests that don't align with my priorities. When I take good care of myself and I'm doing work I'm passionate about, I'm happier and more relaxed.

When we're more accountable to ourselves, we can live a life that's aligned with our own goals, values, and dreams. This energizes us, and we're naturally more productive and less stressed out.

Recently, my kids and I were talking about a family whose last name was Wright, and my seven-year-old son said to me, "Mommy, your last name should be Wright." I asked him why he thought that, cringing inside because I was sure he was going to say because I always think I'm right. Instead, he said, "Because you write so much." I did a little dance of joy because you can count on your kids to speak the truth.

BE PATIENT WITH YOURSELF

Even though I wrote a book on reducing stress and increasing productivity, I still get stressed out. I've created stress for myself while writing this book, irony of all ironies. I set myself unrealistic deadlines (as I often do) and took on too much consulting work when I should have been writing. No one is perfect.

We're all doing our best, learning and figuring things out as we go, so let's go easy on ourselves.

As we pay more attention to the choices we make, we can start to take more personal responsibility. It will take time. Change is unlikely to happen overnight. Most of us are undoing a lifetime of patterns by changing how we prioritize our needs, respond to stress, and shift our mindset from blaming to taking personal responsibility. Be patient and compassionate with yourself as you go through the challenging process of changing your ingrained responses.

CONCLUSION

This is your life—as the brilliant poet Mary Oliver put it, "your one wild and precious life."

If you don't take responsibility for how you're responding to the stress in your life, you'll never be able to change it.

Focus on what you can learn from the past, what you can do differently in the future, and then take action.

You can't control what other people do or how your workplace operates, but you can control how you respond to it. Every choice you've made up until this point has led you to where you are right now. When you take personal responsibility for your actions and responses, get clear on your priorities, and commit to yourself, you'll be able to make different choices and significantly decrease your stress and increase your productivity.

QUESTIONS

1. In what situations do you focus on external events or people rather than focusing on yourself and your response?
2. What can you do differently in the future?
3. What's one situation that you would benefit from taking personal responsibility?
4. How can you prioritize your needs?

ACTIONS

- Say no to one request this week.
- Identify one action you can take to commit to yourself more.
- Identify one situation in which you can take your power back by focusing on yourself.
- The next time you're in a stressful situation or blaming a person or event for your stress, take a deep breath and ask yourself the personal responsibility questions:

1. **Why is this situation so upsetting for me?** This question helps you identify what you're feeling and why.
2. **How did I contribute to this situation?** This question helps you identify how your behaviors might have contributed to the stressful situation and begin to change them.
3. **What can I learn from this situation?** When you focus on learning from the situation, you can concentrate on growth rather than stressing out.
4. **What can I do about this situation?** This question helps you focus on specific solutions and strategies.
5. **What can I do differently next time?** This step helps you identify the specific behavior you need to alter to get different results in the future.

Chapter Two

Take Action

"Action is a great restorer and builder of confidence. Inaction is not only the result, but the cause, of fear. Perhaps the action you take will be successful; perhaps different action or adjustments will have to follow. But any action is better than no action at all."

—Norman Vincent Peale

Most of what I teach in my courses and my books is not rocket science. It's fairly straightforward knowledge that many of us already have. The problem is that even though we know a lot, we don't do anything with that knowledge. If we don't take action and apply what we've learned, it just falls out of our brain. I've been to plenty of courses and read lots of books that were fascinating, and I felt certain I was going to implement what they taught me (and totally transform my life for the better), but life got busy, and a month later, the concepts I'd learned were a fuzzy blur that teetered on the edge of my memory. Two months later, they'd disappeared altogether.

But here's the incentive to actually apply what you're learning here: if we keep taking the same actions, we'll get the same results.

When you're stressed out, that stress is having a negative impact on your mental and physical health and likely on the people you care about as well. If you keep doing what you've been doing, things are only going to get worse. It's time to take action.

IDENTIFY THE SOURCE OF YOUR STRESS

Before we take action to decrease our stress, it's a good idea to get really clear on its source.

What is the true source of your stress?

Often it appears to be something on the surface, but if we dig down, we realize it's more complicated than it first seemed. The first personal responsibility question, *Why is this so upsetting for me?* can usually help us identify the source of our stress.

SUZANNE'S STRESS

Years ago, when I first started my business, I coached Suzanne. Suzanne was a highly organized professional in her late thirties who was feeling very overwhelmed at work. She had five different projects, seven staff, a different deadline every day, and at every weekly meeting, her manager gave Suzanne even more work.

Suzanne was sure that work overload was the source of her stress. Each month, we identified strategies to help her deal with her work overload, including having a conversation with her manager.

After a few months of coaching, Suzanne was even more stressed—she didn't seem to be taking the actions we had discussed, and she was getting frustrated, both with coaching and with herself. I soon realized that I'd misdiagnosed the source of Suzanne's stress, as had she.

Finally, I said, "For the last three months, we've been talking about you meeting with your manager to deal with your work overload, yet you never get around to it. Why do you think that is?"

I should have been asking myself the same question. Suzanne was a highly motivated and productive person. If she wasn't taking action, it's possible I was missing something.

"I know I should, but I don't want to seem like a whiner. I'm someone who gets things done and doesn't complain," she said.

"But you are complaining—you're complaining to me. Is there anyone else in your life you are complaining to?"

She laughed. "My husband is pretty tired of hearing about how stressed I am. I also talk to my friends about what a mess work is."

"So, can we agree that you're complaining?"

"Yes." She nodded.

"And that it's not getting you anywhere?" I leaned towards her.

Smiling as if she were a teenager who'd been busted sneaking out at night, Suzanne said, "You're right."

"You're complaining to the wrong people, but you need to be talking to the right person—your manager—not to complain, but to express your concerns." I was really pushing her because I wanted to see her take action and get some relief from her stress.

"If you don't want your boss to see you as a complainer, one of the best strategies is to start off the conversation taking personal responsibility. What have we discussed as your role in this situation?"

"I know that I just keep saying yes even when I'm feeling overwhelmed because it's hard to say no. And I like to take on challenges."

"Exactly. Anything else you're doing to contribute to the situation?"

"I've never asked why she is giving me all this work. Sometimes I feel really frustrated because it appears that she is giving me more work than some of her other staff. I don't know if it's because she expects more of me, or if she just knows I'll do it, or what. But it bothers me." Suzanne's voice grew stronger as she spoke, and her body language grew more tense.

"So that's your biggest frustration?" I asked, getting a glimpse of understanding that we might have been off track in our first few conversations. I'd been like a doctor who diagnosed the symptom (feeling overworked and overwhelmed) rather than the disease (not knowing what her manager expects of her and feeling unfairly treated).

"Totally. I don't really understand what she expects of me and why it seems different than what she expects of her other staff."

"Would that be an easier way to enter the conversation—to ask about her expectations?" I asked.

"Yes! Definitely. Especially because now that we're talking about it—that's stressing me out way more than the workload. Why do I have so many more projects than her other staff?"

Bingo. She now had identified the real source of her stress: frustration at not being treated fairly. That insight energized her to take action. She committed to having the conversation that she'd been avoiding and getting a clear understanding of her manager's expectations. We planned out the conversation and practiced some ways of bringing it up.

SUZANNE'S RESULTS

When we met the next month, I asked Suzanne, "So, did you have the conversation?" I was happily surprised when her answer was a resounding yes.

"It finally felt important enough to talk to her because I realized how stressful it was to be treated unfairly."

"And, how did it go?"

"I was nervous, so I memorized what we'd practiced. I probably sounded rehearsed, but it was worth it. I said, 'I've noticed that I seem to have about three more projects than everyone else who works for you, and I'm just really curious about why that is. Can you help me understand it?'"

I noticed her hands trembling as she relayed the story. "Was that scary for you?"

"Totally. I was raised to never question authority, just to keep my head down and do what I was told. But it went really well." She smiled, clearly proud of herself.

"Tell me more." I was thrilled that we'd finally found the source of her stress, and she'd been able to push past her fear and take action.

"My manager explained the difference between all the portfolios to me and why so many more projects fell under me. It was the first conversation we'd had in the whole three years that I've worked for her where I really understood everyone's roles. Then she asked if I was finding it too much. I almost said no, but then I told her that I was finding it hard to keep the quality of my work high, and that was really important to me. And you are not going to believe this . . ." She leaned in, her blue eyes bright.

"What? Tell me!"

"She apologized. To me." Suzanne shook her head, clearly still astounded. "She said she knew it was a higher workload than was reasonable, but I seemed so calm about it that she just kept adding more projects. She also said that I was the best project manager she'd ever had, so she did pile more work onto me. She told me she thought of me as her successor."

"Wow. How did that feel?"

"Amazing. I finally know why I have more projects—partly because my role requires it, and partly because she thinks I'm really good at my job. Those are way better reasons than all the ones I'd been making up."

"Way better," I agreed, and we both laughed.

"Then she thanked me for talking to her and said she realized we need to have a team meeting to clarify everyone's roles and portfolios and find a way to distribute the work a bit more evenly." Suzanne sighed and leaned back into her chair. "I'm so glad I finally talked to her. I feel like a ton of bricks has been lifted off my chest."

Suzanne had been able to take action after we identified the true source of her stress: the feeling that she was being treated unfairly. Having the conversation with her manager required tremendous courage based on the way she'd been raised, but she did it. And she got great results: she finally had a strong understanding of her role and her relationship with her manager.

WHAT'S THE SOURCE OF YOUR STRESS?

Think about something that is stressing you out right now that you aren't dealing with.

- Why aren't you dealing with it?
- What's holding you back?
- What's the true source of your stress?
- What would it feel like to resolve this situation?
- What's one action you can take today to deal with this stressor?

If you're having trouble identifying the true source of your stress, ask yourself the first personal responsibility question: Why is this situation so upsetting for me? The answer should help you zone in on the source of your stress.

I have coached so many people who feel hopeless about workplace stress. They feel disempowered and frustrated, and, rather than taking action, they continue to allow the stress to impact them. If there is something that causes you stress at work, identify its source and take action.

JUST DO SOMETHING

Do something! Anything! Taking action will reduce your stress even if you don't get the result you were hoping for. Nobody gets a perfect outcome every time they address their stress, but most people feel more energized and empowered after taking action because they've taken their power back.

You may even feel like a ton of bricks have been lifted off your chest.

If you don't know how to do a task, ask someone to teach you. If you're underperforming or receiving negative feedback, ask for clear direction on what you need to do to improve and then do it. If you're having difficulty working with someone, have a conversation with them to address and resolve your concerns.

If you don't have clarity about your role, job expectations, direction, or priorities, it's okay to ask. Set up a meeting and ask your manager for clarity. Keep asking until you have the information you need. Be sure to do so in a respectful way, approach with curiosity, and recognize that others might be just as stressed out as you are, possibly more.

If your manager can't give you clarity, ask them to find out what you need to know so they can get back to you. And if you still can't get clarity, it means the organization and the people above you don't necessarily have clarity either, so go ahead and make things clear for yourself. Set your own goals, priorities, and direction. Put them in writing. Make sure you keep your manager in the loop, and let them know what you're working on, so they can correct you if you go off track. When you're taking action, you're managing your stress.

Years ago, when I went back to work after a maternity leave, I returned to my organization in a new role, developing leadership programs. My manager was off on a two-month health leave when I started. I had no idea what I was expected to do. I'd returned to work feeling excited and full of ideas, but I was soon feeling frustrated and uncertain as to how to proceed.

I talked to a colleague whose wise advice was: "If they didn't give you direction and there's no one around to clarify things for you, forge your own path." So I did. Taking action reduced my stress and helped me be more productive and engaged. I figured that when my manager returned, it was better to show her something rather than admit I had just spun in circles. When she did return, she was pleased with the work I'd started. We made a few tweaks, and I continued working on the project.

If you aren't getting the direction you need, set goals that feel relevant to the work and move towards them. When you have the courage to take action, your stress will decrease and you'll feel energized.

We can manage many of our stressors by simply addressing them. Focus on the potential rewards of addressing your stressors and that will help you to push through your fear so that you can take action.

ASK FOR HELP

One way you can take action to reduce your stress is to ask for help. I know, worst idea ever, right? It's hard to ask for help. Because we live in a culture that values self-sufficiency and independence far too much, some people even find it embarrassing. But we are tribal people who no longer have our natural tribes, and if we're going to survive, we have to start asking for help.

I run my own business and I have a husband who travels for work, two young children, and no family in town. This means I ask for help on a frequent basis. I ask other consultants to help with teaching when I get big projects; I ask friends to help with picking up my kids or dropping them off when I'm teaching at odd hours; I ask really good friends to come and stay with one of my kids in the middle of the night when I have to take the other one to the hospital. I've gotten very good at asking for help, and it has strengthened and deepened my relationships.

One of the best ways you can ask for help doesn't even involve asking, you just have to say yes when people offer. When someone asks, "What can I do to help?" don't say, "I'm fine, thanks." Delete that response from your vocabulary. Instead, find something they can do to help. Anything. It can be the littlest thing imaginable—helping you with a project, bringing over a meal, taking over one small piece of your work.

By accepting people's offers of help, you are setting a precedent. You are saying, yes, I will let you help me. You are inviting them to be closer to you. If we are in a tough spot, at work or at home, people want to help. When we deny them that opportunity, we aren't strengthening our relationships, we are pushing people away rather than bringing them close.

Now if you are in that awkward spot where you need help and no one has offered, what do you do? You ask. I know that many of you would rather die alone and friendless. I get it. Here are a few strategies to make it easier:

Start small. Ask someone that you are pretty sure will say yes to help you with something small. Then accept their help graciously. Even if things didn't turn out exactly the way you had hoped, be grateful that they helped you. Now keep doing it. Build up to bigger requests as needed.

Be direct and specific. Sometimes we are so uncomfortable asking for help that we don't really come out and ask for what we need. We talk our way around it and then feel frustrated when the person we are talking to hasn't picked up our cues. State your request clearly and calmly and always provide an option to say no.

When I ask people for help, I always end my request with, "If you can't swing it, I have a few other people to ask, so please feel free to say no." If someone says no, I thank them for being honest with me and acknowledge that it's hard to say no. If someone has said no to your request for help, keep treating them the exact same way you always have. Don't judge people for not being willing or able to help you. You have no idea what might be going on for them.

Appreciate and thank people when they do help you. This especially goes for family. Don't take it for granted when a family member helps out. It's a gift. It's amazing. They are giving you their precious time. They have other time pressures and needs, and they are helping you. Thank them. Genuinely and graciously.

Help other people. A friend of mine commented that I was really good at asking for help. I echoed that sentiment back to her as she had frequently asked me to help her out in moments when she was stuck for childcare. She laughed and said that I was the only person she ever asked for help. Why? Because I asked her for help frequently, it freed her up to ask me for help. See what a gift you are giving people by asking for help? You're leading by example, showing them it's okay to be vulnerable and ask for help too. When we help each other, everyone benefits.

Do you have difficulty asking for help? If so, what do you do to make it easier? We all need help. Not one of us can live life well on our own. The more we connect through helping each other, the better our world becomes, one small act at a time. Asking for help weaves our relationships more closely together which helps us all be more effective.

BE COURAGEOUS

Taking action often requires courage. It can be frightening to deal with a stressful situation, make a big change, set boundaries, ask for help, or have a difficult conversation. But it's way better than doing nothing. Many people avoid dealing with difficult people or situations, hoping that the problem will magically resolve itself. It won't. The longer you wait, the more difficult it becomes. We've all lived it. I promise that whatever difficult situation you're dreading dealing with, it's not going to get better with time, it's going to get worse. So, take a deep breath, find your courage, and dive in.

Whatever your workplace stressor is, be it work overload, lack of clarity, or interpersonal conflicts, you can take initial action by having a conversation and bringing up your concerns. It might be scary, but it's better than cringing in the corner, just hoping that things will improve.

You'll find that the more often you have the courage to initiate difficult conversations, the easier they become.

There are plenty of tools and strategies to help you get started coming up in the next chapter, "Have Difficult Conversations."

REFRAME POTENTIAL THREATS AND REWARDS

The reason most of us don't take action is that we associate taking action with pain. We don't want to have a difficult conversation because we fear it won't go well. We don't start that project because we are dreading all the work it entails.

Neuroscience has found that our brains are wired to seek pleasure and avoid pain. Dr. Evian Gordon, the founder of the Brain Resource Company, found that "everything you do in life is based on your brain's determination to minimize danger or maximize reward."[1] This means that we make decisions and take action based on whether we are seeing a threat (pain) or a reward (pleasure).

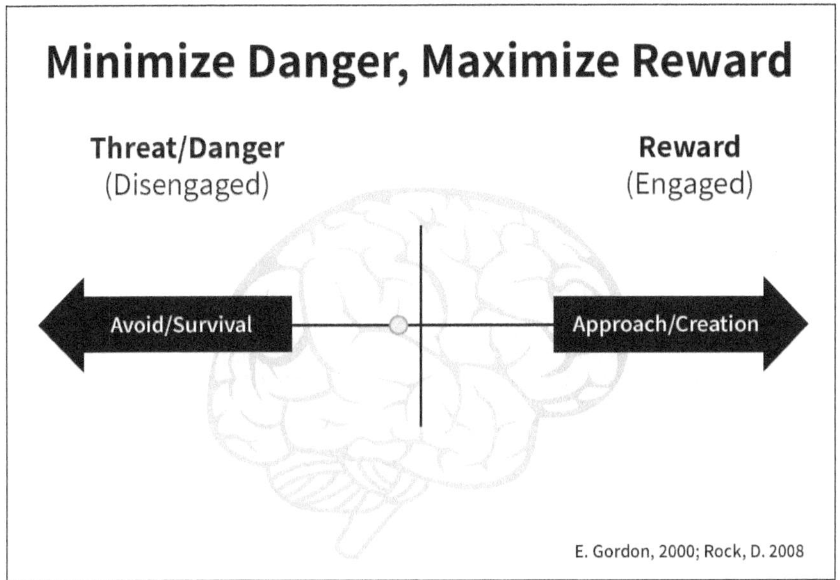

Whether we perceive that a situation poses a threat or a reward can depend on how we frame it.

When we can reframe the situation and envision that taking action will bring us pleasure rather than pain, it makes it much easier to take action.

Let's look at how one of my clients managed to reframe a situation to focus more on the potential rewards than the potential threats of taking action and having a difficult conversation.

HARPREET'S TRANSITION FROM PAIN TO PLEASURE

Harpreet asked me to coach her through dealing with a difficult manager. Her manager needed to be in charge of making decisions, changed direction on Harpreet frequently, was critical of Harpreet's suggestions and ideas.

Harpreet was in her early thirties and had a great deal of confidence. She worked in a high-paced, high-pressure catering company and had worked for difficult people before, but this manager was really getting under her skin. Harpreet didn't feel comfortable with conflict and preferred to go along to get along. This approach had worked for her in the past, but because she was feeling bullied by her manager, she knew she had to have a difficult conversation and deal with the potential conflict that might arise from it.

Having been to my leadership courses, she knew the value of giving feedback but was still very nervous about having the conversation. We started by focusing on how to give her manager specific feedback.

"Okay. You know the model, so let's work through it. Can you identify a specific action impact that you want to give feedback on?"

"It's hard to know where to start. There are so many examples!" She gave a frustrated laugh.

"Is there something that has happened in the last week or two, or anything specific that prompted you to ask for some coaching?" I asked.

"Yes! Last week I'd arranged an event based on his specific directions. We were only a day away from the event when he completely changed everything."

"That sounds quite frustrating, and I can see why you would be really upset. When you say he completely changed everything, that's a bit vague. Can you give me some specific examples of what he changed?"

We talked the situation through, and Harpreet was able to find a way to word her feedback that was both specific and identified the impact. Here's what she came up with:

"When you asked me to use a smaller room for the event as well as switch out some of the menu items the day before the event, I had to work five hours late into the night before the event just to implement everything you wanted. A number of people were very frustrated with me, and I felt that the event wasn't as good as it could have been due to the last-minute changes and the stress and frustration they caused."

"Great, that sounds really clear and helps him understand his impact." I smiled, thinking we were getting somewhere.

"It does, doesn't it?" Her shoulders slumped, she looked down at her lap and sighed.

"What's wrong?" I asked.

"I know that I need to give him this feedback. I just really don't want to. I'm afraid it's going to go badly. I feel really uncomfortable with conflict, and I can't see this ending up any other way."

"What's the worst that could happen if you have this conversation and it goes sideways?" I asked her, zoning in on the possible threats.

"That he will be upset and get angry or defensive. It'll be an awkward conversation, and afterward, he'll be even more difficult and critical. And he'll make my life more difficult at work than he already has. He might even fire me." The words flew out in a stream of anxiety. She was seeing a lot of threats.

"I can see why you'd be nervous about having the conversation; none of those things happening would be a great outcome. But could you survive all those things happening?" I asked that question because I wanted to reduce her fear of the threat. By identifying what we most fear and realizing we could survive it, we relax.

She smiled. "Yes. I could. It might even be a good thing if he fired me. I can't keep working with him the way he is, so I need to speak up. If he fires me, I'll find another job with someone easier to work with." She visibly relaxed.

"Okay, what's the best thing that could happen if you gave him this feedback?" I asked. I wanted to help her focus more on a potential reward than on the threat she'd been concentrating on.

"That he really gets it and stops undermining my decisions and changing things at the last minute just to show that he's the boss. He'll see me standing up for myself, and he'll stop bullying me," she said.

"That would be great, wouldn't it?"

"Would it ever! If he would stop pulling this control-freak stuff, I'd be so much happier. Talking to him might actually get through to him." She smiled and there was a lightness to it that I hadn't seen before.

Harpreet was thinking about potential rewards and threats based on her manager's response. I reminded her that ultimately, she couldn't control how he responded, and, instead, we talked about a potential reward she could control: her ability to step into her power, deal with conflict, and survive.

"Even if you don't get either outcome—he doesn't behave any better or worse—how will you feel if you give him this feedback?"

"I'll feel good, because I've stood up for myself and said what I've been thinking."

"And how will you feel if you don't give him the feedback?"

"Horrible, like I'm letting him walk all over me. Every time he does this to me, I'll just be more frustrated and upset—not just upset with him but upset with myself for not saying anything."

Here was our opportunity to reframe taking action to have the conversation as a potential reward that was completely within Harpreet's control, rather than as a potential threat.

"It sounds to me like you feel pretty nervous about how your manager is going to respond to this feedback, but you also feel pretty strongly that you need to stand up for yourself. Standing up for yourself would be a really good outcome, regardless of how your manager responds," I said.

"Absolutely. I would feel so much better if I finally dealt with this. It's been bothering me for months." She nodded, smiling.

"Can you go into the conversation with absolutely no expectations about him changing his behavior, but just concentrate on speaking your mind, standing up for yourself, and doing what you can to take care of yourself in the situation?"

By framing the situation this way, Harpreet could see a big reward: she'd be taking her power back rather than continuing to let her manager walk all over her.

Her brown eyes brightened. "That I can do. If I focus on standing up for myself, that's enough incentive to get me through the scary parts."

When we left that meeting, I felt fairly confident that Harpreet would follow through.

HARPREET'S RESULTS

When we next met, I was thrilled to learn that Harpreet had been courageous enough to have the conversation she'd been dreading. She told me, "It went better than I expected—he didn't yell at me—I felt calm and powerful when I spoke with him."

She was still astounded that it had gone as well as it did, but a few weeks later, he started pulling all the same behavior again. Harpreet knew that she couldn't change her manager, so she focused on herself and what she could do in the situation. She started looking and found another job within a month. She's never been happier, not only because she's working for a far more reasonable manager, but because she's learned to stand up for herself and face conflict.

YOUR TRANSITION FROM PAIN TO PLEASURE

Think about the other stories I've shared with you about some of my clients. What was stopping them from taking action? Often it was the fear of pain and viewing action as a possible threat. They were motivated to take action by reframing the situation and seeing a potential reward.

George was worried his manager would fire him if he brought up his concerns, but he realized that if he did nothing, his pain would be even greater. Seeing the potential reward of reducing his stress and having a better working relationship with his new manager motivated him to have the conversation.

Suzanne was terrified to have a conversation with her manager—she'd been raised not to question authority. Having that conversation was a threat to her very identity. Yet she had the courage to do it because she could see the potential reward of fixing something that she perceived to be unfair.

- What situation have you been avoiding because it seems threatening in some way?
- How can you reframe it to see the potential rewards?
- Identify at least one step you can take to deal with the situation.

Too many people fall into the trap of feeling anxious and watching the situation get increasingly worse, but they do nothing about it. They put all their focus on the potential threats, rather than on the potential reward of addressing their challenges and improving the situation.

There is always something to be done. We just need to figure out what it is and then have the courage to do it. Focusing on the potential rewards can give us the courage to take action.

CONCLUSION

When we focus on what we can control and how we want to influence a situation and take action towards getting there, our energy and productivity increase immensely. Instead of being drained by the person or situation that is stressing us out, we feel energized by where we're headed and the actions we're taking to get there. The more action we take, the better results we see and the more inspired we are to take further action. Instead of the vicious cycle of stress, it's the energizing cycle of taking action.

The strategy of taking action seems simple, but it can be very challenging. Most of us know what we should do, we just don't want to do it. It's difficult to break unhealthy patterns, give someone feedback, or leave work when there's piles of work still to do. But it's time to take control of the situation.

Think about the action you need to take and then go do it. It's really that simple. Identify what the true source of your stress is, reframe situations so you can see potential rewards, rather than just possible threats. Then take the appropriate actions to reduce the impact of the stressor on you.

There's going to be plenty more action to take in the following chapters, so you might as well start now. If you want less stress and higher productivity, you're going to have to take different actions. You're primed, you bought the book, you made it through two chapters, and you've identified some changes you need to make. Now's the time to strike while the iron is hot.

QUESTIONS

1. What specific action do you need to take to address the stress in your life?
2. What impact will the action have on reducing your stress? Be specific. Write down how your life would be different if this stress were managed.
3. Who can help you stay accountable to this action? Identify one person you can enlist to help you stay on track.
4. What's one situation that you can reframe in order to see a potential reward rather than a threat?

ACTIONS

- Choose one action you know you need to take and do it today.
- Find a small way to celebrate your success in following through.
- Think of a specific situation that is stressing you out and identify the true source of your stress.

Chapter Three

Have Difficult Conversations

"Speak when you are angry and you will make the best speech you will ever regret."

—Ambrose Bierce

Interpersonal conflicts are the most common source of stress that I see in workplaces. It's tough working with people who have different attitudes, approaches, and behaviors than we do. Often, we feel frustrated, misunderstood, or angry. Most of us just want to avoid having a difficult conversation, but the longer we avoid it, the more complicated having the discussion becomes.

When we have the tools and confidence to have a difficult conversation, we can have it sooner which will ensure the discussion goes far more smoothly than if we let things fester for days, weeks, or even months and then try to deal with the situation. This chapter is full of tools to help you prepare for and have all those conversations you've been avoiding.

To prepare for a difficult conversation, it's a good idea to identify the source of your stress, understand how you are contributing to the situation, and consider the possible actions you can take.

You might not think you are doing anything to contribute to the situation, but I guarantee that you are. Even if all you are doing is being silent about your frustrations and not addressing the problem, you are contributing to the situation. To help you think through your part in the dynamics, consider the personal responsibility questions again:

PERSONAL RESPONSIBILITY QUESTIONS

1. **Why is this situation so upsetting for me?** This question helps you identify what you're feeling and why.
2. **How did I contribute to this situation?** This question helps you identify how your behaviors might have contributed to the stressful situation and begin to change them.
3. **What can I learn from this situation?** When you focus on learning from the situation, you can concentrate on growth rather than stressing out.
4. **What can I do about this situation?** This question helps you focus on specific solutions and strategies.
5. **What can I do differently next time?** This step helps you identify the specific behavior you need to alter to get different results in the future.

When we focus on ourselves and take personal responsibility for our role in a difficult dynamic, our intention in a conversation switches from fixing or blaming the other person to improving our interactions.

PREPARING FOR THE CONVERSATION

To prepare for a difficult conversation, we want to think about what our purpose in having the conversation is. When we're focused on the outcome of the conversation, we can prepare what we want to say and even practice having the conversation (you can role-play with a trusted friend, coach, or your mirror) with our intentions in mind. I encourage you to let go of your judgments and assumptions about the person you'll be talking to—it's a difficult conversation because of something that they have done or said, and the discussion becomes more difficult when we layer our own judgements on top of their actions. When we can go into difficult conversations with an open mind and listen to the other person with curiosity rather than judgment, we will usually get a far better outcome.

Another strategy is to start the conversation by taking personal responsibility for our behavior. When we can identify how we have contributed to the dynamic, often we will set the tone for the other person to reflect on their behavior, and the conversation is a lot less bumpy than if we go into it with guns blazing.

It's also really important for us to manage our feelings before we go into the conversation. I've coached so many people who are either nervous or angry or frightened going into a difficult conversation. Rather than taking those feelings into the conversation with you, explore and express them before you enter the conversation. You can write out everything you're feeling or tell the mirror how upset you are or talk through your feelings with a coach or a close friend. When we've addressed our feelings about the issue, we can enter the conversation from a much calmer place.

LISTEN FIRST

If we enter a conversation with the intention to listen deeply to the other person to understand where they are coming from, we can have a much different conversation than if we go into it prepared to make our points and prove that we are right. It can be hard to slow down enough to listen, but when you bring up a concern and then listen to the other person's perspective before trying to get your own point across, the conversation goes way better.

We also need to schedule enough time to have the difficult conversation. Many people are so busy that they try to have important and complicated conversations in a short time frame, which ultimately results in people feeling rushed and not listening well. This can lead to misunderstanding, miscommunication, and sometimes conflict.

If listening is a challenge for you, here are a few reminders of how to listen well:

- Remove all distractions: put your phone away, turn off computer notifications and turn away from your computer.
- Go for a walk or plan the discussion in a neutral, distraction-free environment.
- Schedule enough time for the conversation so you aren't rushed or thinking about your next meeting.
- Let go of your stories and judgments about the person and the situation and listen with curiosity and an open mind.
- Paraphrase what you've heard to ensure you've understood correctly.
- Acknowledge the feelings the other person is expressing.
- Ask questions to keep yourself focused on the conversation and ensure you understand the speaker.
- Enter the conversation with the intent to listen to the other person with the goal of understanding their perspective (rather than listening with the intent to prove your point).

When we can approach a difficult conversation with an open mind and the intent to listen to the other person, it will often transform into a much easier conversation than we envisioned.

YOUR TRIGGERS

We all have our own histories and unique experiences that make us react more strongly to some situations or individuals than other people might. These are often called *triggers* as they trigger automatic reactions in us.

For example, years ago, I worked for a man who was a very distant and distracted manager. One of my coworkers absolutely loved working for him as she liked the autonomy she had. While I also appreciate freedom and autonomy, there was something about this manager's style that I found upsetting. I often felt dismissed and hurt after our interactions. After one of our more difficult meetings, during which he was confused about what projects I was working on—even though we'd discussed the projects in detail a few days earlier—I asked myself the first personal responsibility question, "Why is this so upsetting for me?"

As I sat with the question, I realized that I felt similar to the way I'd felt as a child when I'd told my father about things that were really important to me, and he didn't really pay attention so he promptly forgot. My father was very distracted while I was growing up, and this manager had similar behaviors. I reacted to his behavior quite strongly because it brought up old feelings. Because I'd taken some time to think about what was so upsetting for me in our interactions, I realized this was my issue and was able to deal with it myself rather than have it interfere with our working relationship.

When I went into meetings with my manager, I expected him to be unprepared and distracted, and I didn't take his lack of attention to my work personally. I knew he was really busy, and he trusted me to get the work done. Changing my perspective made our working relationship far less stressful.

Asking the first personal responsibility question is a good way to help you identify if you might be feeling triggered and bringing some of your own interpretations or past issues to the interaction.

Is there someone at work who you have a very strong reaction to?

Why is that person so upsetting for you?

Are there ways that you need to adapt your approach to working with this person?

MANAGING YOUR EMOTIONS IN THE CONVERSATION

When we're in the midst of a difficult conversation, it can be hard to remain calm, but staying emotionally steady is going to create the best outcome in the conversation. Here are a few tips to help you bring yourself back to a place of calm if you find yourself getting emotional. We will discuss more general strategies in the "Manage Your Mental and Emotional State" chapter, but these ones are useful for calming yourself down in the moment:

- Breathe deeply, take three deep breaths—this is magic, just try it now and see how much more relaxed you feel.
- Remind yourself that you have no idea what the other person is going through.
- Don't take the other person's behavior personally.
- Identify what you're feeling—simply labeling the emotion in your mind will reduce the emotion.
- Put things in perspective—How much does this really matter? How much will it matter next week? Next month? Next year?
- Notice the physical signs of escalating feelings and change your posture to a more relaxed posture (unclench your fists, relax your shoulders, unclench your jaw, etc.).
- If necessary, leave the situation temporarily to get grounded and come back when you are calmer.
- Focus on what you can control: your response. If you get emotional, the other person won't remember what you said, only that you were angry, sad or upset, so your message will be lost.
- Ask questions or discuss facts. This moves you from the emotional side of the brain to the rational side of your brain.

TALK TO COWORKERS, NOT ABOUT THEM

An unhealthy workplace behavior that I see frequently is when one person has an issue with another person, but they don't talk to them, they talk about them.

If you do that, stop. It doesn't resolve the situation; it actually makes the situation worse and contributes to a culture of gossip and negativity. If you're really frustrated and need a listening ear, talk to someone outside of work who can keep the conversation confidential. If it's a situation that has workplace implications and you need to involve your manager, your union rep, or HR, do so after you have thought through the situation and you are clear on your part in it and the kind of support you need.

Many people, consciously or unconsciously, choose endless, sleepless nights over having a difficult conversation. They talk to everyone in the world about the problem except the person they have the problem with. Please stop avoiding tough conversations. Instead, prepare for them.

FOCUS ON PRESERVING THE RELATIONSHIP

Dealing with interpersonal conflict requires a genuine desire to resolve the situation and find a good outcome for both of you.

The point of conflict is not to determine who is right or wrong (a trap I sometimes fall into) but to find a way to stay in relationship with each other.

If we can approach a difficult conversation with the goal of staying in relationship with the other person and discussing our perceptions as perceptions rather than facts, the conversation will go more smoothly. Both people need to work at it, and, of course, you can only do your part. But you'll often find that if you do your best to make it work, the other person will follow your lead.

Trust me, I know that there are people out there who are almost impossible to work with. They seem to delight in making life difficult for others. I'm sorry if you have to work with someone like this—it's awful. I've lived it and it nearly broke me. I'd come home every day feeling frustrated and stressed out and dreading having to work with this colleague the next day. Then I figured out how to have difficult conversations and deal with my challenges in a healthy and professional way. Believe me, that person was never my favorite person in the world, but dealing with them became much easier after I had the courage to have a difficult conversation. Even just having the conversation was enough to change the dynamic between us, and I felt more relaxed.

Think about some of those people who cause you a lot of stress. Wouldn't it be nice to reduce their impact on you? There are two ways to do this. You can choose to not take their behavior personally and ignore it, shrug your shoulders, and think "Oh, that's just Amy, doing her thing, nothing to do with me." This is the approach to take if the behavior is designed to get a reaction from you or if it's really just not worth getting that upset about. When you stop reacting and taking the behavior personally, your stress levels will decrease.

The other response is to address the behavior. This is the approach to take if you want to let the other person know how they are impacting you. Your goal in this conversation is to make changes in how the two of you interact. A common progression is that people try the first strategy of letting the behavior roll off their back; then if they realize they can't let the behavior go, they choose to have a conversation to give the other person some feedback.

REFRAMING FEEDBACK

One way we can become more comfortable offering feedback is to reframe it. We often perceive a feedback conversation as a threat, something that will cause us pain. Usually when thinking about giving someone feedback, we feel a pit in our stomachs and dread coursing through our veins. We're worried that we might upset the other person and possibly damage our relationship with them or make things even worse.

What if we reframed the whole idea of feedback? When we give someone feedback, it's because we want to improve our relationship—otherwise we wouldn't bother. When we can stop being fearful of hurting the other person and can recognize that our true intent is to help them, feedback conversations feel less frightening.

When you tell someone that their fly is undone, they're genuinely grateful as you've saved them from embarrassment! A coworker might feel the same level of gratitude when you let them know about a workplace behavior they've been engaging in that's having a negative impact.

We can also reframe a feedback conversation to see the potential reward of taking our power back by dealing with our stress.

TIMING AND THE DIFFICULT CONVERSATION

When preparing to offer feedback or to have a difficult conversation, it's important to consider the timing. In an ideal situation, you'll want to offer feedback as soon after the incident as possible. It's possible to give feedback within a few minutes or an hour of an interaction, but only if you feel calm enough to have the conversation respectfully and if you sense that the person is able to be receptive and listen to the feedback.

If you need some time to recover or prepare and you sense the other person might have the same need, I recommend the twenty-four- to forty-eight-hour rule: give yourself a day or two to process the events, consider your approach, and get yourself into the right mind frame to address the issue. Don't leave it any longer than that because the associated stress and worry just builds up and the situation becomes harder to deal with. Ask the person when a good time to talk would be and approach the conversation with a genuine desire to resolve the situation.

THE AIID MODEL

We can also have conflict and challenges with people that we enjoy working with, and we need tools to resolve these challenges as well.

If you decide to have a feedback conversation, either with a difficult person or your work spouse, I encourage you to use the AIID feedback model. I've taught this approach to thousands of people, and I've seen it dramatically change their relationships for the better.

Framework for Feedback - AIID

A	**Action** – identify the specific action you are giving the person feedback on
I	**Impact** – share the impact that their action had on you
I	**Input** – ask for their input
D	**Desired outcome** – together, come up with a desired outcome to be able to take action on the feedback

A stands for Action. The first step of the AIID feedback model is to identify the specific action that is problematic. Here, you have to be as specific as possible—being vague is tempting because you may feel nervous, but being specific is stronger and more clear. Think about the last time you got frustrated with someone at work—what did they do specifically?

For example, if one of your coworkers or staff members is always late, you don't want to be vague and say, "You're always late these days." That broad and judgmental statement is likely to make the person feel defensive. "Always" and "never" are words best avoided in any conversation.

Instead, choose a specific action or behavior that has occurred in the recent past (ideally in the past day or two, and no more than one week ago) and describe it as specifically as possible. You could say, "For the last three days, you have come in fifteen minutes late . . ." or, "I noticed you came in twenty minutes late four times last week; I'm just wondering if everything is okay?" This specific feedback is much easier to receive. I've used a very simple example here, but if you think back to George, he used this model to give his manager feedback on the specific ways he was feeling micromanaged. You can use this model for any kind of feedback, just remember to be as specific as possible when describing the **Action**.

I **stands for Impact.** After you have clearly stated the **Action**, you need to share with the person the **Impact** that their action had on you. This is key. So many people make significant changes to their behavior after they became aware of its impact.

In this situation, you could simply say, "We can't get started until you are here, so we start our days late." Or, "When I'm waiting for you to arrive, I feel frustrated because I've worked hard to arrive on time." This approach helps the person understand how you feel in response to their actions, and we can usually connect with one another's feelings.

....

Being aware of our tone in these conversations is really important. We want to have an open and curious tone. That's why it's a good idea to address issues as soon as they arise.

....

We usually feel more frustrated as the situation goes on, but if we speak to someone about a challenge as soon as it arises, it's easier to maintain curiosity and open-mindedness.

Understanding our impact on others can generate insights that will propel us to take action and change. In one of my leadership classes, I give students an assignment to go and ask five people for feedback. One of my students had a profound realization when people told him that when he was sarcastic it made them shut down and they did not want to bring issues to him. When they shared how he made them feel (anxious, worried about his response), he had a much better understanding of his impact.

He had always known that he was sarcastic and until then he had prided himself on it, thinking it made him funny and approachable. When he saw that he was having a totally different impact than the one he'd intended, he cut out all sarcasm because he wanted to be approachable.

The second *I* stands for Input. This is the step we most often forget, but it's so important. Without asking the other person for their **Input**, we haven't really communicated, we've just told them about the **Action** and the **Impact** it's had on us.

After you've shared your feedback, it's time to stop talking and listen.

At this stage, you ask the other person for their **Input**. There are two questions you can ask. The first question is something along the lines of "What's up?" or "What's going on?" Again, we need to be so aware of keeping our tone light and curious in this discussion. When we ask the person what's going on for them, and truly listen, we can get to the root of the problem and work towards solving it. The next question is: "What do you think we can do about it?"

The most important thing to do now is to listen to the other person.

Keep in mind that they might be feeling hurt or defensive, so it could be difficult for them to engage in the conversation.

Give the other person the opportunity to share their perspective and ideas. After you have listened to them, you can share your own ideas. Often people will come up with far better solutions than you will—and most importantly, they will be committed to them because they suggested them. If I were to suggest to a staff member or coworker who was always late that they just set their alarm twenty minutes earlier, how do you think they would respond? Most of us know how best to solve our own problems, we just need someone to listen and talk things through with us.

D **stands for Desired Outcome**. When having a feedback conversation, it's important to make sure both of you are clear on the desired outcome based on the feedback given. It's valuable to come up with this outcome together so that you are both invested and it doesn't feel like one person is telling the other what to do (yes, this works well even when you are a manager speaking to an employee). In the example of the coworker being late, the **Desired Outcome** seems fairly obvious: that they arrive at work on time. But your discussion might land you somewhere totally different. For instance, you may realize that due to their circumstances, they need to start and finish their work day half an hour later.

....

Go into the conversation with a curious, open mind, and you'll be surprised at where it can lead.

....

Usually the **Desired Outcome** will grow organically from having listened well to one another.

After you have both agreed on the **Desired Outcome**, set a time to follow up and see how things are going. If things are still off track, you can discuss other solutions. If things are on track, you can focus on what's working and build on that.

GIVE FEEDBACK FREQUENTLY

Whenever you have a challenge with someone, give them constructive feedback. The more comfortable and practiced you become, the easier it is to do. Often, when we let someone know about the impact of their behavior on us, that is enough for them to make a change.

Other times, they won't change no matter what we say or do. But if that is the case, you've done your best; you have taken action to reduce your stress. If you've given someone feedback and things haven't changed, you can simply turn your attention to managing how you respond because that's the only thing you can control in the situation.

Who do you need to have a feedback conversation with?

Who have you been avoiding sharing constructive feedback with?

Take a moment right now to think about how you would frame the specific action and impact to help you prepare for the feedback conversation. Here's a basic example:

Specific action: When you interrupted me three times during that conversation.
Impact: I felt frustrated and I didn't feel like my opinion mattered.

After you've identified the action and impact you want to discuss, set yourself a deadline within the next few days to go and have the feedback conversation you've been avoiding. I know it can be hard to work ourselves up to the conversation, but the sooner you do it, the less stressed you will feel. In the future, do your best to stop avoiding these types of conversations—the next time something feedback worthy happens, push yourself to give feedback within one to two days.

Remember to approach the conversation with an open mind and listen to the other person's perspective. I regularly give an assignment to students where they have to have feedback conversations they've been avoiding, and they always return to class feeling relieved that they had the conversation. Almost all of them find that the conversation goes far better than they anticipated.

The more frequently we give feedback, the more comfortable we become having those difficult conversations.

HOW FEEDBACK CAN HELP YOU

I know you're not a difficult person at all, neither am I. We are perfect, and all those people we work with are difficult. I get it. But on the rare occasion, it's just possible that we might also be a teensy bit difficult.

If you can find the courage to ask your coworkers and your manager for feedback, you might learn a few things that will help you grow. In addition to improving your relationships, asking for feedback has plenty of career benefits. As Sheila Heen and Douglas Stone share in their book *Thanks for the Feedback*, research has found that "feedback-seeking behavior has been linked to higher job satisfaction, greater creativity on the job, faster adaptation in a new organization or role, and lower turnover. And seeking out negative feedback is associated with higher performance ratings."[1]

Asking for feedback might be really good for us, but it's kind of terrifying. The first time I asked someone for feedback, I felt like I was going to throw up. The second time, I felt slightly less nauseous. Now, I just get a few butterflies. If you can muster up the courage to do it, you'll have my utmost respect.

We all want to be loved and accepted just as we are. Feedback hurts because it's the opposite of that. But if we can focus on our desire to learn and grow rather than our need to be accepted, we can take feedback in much more easily.

Just like when we are giving feedback, we want to be as specific as possible when asking for feedback. Maybe you want to improve your communication or presentation skills, or you would really like feedback on how to be a better listener.

Instead of saying, "Can you give me some feedback?" say, "Can you give me some feedback on how I can be a better listener?"

When someone is giving you feedback and you feel tempted to punch them in the face and then explain all the reasons they're wrong, know that your reaction is totally natural. We're hardwired to defend against feedback. Instead of a throat punch, smile and thank the person for sharing their feedback as you know it takes courage. Then see what you can learn from what they have offered you.

Likewise, when giving feedback, be prepared for a defensive reaction. When it happens, acknowledge that it's hard to hear difficult feedback, and express that you appreciate that the person has listened to your concerns.

Who are three people you could ask for feedback?

What specific feedback questions will you ask them?

I'd encourage you to choose at least one or two people from your personal life as well as your workplace. The first time I asked for feedback on my listening skills, everyone I asked thought I was a very attentive and focused listener except . . . wait for it . . . my husband. He was right: I was using up all my attentive listening at work. I was so grateful I'd asked (and listened openly to his response), and I'm a much better listener at home now because I really want my family to feel listened to and valued.

Give the people you've selected a heads up, so they have time to think about your questions. When asking for feedback, we want to give the other person time to prepare so that they can offer us useful feedback.

We also want to have one-on-one conversations. One of my clients complained to me, "Every week in our staff meeting, I ask my staff for feedback, and they just smile and say everything is good."

I laughed and explained, "That's because they are nice people. They don't want to say anything negative to you in front of others."

Her eyes opened wide. "You're so right. That would have been really awkward if they'd been critical of me in front of the team."

When she scheduled some one-on-one meetings where she asked for specific feedback, she was able to get meaningful feedback that helped her adjust her management style.

If you've decided to ask someone for feedback, you might want to send them an e-mail and let them know you'd love some feedback. Include your specific feedback questions and ask them to meet with you to discuss their responses.

Here is an example e-mail that I often have my clients send to their staff when they are seeking feedback on their management style.

> Hi, John. I'd really value your feedback on how I'm managing you. I have a few questions that I'd love you to consider before we meet:
>
> 1. As your manager, what would you like me to do more of?
> 2. As your manager, what would you like me to do less of?
> 3. As your manager, what would you like me to keep doing?
>
> And, of course, if there is anything else that comes to mind, I'd love to learn from your feedback. I'm genuinely interested in hearing how I can support you

as your manager, so please be as open and honest as possible.

Please don't e-mail your responses. I'd prefer to meet in person to discuss. Can we meet next week?

You could easily take this sample and insert your own questions into it to help you open up the feedback conversation. Asking for feedback takes courage, but when you have those conversations, you'll learn a lot and build more trust in your relationships. There are two keys to building trust through feedback conversations: don't get defensive and act on the feedback you've received.

TO GIVE FEEDBACK OR NOT

When I'm assessing whether I should give another person difficult feedback, I consider how much energy I'm putting into the issue:

- Is it keeping me awake at night?
- Is it impacting our working relationship?
- Is it impacting the work we are doing?
- Am I talking to a coach or trusted friend about it?
- Do I complain about this person to my husband on a regular basis?

If the answer to any of these questions is yes, I always choose to give feedback. Giving feedback is an action I can take to resolve the situation. I give feedback, then let go of the outcome. I hope that the other person will change, but I can't control that.

We encounter all kinds of challenging situations and personalities at work and in our lives. Some people are outright jerks, others are just going through a difficult time themselves. Some people are genuinely unaware that their behavior is causing any problems. When we give those people feedback, we are actually doing them a favor by letting them know about the impact of their actions.

If we want to reduce our stress, we have to figure out ways to reduce the impact that difficult people have on us. We can't control other people, so we have to focus on what we can control: ourselves and our responses.

The way we interact with others has a huge impact on our productivity. We'll talk more about this in Chapter Eleven, but for now, think about what you can do to ensure you have strong working relationships. The better your relationships are, the more effectively you'll be able to work together.

THE VALUE OF POSITIVE FEEDBACK

On the note of building positive relationships, the AIID feedback model can also be used for providing positive feedback. We're often so busy that we forget to make the time to point out what we appreciate about one another.

I encourage you to give positive feedback as often as possible. When you notice things going well or feel appreciation for someone, acknowledge it by giving them positive feedback. Taking two minutes to share a specific action someone took and the good impact it had on you will go miles towards building strong relationships, both at home and at work.

It can be a quick conversation, a two-line e-mail, or a thank-you card, depending on the situation. Giving positive feedback doesn't take much effort, but it can have a powerful impact on our relationships and the people that we work with. Building and maintaining healthy relationships is always preferable to having to fix them.

Please give positive feedback in a separate conversation than when you're offering constructive feedback.

Our brains are hardwired to remember only the more negative aspects of a conversation, so the positive feedback gets forgotten too easily if it's delivered at the same time as constructive feedback.

You don't want to be the person who offers only critical feedback—you know, the one that people cringe when they see her coming? Even if it's your natural style to be more critical, think of the ways you could provide positive feedback and the great impacts that could have on your relationships. As a bumper sticker I saw recently said: "Wag more, bark less."

Giving positive feedback doesn't just help build our relationships, it also significantly improves productivity. Research conducted by Marcial Losada determined that we need to have a ratio of three positive interactions for every negative one in order to make a corporate team successful.[2] Interestingly, John Gottman, researcher and marriage expert, found that to keep a healthy marriage, the ratio was five positive interactions for every negative one.[3] The research is in: be nice to your coworkers and even nicer to your spouse.

Losada used the three-to-one formula with a global mining company that was losing money. He told team leaders they had to give more positive feedback and encourage more positive interactions. And do you know what happened? The company went from losing money to making money. They improved their performance by over 40 percent.[4] I love this research because it shows the very tangible result that we can get from sharing positive feedback and engaging in positive interactions.

Providing positive feedback can have incredible impacts on our team's productivity, on our relationships, and on our work. It takes no time at all, and you can make someone's day by sharing your positive feedback with them.

This doesn't apply just to work. Think about all the people you encounter in your day: your friends, family members, the server at the restaurant. Sharing positive feedback with others builds stronger relationships and connections, helps improve productivity, and increases happiness.

Who can you share some positive feedback with today?

Take a moment right now to think about how you would frame the specific action and impact to help you prepare for the feedback conversation. Here's a simple example:

Specific action: When you stayed late to help me work on that project.

Impact: I felt really supported and even more motivated to get the work done.

Take some time to have a positive feedback conversation in the next week and notice the impact it has.

CONCLUSION

Nobody loves having a difficult conversation. But the sooner you have the conversation, the easier it will be. You've now got plenty of tools to enable you to have a difficult conversation, remember to listen well, maintain your calm, reframe feedback conversations, find ways to reduce the person's impact on you, use the AIID feedback model to guide you through a tough conversation, and focus on the one and only thing you can control in these situations: your actions and responses.

The more often you have difficult conversations and deliver difficult feedback, the easier it will get.

And remember, we're all difficult at times. Maybe asking for some feedback and reflecting on your own behavior might help you be a little less difficult for some of the people you work (or live) with.

QUESTIONS

1. What feedback conversations have you been avoiding?
2. Why have you been avoiding them?
3. How can you reframe the conversation so you don't see it as a threat but can see the potential reward in it?
4. How can you be a better listener while having difficult conversations?
5. What one action can you take to better prepare for difficult conversations?

ACTIONS

- Plan and role-play the difficult conversation you need to have.
- Let go of all your judgments and assumptions before entering the conversation.
- Use the AIID Model to identify the specific action and impact you want to give feedback on.
- Book a date in your calendar and have that feedback conversation you've been avoiding. Use the tools that will help you listen well and maintain your calm.
- Have a positive feedback conversation in the next week. Notice the impact it has on your relationship.

Chapter Four

Put Stress in Perspective

"If you change the way you look at things, the things you look at change."

—Wayne Dyer

When we think of stress, we tend to focus on its negative impacts, but if we had no stress in our lives, we'd likely have very little motivation and satisfaction. The stress we experience is often a result of living full and engaging lives and striving to achieve our goals.

When we can change our perspective, we can see that stress isn't the enemy; we just need to have the right amount of stress in order to be productive and healthy. As neuroscience has found, "the prefrontal cortex needs just the right level of arousal to make decisions and solve problems well. That level is quite high but not too high. Positive stress helps focus your attention."[1] In other words, when we have too little stress, we lack energy and purpose; when we have too much, we become overwhelmed and anxious.

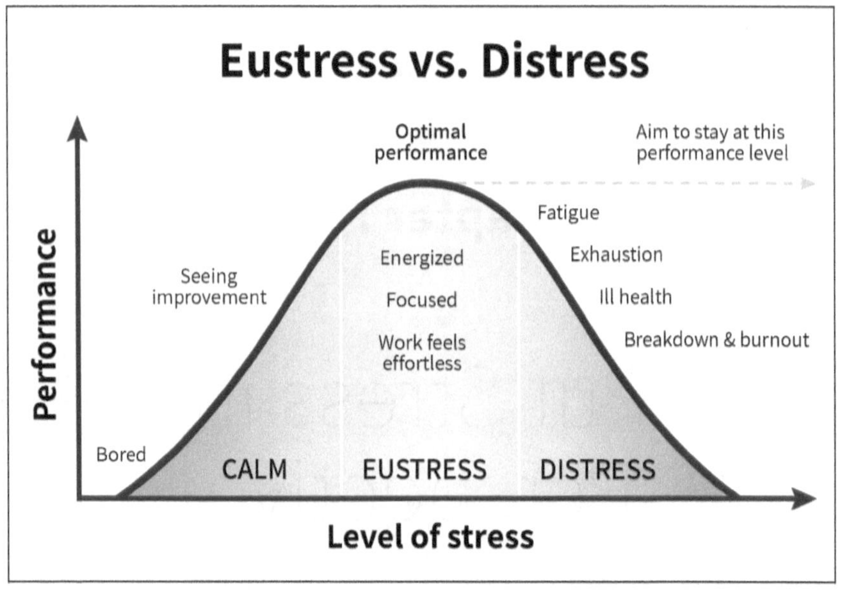

Work will always have elements of stress, and we actually need a healthy level of stress to keep us motivated to get work done.

This is called *eustress* or "good stress." This good stress gets you out of bed in the morning because you have bills to pay, and a boss who will be angry if you don't show up. It motivates you. We don't want to eliminate this energizing stress at work because it keeps us engaged, makes us highly productive, and ensures we deliver on our commitments.

While a little bit of stress is good for us, too little or too much stress is bad. Each one of us has a different threshold for stress. Look around the office and you'll see what I mean. When the photocopier breaks, some people start crying. They have a lower threshold for stress. Judge not. You have no idea why they reacted that way or what happened before that photocopier breakdown.

When we have just enough stress, we're highly productive. This is the sweet spot called *optimum stress* that we hope to find for ourselves. I have this great talent for finding that sweet spot for a few months, then taking on just a bit more work, and then a bit more until I'm a frazzled, stressed-out mess. Then I start all over again. Figuring out how to manage our stress so we can live a happy, healthy, productive life is definitely a lifelong journey, especially because our stressors keep changing.

We've all experienced this wonderful state of optimum stress: we're on fire, getting lots done, full of energy, and really enjoying ourselves. The challenge is noticing when our optimum stress becomes less than optimal. Too often, we are operating just at the edge of optimum stress, and when we start to tip over into overload, we ignore the warning signs. Instead of slowing down and managing our stress, we power through.

When I'm operating at optimum stress levels, I'm highly productive. I end each day feeling energized by all that I've accomplished and excited about what I'll be working on the next day.

How about you?

Think about a time when you've had optimum stress levels. What were you doing? What was your life-work balance like?

How can you replicate some of those elements in your life now?

I'm hoping that someday I'll be able to report on what it feels like to have too little stress in my life, but so far, I couldn't tell you. I imagine you're not in that situation either because most people who buy books on managing their stress tend to be in stress overload.

When I'm operating at stress overload levels, my brain races, I can't stop thinking about everything I need to get done, it takes me hours to fall asleep, and I wake too early. I often get a sore neck and tight shoulders. I can be short and irritable with my family, and I feel like I'm running through every day but getting nowhere. At the end of the day, I'm drained and dreading the next day, wondering how I'm possibly going to get everything done.

How about you?

How does stress overload impact your body? Your relationships? Your sleep? Your productivity?

Rather than powering through when we're in stress overload, we need to change our perspective.

It's not normal to be overwhelmed all the time, and our response should not be to just keep going until something gives.

Instead, we need to notice our stress signs and take action to manage our stress the moment we notice it reaching—or passing—the tipping point. Ideally, we want to pull our stress levels back as soon as we notice signs that we are feeling stressed out or anxious. The sooner we deal with our stress, the easier it is to manage. Too often we have the perspective that being highly stressed out is typical. It's not—it just seems that way because everyone we know is usually super stressed.

Most of us know our individual signs of a rising stress level: a kink in the neck, impatience, irritability, difficulty falling or staying asleep, headaches, or a deep desire to lock yourself in a room with a good book and a box of chocolate (okay, that one may be unique to me).

What are your indications that you're no longer operating at optimum stress levels?

Make a list and start watching for your stress signs. You can also keep track throughout the day, ranking your stress levels from one to ten and noticing what caused them to change. Chances are that you're living with many signs of stress overload right now—and now is the time to make a change, before you begin to experience even more physical and mental health impacts of being stressed out.

Stress is like any illness: if we can catch it early, we can reduce the negative impacts.

Unfortunately, many people let their stress pile up until they end up burned out and exhausted. There are negative consequences of ignoring your stress, including major health issues like relationship breakdown, job loss, diabetes, heart disease, and obesity.[2]

We live in a culture that values powering through and pushing ourselves beyond reasonable limits. We seem to think that working ourselves to the point of severe stress and potential physical and mental health problems shows great dedication and loyalty. That's old thinking.

What shows great dedication and loyalty, to your employer and to your family and friends, is taking really good care of yourself so you can maintain a highly productive, positive, and engaged presence at home and at work.

When we are relaxed and healthy, we are far more creative, productive, and pleasant people. Ask yourself the following questions to help you switch your perspective on stress:

- What are the signs that I'm highly stressed and powering through?
- How effective am I at work when I'm powering through rather than taking some time to recharge?
- What am I like at home when I'm powering through rather than taking some time to recharge?
- How have I taken care of myself during stressful times in the past?
- What are three simple actions I can take to reduce my stress?

Let's stop powering through and, instead, find ways to recharge and take care of ourselves in order to bring life back to optimum stress levels. As you'll learn in the next chapter, when we take the time to recharge, we are actually more productive.

Being stressed out doesn't help us get more work done or be a better employee. Taking time to care for ourselves does. What are the little actions you could take today to reduce your stress and bring it back to optimum stress levels?

It might be as simple as leaving work on time, actually taking a lunch break, asking a friend or family member to help you out in the evenings or on the weekends, or making time to go for a walk during your workday.

Being proactive in managing our stress is the best way to serve our employers, our families, our friends, and ourselves.

QUESTION YOUR PRIORITIES

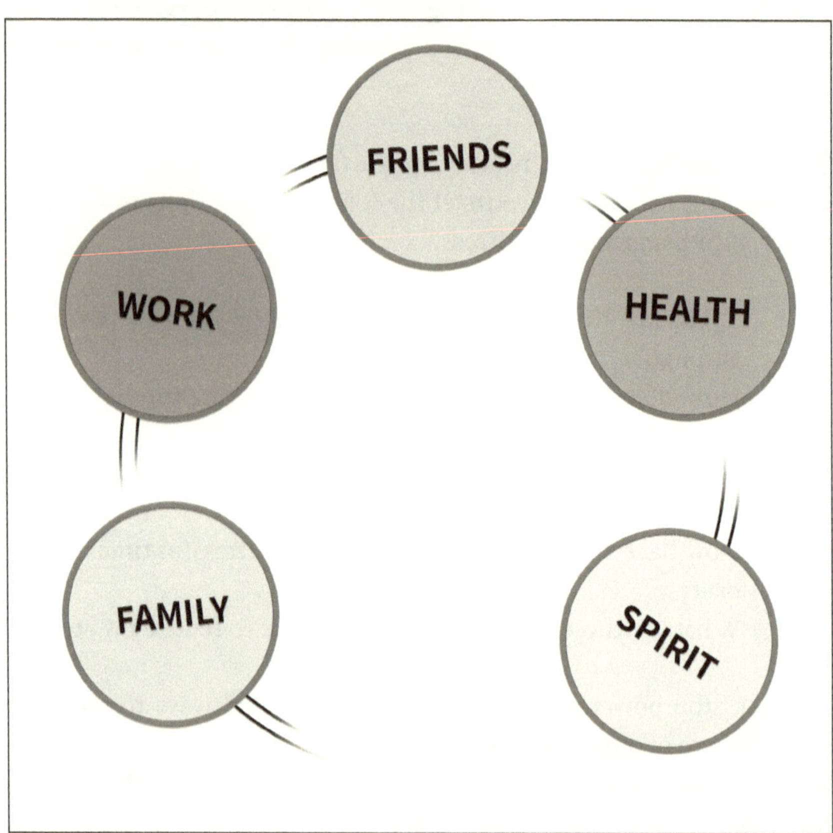

Some of you may have heard the analogy that we are all juggling five balls in life. Four of these balls are fragile. They will break if we drop them. Only one of them is rubber. It will bounce. Which ball do you think is rubber?

It's work.

That sucker will bounce. You can drop work and pick it back up again. Even if you get fired, you can find another job.

This might seem like a strange thing to say in a book focused on work, but one of the most important things we can do to reduce our stress is to put work in perspective with the rest of our lives.

Looking at the big picture of our lives not only reduces our work stress, but it helps us prioritize what matters most to us. My husband often gets stressed about work and he can't sleep. When he finds his mind buzzing with all of his stressors, he goes and sits in our kids' room for a few minutes watching them sleep. This simple act grounds him and reminds him of what is most important. With that perspective, his work stressors don't seem like such a big deal, and he lets them slip out of his mind, which enables him to sleep.

As a wise friend of mine once told me when he was explaining how he prioritized family and work, "There are plenty of jobs, but I only have one family."

A few years ago, I stopped by to visit some clients that I hadn't seen in a while. One of the guys had been off for six months because he'd had cancer. He had the poster of the five balls on his office wall, and it struck me more powerfully than it ever had.

He told me he was thrilled to be back at work, but he'd stopped working like a lunatic because he knew that his health, his kids, his relationships, and his life were way too important to sacrifice to his job.

Even though work is the bounciest ball out there, we often treat it as the most important ball. We miss our children's science fairs, concerts, and soccer games; our friends' dinner parties and birthdays; our parents' visits; and a million special moments that we can never get back because our culture values work over everything else.

Our work is not more important than our health, our relationships, and our lives. I promise you that.

Many of you, like me, have learned the hard way what's most important. I was lucky in many ways, because when I was eleven years old, my mother had stage four cancer. This might not sound very lucky, but hear me out. She was given a 10 percent chance of survival. She beat the odds by telling the doctors to double the recommended dose of radiation. She refused to die then, but since that time, I sensed my mother was living on borrowed time. That made me lucky because I took every opportunity to spend time with her; I knew our time was precious. When she got Alzheimer's nineteen years later, I had no regrets. I'd made my relationship with her a priority throughout my life. We'd lived in different countries and had our own lives, but we spoke every week on the phone, and I visited her in Mexico at least two or three times a year.

My mother visited me in Vancouver every summer and we spent quality time together—we talked and laughed and shared our favorite books and went for slow walks. Whenever she needed me, I was there. Because I suspected and feared that she would not be with us until the ripe old age of eighty-three, as her mother had been. I was right. She was fifty-nine when she died.

We don't have to wait for big wake-up calls like a personal health crisis or an ailing family member to make a change. We can find perspective in the little moments.

What gives you perspective in your life?

Losing my mother changed me. Our journey through Alzheimer's changed my perspective on life. One of the main reasons I chose the slightly scary path of consulting (no benefits, no holidays, no sick days, and no certainty of a paycheck) is that it gives me the flexibility to spend more time with my kids. Because no matter how much satisfaction my work gives me, I know it's not the most important thing I do in the world. The most important task I have in this world is to love my people and to show them that love by spending time with them, by being there when they need me, and by being fully present.

For those of you who tend to torture yourselves with guilt about how much more time you spend at work than with your kids, don't. Research has shown that when it comes to time with our kids, quality time (being fully present and engaged with them rather than being on our phones or distracted in some other way) is far more important than quantity: "Building relationships, seizing quality moments of connection, not quantity . . . is what emerging research is showing to be most important for both parent and child well-being."[3]

And get this: when we are stressed out, it's really bad for our kids. The first large-scale longitudinal study of parent time "found one key instance when parent time can be particularly harmful to children. That's when parents, mothers in particular, are stressed, sleep-deprived, guilty and anxious."[4]

Of course, it's mothers in particular. Thanks for the added pressure there. Why is it always the mother?! If there was ever a reason to get your stress under control (perhaps by taking a night away from your kids), this is it.

I still remember the first weekend I took away from my kids—my daughter was ten months old; my son was almost three years old. A friend and I booked a weekend at an Airbnb so we could write and have uninterrupted conversations (something that hadn't happened in almost three years). I left home feeling frazzled, drained, and irritable. I returned home feeling relaxed and happy, and more like myself than I'd felt in months. And something amazing happened. I really, really loved my kids when I got home. I was so happy to be with them. I was the best mom ever, for at least two days. Then, you know, life happened. I can't recommend a weekend away enough for reminding you how awesome it is to have kids. Or to have parents. Or needy friends. Or a demanding job. Or whatever wonderful but challenging thing you have in your life that both fills you and drains you. Give yourself some time to take care of all the five balls in your life, not just work.

PUTTING WORK IN ITS PLACE

For me, a good life includes work. I love work. I'm not suggesting you give up your job or turn into a total slacker. I'm just suggesting you question where it fits in your list of priorities. I feel so grateful to be able to work, both for the income and for the satisfaction and growth it provides. Work is my happy place, where I feel competent and capable (unlike parenting and writing, where I often feel like I'm stumbling around in the dark, hitting my shins on things, and trying not to swear). When I'm working, I'm giving and growing and learning, and that makes me incredibly happy. Yet, when I look back on those years when my mom was sick, I'm far prouder of the daughter I was to her than I am of the award-winning Mental Illness First Aid program I built.

Work is important and satisfying and rewarding and necessary, but do not fool yourself into believing it deserves all of you. You have to hold back some of yourself for your family, your friends, and yourself. We can't be with our loved ones in every instance that they need us, but we have to make the effort to be there when it feels important to us.

- Who are the people in your life that are most important to you?
- What little adjustments can you make to free up a bit of time and space so you can spend more time with them?

We can't do it all, and we have to make choices between the demands of our personal lives and the demands of our work lives. It's unrealistic to expect that we can choose the demands of our personal lives every time. That's reality, and there's no reason to feel guilty about it, unless you know you aren't living by your own values and doing what feels right for you; in that case, you need to take action and make different choices.

When we look back on our lives, we will value the love we gave and the relationships we had as our greatest treasures and as our greatest contributions to the world. Hopefully, some of those wonderful relationships and some of that sense of contribution will have happened at work, but work has to stop being our top and, often, our only prior-ity. Clarifying our priorities helps us become more effective at work as well. Committing to get home by five to have dinner with our family and knowing we aren't going to work at night pushes us to work more efficiently during the day. You'll get plenty of tools to increase your productivity in Chapter Eleven to make sure you can get all your work done and relax in the evenings.

RELAXING OUR EXPECTATIONS

Most of us live with more demands and pressures than ever, and it's impossible to live up to all the expectations we have of ourselves. So, let's give up on them. Let's have an expectation revolution! My goal for this year is to be content. I'm going on an expectation moratorium. This year, I'm planning to just relax and appreciate my life. Sure, I want to do some great work and writing along the way, but I'm tired of all the pressure and expectations I put on myself. It's freeing to be okay with being a decent parent, a good consultant, a good-enough writer. I'm letting go of striving for excellence and instead enjoying competence. This shift in mindset has significantly reduced my stress.

How about you?

- What are the unrealistic expectations you put on yourself?
- How can you lighten the load a little?
- Are there a few expectations you can let go of (particularly ones that don't belong to you, but to others)?

Maybe you don't want to throw all your expectations away as I have. Maybe that's too radical a step. Or maybe you do. At the bare minimum, many of us could benefit from relaxing our expectations of ourselves.

Whatever you choose, if you can find a way to take just a little bit of that self-induced pressure off of yourself, I think you'll find your stress levels slip down a few notches. Just go with the flow, appreciate and enjoy your work and your life and see what happens.

You'll still get a lot accomplished, maybe even more than when you were putting all that pressure on yourself. So far, I've managed to continue to deliver great work and be more relaxed in the process.

KEEP YOUR STRESSORS IN PERSPECTIVE

To keep my current stress in perspective, all I need to do is to look back. I've had some very stressful times, as I'm sure you have. Sometimes recognizing how manageable and simple your stressors are now, in contrast to what you've faced in the past, can help reframe your relationship with your current challenges. It's also an excellent reminder that you have the resources and resilience to get through difficult times.

My husband also went through a heartbreaking time a few decades ago. He was working as an engineer at a company that designed and installed industrial boilers. He was taking time off to be with his father, who had just had an aneurysm, when his sister suddenly became ill and died within a few weeks. It was his first job after graduating university; he had only been working there a matter of months; and he was working on large proposals with short deadlines. When he spoke to his boss to express his concern about all the time he'd had to take off from work, his boss responded by saying, "It's only boilers."

This man had perspective. He knew what was most important in life, and it wasn't work. It was being with the people you love when they need you. Time is precious, and it becomes more precious in crisis. I'm so grateful that my husband's boss had the wisdom to offer him this perspective because it gave him the freedom to spend time with his family when they needed him.

When I'm feeling stressed about some of the less important things in life, I remind myself "It's only boilers."

Work can cause me a lot of stress when I allow it to, but when I switch my focus to the fact that everyone in my family is healthy and doing well, I remember how minor the work stress is in the grand scheme of things.

In fact, all the stressors I have currently are the result of good things: my husband travels because he has an interesting job that he loves. I've always wanted kids, and now I get the gift of their brilliant stubborn little spirits; when I am feeling frustrated, I remind myself of how sad I would be if I didn't have them in my life. My job is stressful because I'm busy, and I have so many wonderful clients and so much interesting work. I have so many stressors to be grateful for—it's all about perspective.

What are some of the stressors that you're grateful to have in your life?

YOU ARE NOT YOUR WORK

Part of why work becomes such a priority for us is that in our culture, our success and status are tied to work. I taught English in South Korea for a year, and I was always surprised by the first questions people would ask me: "How old are you?" and "Are you married?" Those were the questions used in that culture to determine status. Here in North America, we ask: "What do you do for a living?" because we believe that helps us determine another person's character and status. It doesn't, any more than age or marriage does. But it illustrates what we value in our culture and how we define ourselves.

Work is a significant and important part of our identities, but it is not who we are. A lifetime ago I was a cashier, a wilderness guide, a receptionist; now I'm a leadership coach and consultant. Maybe in another decade, I'll be a nanny or a clerk in a bookstore or a bestselling author. Not one of these jobs, or even the collective of them all, defines me. Who we are is far bigger than the work we do. When we remember this, it can help us relax and keep our work in perspective.

MAKE TIME FOR YOURSELF

Think about the five balls you are juggling: work, friends, health, spirit, family. Work is not who you are. Spirit is who you are. Some people feel uncomfortable with the word *spirit*. I think of it as the essence of who you are. What makes you happy? What fills you up? For each of us there will be a different answer. For me, a night of dancing makes me happy; for my husband, that would be his worst nightmare.

- How about you? What fills your tank?
- List three things that recharge you.
- Think about three things that make you happy.
- Choose one of these things to schedule into your next week.

Do you long to go to yoga, sleep in on a Sunday morning, savor a sweet, milky cup of tea, share a night laughing with friends, do a crossword, disappear into a good book, dance in your living room? That's clearly my list—what's yours? Do you want to go for a hike, build a model airplane, go to a chess tournament? What quirky wonderful loves do you have that make you essentially you?

What would happen if you left work just fifteen minutes early or took an actual lunch break and spent a bit of time each day filling up your tank? Research has found that the best way to increase our productivity and decrease our stress is to focus on our happiness—we'll cover this in more detail in the next chapter.

We tend to put ourselves last on the list, but if we don't prioritize ourselves—our spirit and our health—we are of no use to anyone else.

After you've determined what's most important to you, start creating a life that reflects that. If you love to run and you haven't run in years, find a way to start running again. Run so much that your kid tells you that your last name should be Runner. Go for it. You'll be happier, less stressed, and more productive.

5 BY 5 RULE

If it's not going to matter in 5 years, don't spend more than 5 minutes being upset by it.

Do you ever think back to something that you were losing sleep over a few months or years ago and wonder why it was such a big deal? Do you remember the H1N1 virus from years ago? It was the flu that was going to kill us all. When H1N1 was a threat, I had a job developing educational resources for health-care providers.

I had to cancel my vacation plans to design and deliver province-wide training on how to prevent the spread of H1N1 in health-care providers. As you can imagine, there was serious pressure and a lot of late nights and working weekends.

Everyone around me was highly stressed, not just by the workload but the worry that the we were all going to be taken out by the deadly flu. It was a super stressful time but now whenever we look back on it, my husband and I laugh about the H1N1 ridiculousness. This illustrates that at some point in the future, a person or situation that, at the time, feels like it might break you will become just a fuzzy memory. Think back to your life five years ago. Can you remember what was stressing you out then?

Sometimes we work ourselves up into such a frenzy that we lose perspective. The little things grow large and terrible in our minds. If we catch ourselves, we can recognize that whatever is stressing us out is really not that big a deal and let it go. That's how we reduce our stress.

When we have true perspective and know what's important to us, we can change our response to seemingly stressful events from total stress cadet to Zen Buddhist in training.

If you're having trouble keeping your stress in perspective, try the following:

- Think back to a more stressful time in your life. Let yourself feel how much easier your current stressors are.
- Notice what's working well in your life that wasn't working well before.
- Consider someone else's stressful life (even if you don't know the person. Perhaps you have only heard or read their story). Notice how good your life is in contrast.
- Focus on what you have to be grateful for and the resources and resilience you have to help you get through whatever you are facing.

When we have perspective, we can change how we respond to stress. I'm not saying that I don't ever get stressed out. I do. But when I get a little perspective, it significantly reduces my stress.

CHANGE YOUR STRESS RESPONSE

Stress is a natural response to challenges; it's hardwired into us. We are evolutionarily predisposed to perceive and manage threats. This is how we, as a species, have survived. It's natural that we are still responding in a way that is hardwired into our brains. But it doesn't help us the way it once did. There are no longer lions chasing us, there's just the annoying person we have to work with every day. If we have a huge stress response to our annoying coworker, we're setting ourselves up for unnecessary angst. And for what? That person's not worth it.

We all have challenges, and we all have stress in our lives. That's reality. Some of us have way more stress in our lives than others could even imagine and are able to handle it, while others have minimal stress but react strongly to it. Everyone has a different optimum stress level. Instead of judging others for their stress responses, focus on your own stress response and consider ways that you can respond differently.

There will be many life events that are beyond our control and the only power we have in any situation is choosing how we respond to it. We could get sick, people we love might get hurt or die, we might lose jobs and relationships, and, at times, we may even lose our own way. Life can be heartbreaking.

However, we always have a choice about how we respond to our challenges, and we can use that choice to respond in healthy ways.

Even if you are going through the most stressful time of your life, remind yourself of all the other stressful times that you have come through and all the resources you have to get you through this time. You're tough. You'll make it. During the impossible times, we have to be compassionate with ourselves and prioritize taking care of ourselves, so we can cope with all our stress.

We choose our response to everything. Often, our response to stressors becomes so hardwired that we don't recognize it as a choice. The beauty of becoming more self-aware is that we can make a different choice about how we respond to our challenges. We can recognize our hardwired stress response, take a few deep breaths and calm down, reminding ourselves that there are no lions chasing us. Or we can throw up our hands, freak out, and run around telling everyone about how terrible things are. Or we can focus on what we can do about the situation, take action, then move on, and let it go. That's stress-reducing behavior.

We always have a choice in how we respond, and we'd be wise to use it. Remember that research "found that it wasn't the number of stressful events but how a person perceived their stress and then reacted to it emotionally that was associated with increased risk for heart disease and death."[5] Our stress response is killing us. This is why it's so important that we bypass our hardwired stress response and calm the heck down.

I had a life-changing shift in perspective about how to manage stress when I was eighteen. I was working at a summer camp, leading wilderness camping trips in northern Saskatchewan. This was a long time before cell phones existed. We took groups of kids into the wilderness for three to fourteen days and had no way of communicating with the outside world.

I worked for Gary, a very calm twenty-three-year-old. One day, I was at the base camp in the Qu'Appelle Valley coordinating the local out-trips. At the time, two counsellors and fourteen kids, aged nine to twelve, were out on a three-night canoe trip. The forecast came in for a serious storm: lightning, thunder, torrential winds, and rain; we needed to get the kids off the lake. Luckily, we knew where their campsites were and when they were expected to reach each site. Early that morning when we heard the forecast on the radio, Gary and I set off in the clunky old green camp pickup truck. We drove to the campsite that the campers should have been staying at the night before. There was no sign of the canoes or the kids.

The winds whipped up, and the rain started coming down; lightning struck the lake repeatedly, and my panic levels started rising. We drove along the lake towards the campsite that they should have headed to. No sign of them. I went into full-blown panic. Every *what if* imaginable came to mind. I have a very vivid imagination and, when I was in my teens, I was prone to drama. I worked myself up into quite a state, imagining attending the funerals of those children, facing their devastated parents.

Gary spoke in a steady voice, "We'll find them. They're fine. The counsellors are smart. They got off the lake somewhere. Panicking isn't going to help. Now let's think, and let's find them." He was right. Stressing out wasn't helping. Panicking was even worse. His calm manner helped me get grounded and focus.

We talked over the possible options, looked at maps, and then drove slowly along the road, keeping our eyes peeled for the canoes along the shore. I caught a flash of silver as we drove and nearly jumped out of my seat. Gary pulled the truck over to the side of the highway. We crashed our way down through the scrubby bushes to a small, protected area and saw that the boats had pulled into a little stretch of beach. The kids were huddled under a tarp that the counsellors had set up. They were cold and wet, but they were okay. We drove them back to the camp and everything was fine. Absolutely fine.

From that moment forward, I worked to respond differently to stressful situations. Whenever I felt my high-stress response kicking in, I asked myself, "What would Gary do?" I knew that staying calm would result in the best possible outcome. Eventually, I no longer needed to ask myself what Gary would do because responding to stressful situations with a calm manner became my natural response.

This ability to remain calm and think rationally about solutions in times of stress has served me incredibly well over the years. I've been able to maintain my calm during terrifying trips to the hospital with various family members as well as the highly stressful work situations that arise when you are a consultant who is called in to deal with difficult workplace dynamics.

We can't kick into high-stress response every time something difficult or upsetting happens. The physical and mental health impacts of being regularly and highly stressed out are far more dangerous to us than any of the events that we are responding to.

Our high-stress response is also destroying our productivity. Neuroscientist David Rock explains that "the threat response is both mentally taxing and deadly to the productivity of a person—or an organization. Because this response uses up oxygen and glucose from the blood, they are diverted from other parts of the brain, including the working memory function, which processes new information and ideas. This impairs analytic thinking, creative insight, and problem solving; in other words, just when people most need their sophisticated mental capabilities, the brain's internal resources are taken away from them."[6]

We don't think as clearly when we are in high-stress mode, so finding our calm in the midst of chaos is the best way to get through whatever is happening. An easy way to calm ourselves down in the moment is to take long, slow, deep breaths.

Take a moment to think about the ways that you respond to stressful events.

- Think of a time when you had a high-stress response. How could you respond differently today?

- List three things that help you maintain your calm.
- List three things you do that increase your stress response.
- What is one replacement response that you can implement the next time you feel yourself getting highly stressed (take three deep breaths, laugh, let it roll off you, remind yourself "It's only boilers," ask yourself the personal responsibility questions)?
- Is there anyone in your life who is always calm and steady that you can learn from?

DON'T TAKE THINGS PERSONALLY

Believe it or not, most of the things that happen at work aren't about you. There are big organizational systems at play that impact many elements of your workplace, but even when they affect you, they are very rarely about you.

I've worked with an alarming number of people over my career who think that management sits in a room and thinks up ways to make their lives miserable. They really do believe this. And I've worked with their managers, so I know that while they may not always have the best ideas, they aren't out to get people. I've never heard any manager say, "Let's introduce this scheduling change because that is just going to destroy Brian's life. He's never going to see his wife or kids and that'll make him miserable. It'll be awesome," while giggling gleefully and rubbing their hands together.

It just doesn't work that way. You aren't the star of anyone's show but your own. In addition to organizational issues, we often take other people's behavior—what they say and do—personally. Don't.

Guaranteed, 90 percent of the time it's not about you, it's about them.

I can't tell you the number of people I see caught up in the drama of interpersonal conflict at work. They waste countless hours, days, and sometimes even months or years of their lives obsessing about other people and how they are behaving. The great irony is that if they spent half as much time taking personal responsibility by thinking about their own work or how to improve themselves, they would be wildly powerful and productive.

If you find yourself in conflict with a coworker, think carefully and consider if there's anything you might have done to contribute to the situation or dynamic. Identify what you've done (if anything), do something to rectify the situation, then let it go.

If the situation escalates, use the feedback model to tell the person about the action and impact of their behavior, and discuss a way to work it out. A great way to start this conversation is: "I know I might be totally off-base here . . ." or: "I'm really confused about what's going on, and rather than make up stories in my head, I thought I'd come talk to you."

I've mediated so many workplace conflicts because people were taking things personally. I once worked with a team that was in conflict because one of the team members was quite controlling, and the manager did nothing to prevent it. The controlling coworker, let's call her Joan, was a perfectionist and did most tasks herself because she believed no one else could possibly do them to the same standard that she did.

How do you think Joan's coworkers responded? Did they say, "Oh, that's just Joan, being a perfectionist, nothing to do with me."? No. They said, "She doesn't trust me," and, "She's holding a grudge from that time three years ago when I screwed up that project," and, "She thinks my work is inferior," and, "I think she's trying to get me fired." In short, they made up stories—stories in which they were the main character. How many of us do that? We are never the main character in another person's story; they are.

Don't get caught up in another person's drama. It doesn't serve you, it doesn't serve them, and it doesn't serve the work. Recognize that people engage in a lot of unhealthy behaviors, especially when they are unhappy. Most of the time, it's not about you.

Your job is to figure out how you can work with a difficult person and still be professional and productive. You don't have to be best friends; you just want to minimize the amount of stress they cause you. Be the bigger person. Use the feedback model, find ways to change your stress response, and don't get caught up in the drama. You'll find that when you change the way you engage with the person, the dynamics will shift.

VIEW DIFFICULT PEOPLE AS TEACHERS

There are often people who are incredibly difficult to work with in our workplaces. If we can switch our perspective and start considering these people our teachers, we'll react less strongly to them. Sometimes, they have a specific lesson for us. Other times, the lesson is simply to learn not to engage in the drama and difficulty they are creating.

Is there someone at work who you could start considering a teacher instead of a jerk?

What would it feel like to look for the lessons you can learn from this person, rather than raging about them?

Think of one person who was a really difficult person in your past, what lessons were you able to learn from interacting with them?

If you can switch your perspective, you'll often be amazed at all the ways this person is legitimately teaching you to engage differently. It can transform your relationship with them to view them as someone to learn from rather than someone to run from. Instead of cringing when we see them walking towards us, we can smile and think, *Here comes my teacher, I wonder what I'll learn today.*

Maybe you'll learn to take a deep breath and let things roll off you, or maybe you'll learn to be compassionate or to stand up for yourself. When we can look for the learning in the situation rather than the stress, we'll find it.

One difficult person I've worked with recently has taught me that I need to be very clear and assertive regarding my boundaries. There is always something to be learned from the challenges we experience: it might be how we want to behave, think, or engage differently.

Take a minute to think back on a difficult interaction you've had recently and identify what you learned from it. Who are some of your best teachers? What might change in your relationship if you started viewing them as teachers? Often when we shift our perspective, we can engage with them with a more lighthearted and calm perspective.

I had a client who was terrified of conflict while his manager thrived on creating it. He had no idea how to deal with his manager, and he spent every day feeling anxious and upset. His productivity was dropping, his stress was through the roof, and he knew he needed help.

When he told me all the stories about his manager, I laughed and said, "I think you're getting a PhD in how to deal with conflict."

He was able to laugh too, and he recognized that it was time he learned these particular skills. "Well, I kind of need it. I let people run all over me, not just at work but at home too."

That perspective made for a very different approach. By viewing the situation as a learning opportunity, my client was able to learn some tools and find the courage to have the difficult conversations he needed to have with his manager.

It wasn't easy, but it was a lot easier than spending all day feeling upset and angry at another person who he had no control over. He learned strategies that made him better at handling conflict, not only with his manager but in other work and life situations. He grew, where before he had been withering. After a few months of practicing all his new skills, he reported with delight, "I'm totally comfortable with conflict now. Yesterday my manager pulled some of his BS, and I just calmly looked at him and said, 'I disagree with you.' I had no butterflies, I just did it. It didn't even feel scary. I'm good with conflict in a way I never thought I'd be. I thought I'd go to my grave having spent too much of my life giving up what I wanted so I could avoid conflict. Now I don't have to!"

I'm not a high-fiver by nature, but we high-fived that day.

ACCEPT REALITY

Often much of our stress comes not from the event itself but from our feeling that it shouldn't have happened. We can waste countless hours and precious energy being upset that something has happened, or is happening, rather than accepting reality. It's reality, it *is* happening. The more time we spend being upset about reality rather than accepting it, the more pointlessly stressed out we are. It's time to access our inner Buddhists and surrender to what is.

I often go into workplace situations where people are not happy to see me. I mean really, how many of you are thrilled to do some team building or to be sent to a leadership class? When I accept the reality that people don't want to be there, I can relax and meet them with acceptance, rather than trying to convince them how worthwhile it will be to spend time with me.

This ability to surrender to the reality of the situation has served me really well, and it's enabled me to connect with people in a way that I otherwise wouldn't have. I once went into an organization that had a reputation for having some difficult staff to deliver a five-day leadership program that all the staff had been mandated to attend.

In the introductions, one woman said, "I did this course three years ago, but I must have failed because they sent me back." Another guy said, "I have twelve projects right now, and I'm behind on all of them. But I'm stuck here for the next five days." That was the tone of almost all the introductions. People were not happy to be there.

I accepted that reality and surrendered to it. After thirty people had introduced themselves, expressing various levels of dissatisfaction with having to spend five valuable days doing this leadership crap, I responded by saying, "I get it. You don't want to be here and it's frustrating, especially when you have so much work to do. But you're stuck here, so if you're willing to make the most of the time and give me your full energy and attention, I promise I'll make it the most valuable class you've ever attended."

At the end of those five days, the entire class gave me a thank-you card. Some of those students still e-mail me. In that situation and many others, I've had far more success by accepting reality than fighting against it.

Is there a situation that you can think of where you've been fighting against reality?

How much less stress would you have if you accept the reality of the situation?

How much more productive could you be if you accept the reality of the situation?

When we can accept the reality of a situation, we can put our energy into how we're going to deal with it rather than fighting reality.

LEANNE'S DENIAL

Leanne was a midlevel professional in her early thirties who'd just been fired from her job. Leanne had been in the same role for nearly fifteen years, and, although she'd been having difficulties with her new manager, she was utterly shocked that she'd been fired.

Within two minutes of meeting her for the first time, Leanne was raging, "Do you know I had absolutely no idea it was coming? I mean, I knew my manager didn't like me, but come on, you don't just *fire* someone. They should have offered me coaching or told me what the issues were. I can't believe they just up and fired me like that."

"Wow, that sounds tough. So, what's next?"

"You mean other than suing them?!" she laughed bitterly.

"Well, yes. I was thinking along the lines of your next job or where you'd like to go."

"I don't know. Did I tell you my manager had it in for me the minute he started? It was like someone had told him that his mandate was to make my life hell, then fire me. I gave my life to that place; I've been there since my twenties. It was one of my first jobs."

It had been six weeks since she'd been fired, and she was so not ready to move on.

Finally, after at least ten minutes of listening and validating how upset she was, I said, "I can hear how hard this experience has been for you, but it seems like you might be making it a bit harder on yourself."

Her head snapped back as if she'd been slapped. "What do you mean?" she asked, her green eyes fierce.

"What would it feel like to accept the reality that you've been fired?"

She got really quiet. "I guess it would feel better than being angry all the time."

"That's what I mean. It's important to let yourself feel angry and hurt and have a good cry, but then you have to accept reality. You're making this experience harder by being angry about what happened, rather than accepting it. They fired you over a month ago. Do you think maybe it's time to start looking forward instead of backward?"

She glared at me, and I took a sip of my tea and looked calmly back at her. Then she said, "I just need a bit more time to be angry."

"Absolutely. Your choice. Just recognize that it's a choice."

"Give me ten minutes to vent, and then I can start talking about the future."

I smiled, set a timer on my phone and said, "Go for it, really go for it, and, if possible, dig underneath the anger to see what else you might be feeling."

Her eyes immediately welled up with tears. "I'm terrified. My severance package will give me about six months to live on, but what if I never find another job? Or one that pays that well. I never went to university, and I know that to get a job like that today, I'd probably need a degree."

"That sounds really scary," I said. She started to cry. I handed her a tissue. "What else?"

"I'm worried about what everyone will think of me. I was a really good employee for so long. And now that I've been fired, people are going to think I'm an awful employee."

"I can see why you'd be worried about that." I nodded.

"And I'm going to miss my friends. I worked with some of those people for almost twenty years."

"Oh, that must be so hard," I said. She really cried then. I handed her more tissue.

We kept going for another six minutes, she talked about everything she felt—she realized she'd been using her anger to hide her fear and her shame and her sadness. Any kind of loss can bring up grief, and our first reaction to grief is often denial. When Leanne allowed herself to feel all her feelings, not just her anger, she could finally move on.

After the ten minutes were up, we took a break and then came back to our conversation. She started off, "They fired me. I'm mad, and I'm sad, and I'm scared, but I'm not going to sue them. Nothing is going to change. I can't go back and fix things. So, I need to find another job."

I wanted to do a dance of joy! She'd found a way to stop looking back, primarily by acknowledging and validating all of her feelings. Now, we could look forward. We worked together for a few more sessions, and within three months, she was happily employed somewhere new, making friends and using what she'd learned in her previous job.

I meet too many people who spend their days feeling frustrated because they aren't accepting reality. Every day they have the same experiences, and instead of accepting that those experiences are their current reality, they rail against them. I've been there. I think I spent the first three years of my son's life not accepting the reality that the kid didn't sleep through the night. Ever. I just couldn't accept it.

If your boss is a nightmare and you've given them feedback and had a few difficult conversations with no results, you need to accept that they will likely continue to be hard to work for. If the organization you work for is a bureaucratic mess, that is unlikely to change. It's up to you to accept the reality and then make your choices accordingly.

I've seen the impact of stress fall away when people have accepted reality.

I've worked with coaching clients who have completely shifted their response to a stressor after they've accepted it; they've gone from righteous rage to laughter, from being super stressed to being able to shrug their shoulders and refuse to get caught up in the drama of the situation.

I've said to many of my clients, "It's clear that you work in a highly dysfunctional workplace. That's your reality. Now the question is, do you want to stay within that reality, accept it, and find ways to function within the dysfunction? Or, do you want to make a different choice and find a different reality?"

Everyone's answer is different. Some people choose to accept their current reality and put their energy into operating within those circumstances. Others decide they don't want to live with their current reality, and they commit to making a change.

Accepting reality and making the right choice for you is so much healthier and less stressful than being upset and frustrated by what's happening every single day.

CONCLUSION

We will likely have some form of stress in our lives at any given time, so our best strategy is to keep our stressors in perspective. When we can change our stress response, clarify our priorities, and find ways to learn from our challenges, we can significantly reduce the amount of stress we experience. Identify what optimal stress looks like for you, don't take things personally, accept reality, and respond accordingly.

If you let go of the things you have absolutely no control over, avoid the workplace drama, and focus on your choices and responses, you'll be less stressed. Focus on what really matters, take care of yourself, keep your stressors in perspective, and you'll be *Working Well.*

QUESTIONS

1. What is one way that you could change your stress response today, and how would that benefit you?
2. Consider the five balls: Health, Spirit, Work, Family, Friends, which is most important to you?
3. Do your actions reflect your priorities? If not, what is one small change you can make?
4. Who is a good teacher for you? What have you been learning from them?
5. Are there any ways that you aren't accepting reality? What could you do differently?

ACTIONS

- Identify your signs of negative stress.
- Identify and implement a calm replacement response instead of your natural stress response (taking three deep breaths instead of panicking).
- Identify one simple action you can take when you notice you've slipped from optimum stress to negative stress (leave work on time, set boundaries, spend less time on your phone, identify and manage your priorities, etc.).
- Take action to change your perspective or reshuffle your priorities as needed.

Chapter Five

Take Care of Yourself

"Caring for myself is not self-indulgence, it is self-preservation, and that is an act of political warfare."

—Audre Lorde

Prioritizing self-care is a fundamental aspect of reducing your workplace stress. If you don't take care of yourself, you're going down. That's the unfortunate reality. You need to look after your physical, emotional, and mental health. If you can't do it for yourself, do it for the people who care about you and depend on you: your kids, your friends, your family, and your coworkers.

I have seen stress turn to burnout and burnout turn to serious mental or physical health conditions too many times. I don't want that to happen to another person. Please take care of yourself. If you don't, something will give and that something will be you. And when you give, everything else around you will fall apart. I don't care how passionate you are about your work or how dedicated you are to your family; you are not doing anyone any favors by not looking after yourself.

When you don't take care of yourself, you can't take care of anyone or anything else. In fact, other people will have to start taking care of you.

If you get sick, you'll spend even more time trying to heal than you would have spent taking care of yourself in the first place.

Save the people who care about you from the heartbreak and burden of seeing you suffer. Lead by example and save them from following in your footsteps. The more of us who start setting good life-work boundaries and taking care of ourselves, the more common it will become.

RESPONDING TO OVERWHELMING DEMANDS

It's not easy to take care of ourselves with all the demands on us. For those of us who have children, the demands of parenting have grown exponentially. The expectation to volunteer at school and sport events and help our children with complicated science fair experiments and homework, in addition to managing their extracurricular lives, setting up their play dates, and scheduling their after-school activities while making sure they are not *too* scheduled, is overwhelming. Not to mention making their lunches. Don't even get me started on that. Those lunches are the bane of my existence.

For those of us with aging parents, there are appointments to take them to, plans to make for an uncertain future, and financial stressors and obligations. In some situations, we have to step in and manage our parents' care and their lives when they are no longer capable. Our families can be filled with stressors that we have no control over.

And our workplaces are putting more demands on us than ever. Many of us live in fear of downsizing, and we're all overwhelmed by e-mail and the expectation to be available at all hours. Everyone I know has been told they need to do more with less. Between life and work stressors, it's no wonder that so many people are struggling to manage everything on their plates.

Then there's our phones—the gateway to working twenty-four hours a day. The pressure never ends.

Most people's lives remind me of when I was a kid and I used to play *Asteroids* on Atari. It was a very simple game in which your only goal was to shoot down as many asteroids as you could before they landed on you. As the game progressed, the asteroids came faster and faster.

We are being bombarded by asteroids that are coming at us much faster than we can shoot them down. Most of us ignore the toll the effort is taking and just keep powering through, shooting as many asteroids as we can and hoping we won't get clobbered. This is not sustainable. We need to slow down, realize the impacts of all this stress on us, and make different choices in our lives.

I learned the importance of self-care during those long years of my mother's illness. Alzheimer's is a devastating and demanding disease. The landscape and needs are constantly shifting, and I was always running to catch up to the next crisis. If I hadn't taken care of myself, I wouldn't have been able to care for my mother.

Now that I'm insanely busy with work and parenting, it's easy to forget how important it is to take care of myself. I used to go for weeks without exercise or making time to see friends. Then I'd notice how cranky I was getting and plan a night out with friends.

Lately I've been much better at scheduling self-care into my life because of all the research that shows that self-care not only makes us happier and healthier, it also makes us more productive.

Some of the ways I've scheduled self-care into my life include planning walking dates with friends, dinners out with my husband, and scheduling a weekly yoga class. When we schedule it into our lives, self-care happens.

When I take care of myself, I'm happier. Everyone benefits. I show up to my relationships as a far better version of myself than when I'm overwhelmed and stressed out.

- What do you need to start doing to take care of yourself?
- What is one small action you can you take to nurture yourself today?
- How does taking care of yourself improve your relationships?

- How does taking care of yourself improve your work?
- How can you start scheduling self-care in your week the way you plan everything else?

....

When we take care of ourselves, we are *Working Well.* We can be the absolute best employee and give our all at work because we have recharged and looked after ourselves. We can be loving and present parents, spouses, children, and friends because we have filled ourselves up, so we have enough energy, love, and attention to give others.

....

When we aren't taking care of ourselves, our batteries get drained—we behave just the way our phones and computers do when they're drained. There are glitches, things go more slowly, tasks that should feel easy feel impossible. Just like our phones and computers, we need to switch off, disconnect and take a break.

GET HAPPIER

There is excellent research that makes a compelling case for taking care of ourselves and focusing on our own happiness. Shawn Achor, Harvard researcher and author of *The Happiness Advantage*, found that happier people experience:

- 23 percent reduction in stress
- 31 percent increase in productivity
- 39 percent better health
- 34 percent more positive social interaction

Further, he observes that "data abounds showing that happy workers have higher levels of productivity, produce higher sales, perform better in leadership positions, and receive higher performance ratings and higher pay."[1]

If you need a reason to prioritize your happiness, this is it. When we are happy, we naturally have better relationships, our health improves, our stress decreases, and our productivity increases.

Often, the way we go about finding happiness is completely backwards. Most of us see happiness as the result of achieving a specific goal. We think, *Once I get a new job, finish this project, find the perfect partner, get in better shape, then I'll be happier.*

I've certainly fallen into this trap, and I'm pretty sure I'm not alone. We get caught up in believing that if we can just achieve a goal, figure out a problem, or deal with a stressor, we will be happier. But it turns out, that's backwards. If we choose to be happy first, we're more likely to succeed. If we can find a sense of happiness within us that isn't dependent on external circumstances, everything flows more smoothly.

Achor's research found that:

> happiness fuels success, not the other way around. Your brain works significantly better at positive than at negative, neutral, or stressed. Every single business and educational outcome improves when we start at positive rather than waiting for a future success. Sales improve 37% cross-industry, productivity by 31%; you're 40% more likely to receive a promotion, and nearly ten times more engaged at work; you live longer, get better grades, your symptoms are less acute, and much more.[2]

Happy brains deliver amazing outcomes. But here's the tricky part: research has found if we pursue happiness, we become less happy.

What? The research says we should find ways to be happy, but we shouldn't try too hard at it? Pretty much. Happiness is like that quintessential butterfly. You've just got to sit there and let it land on you.

I read *The Happiness Advantage* in November of last year and was amazed to learn about all the positive impacts happiness could have on my life. When I met with my goals group in January, I chose the goal of being happier. No one was very pleased with me setting this goal. It was too vague; it would be hard to measure; it was not at all what a proper goal should look like. I persevered and stuck with my nebulous goal of happiness. The year 2018 is over, and the results are in.

I have a much closer relationship with my husband—we prioritized spending more time together, and that has been awesome. I'm really enjoying my time with my kids—I feel more relaxed with them, and we're having more fun together (until I ask them to clean up their rooms). I wrote two books this year. I had at least two new clients through referral every month. I earned fifteen percent more this year than the previous one. I took a total of ten weeks off, worked four-day weeks, and I have accomplished far more than I did in previous years when I was working all the time. When you look at those results, it seems pretty clear that focusing on your happiness will be the best productivity tool you ever use.

I didn't know about the research that says if you turn happiness into a goal, you put too much pressure on yourself and your time, which means you don't feel as happy. I treated this project like every other project in my life and put way too much pressure on myself. I had moments of being happier, but they didn't happen when I was planning out my weekly happiness activities (date with husband, visit with friend, yoga at least twice a week, take kids somewhere fun, and so on).

My happiest moments were when I just relaxed and let go—when I took a true vacation and didn't try to accomplish a damn thing and was really present in the moment, when I laughed with friends, lay down at the end of a hard yoga class, had a client tell me that I was a miracle worker, watched my kids dress up and be goofy. When I just relaxed and took in what was happening in the moment, I was genuinely happier than when I tried hard to be happier.

I'm about to give you a whole bunch of fantastic research-proven strategies to get happier, but please learn from my mistakes. Don't make happiness your goal, instead let it be your way of life.

What's so amazing is that the choice to be happy is all within your control. As Shawn Achor found in his research, "only 10 percent of our long-term happiness is predicted by the external world; 90 percent of our long-term happiness is how our brain processes the external world."[3]

This is why Negative Nancy and Bitter Bob are never happy, not because of their external circumstances but because of their internal worlds. If you're a Negative Nancy or a Bitter Bob, you've got the ability to make a significant change in how you view the world, simply by focusing your attention in different ways. All the research-based strategies in the upcoming section will help you with shifting your mindset.

What are the little things that make you happy in the day-to-day? Often, they are the same things that we do to take care of ourselves.

Think of three things that make you happy and find ways to implement them in your day.

The little things that make me happy almost all revolve around people: having a cuddle with my kids in the morning, sharing a quiet glass of wine after dinner with my husband, working with clients that I love, seeing good friends.

When we can take little actions every day that build up our happiness, we're going to be more relaxed and more productive. We'll have better relationships and more success in every aspect of our lives.

When we spend time with people we enjoy being with, doing activities we love, that's when happiness spontaneously arises.

Hopefully, some of the following strategies will help you remember ways you can let that beautiful butterfly land on your shoulder rather than chasing it.

BUILD POSITIVE RELATIONSHIPS AND SPEND TIME WITH FRIENDS

We intuitively know that spending time with good friends makes us feel happier. After a night of sharing stories and laughter with my friends, my tank is full. Numerous studies have also found this to be the case, including Harvard's longest running study on longevity and well-being that found that friendship was the biggest contributor to living a long and happy life:

"The surprising finding is that our relationships and how happy we are in our relationships has a powerful influence on our health," said Robert Waldinger, director of the study, a psychiatrist at Massachusetts General Hospital and a professor of psychiatry at Harvard Medical School. Close relationships, more than money or fame, are what keep people happy throughout their lives, the study revealed. Those ties protect people from life's discontents, help to delay mental and physical decline, and are better predictors of long and happy lives than social class, IQ, or even genes.[4]

How's that for a reason to book a night out with your friends? Or to build stronger working relationships with your colleagues? Having good relationships at work and at home makes us happier, and that yields amazing results. When our coworkers become our friends, our work lives are not only more pleasant, we are also more productive.

Friends make us happier and healthier. I often feel much better after a walk or even a phone call with a friend. I feel listened to, understood, and I'm often able to laugh about some of the elements of life that have been stressing me out.

The challenge of living such busy, demanding lives is that we aren't making enough time for our friendships. We do far too much socializing through social media and far too little socializing in our living rooms. I once had a client who explained that she was so busy that all she could do to maintain her social life was to spend half an hour every night on Facebook. This horrified me because recent research has found that "the more we use social media, the less happy we seem to be."[5]

So many of us feel too busy to make time for our friends, and we don't prioritize maintaining our friendships. Can you relate to this?

Get off social media and go out with a friend. Please. It'll make you happier. It'll make them happier, and it'll make everyone who deals with both of you happier.

My client and I had a long conversation about what she was denying herself and her friends through focusing her social time on Facebook rather than real-life interactions. She committed to going out with friends one night a month and replacing her social media time with phone calls to friends. After a few months, she felt a marked decrease in her stress levels. She was still insanely busy with too much on her plate, but by putting friendship back on her plate, she was less stressed and happier. This allowed her to manage all of her stressors better.

- How often do you see your friends?
- How do you feel after you see your friends?
- How can you make more time for your friendships?
- What do you need to do to carve out at least one night a month to spend with friends?
- Can you fit in one ten-minute phone call to a friend once per week?
- If you feel you don't have many close friends, what is one action you could take to start developing friendships?

We will talk more about building positive work relationships in Chapter Nine because having friends at work is a key element of increasing our productivity and decreasing our stress. Many of my close friends are people that I met at work.

GET MORE SLEEP

Arianna Huffington explains in her book *Thrive*: "We have all the data now that shows how [sleep deprivation] affects every aspect of our health. This includes everything from a suppressed immune system (it might be why you're always getting a cold), hypertension (less snooze means a harder time processing stress), and obesity (the sleepy crave bad carbs and sugars)."[6] Sleep is crucial to our well-being on so many levels. Yet it's the first thing we give up when we are stressed out.

I know how challenging it can be to get enough sleep. Seven years of parenthood-related sleep deprivation has made me all too aware of the negative impacts of missing out on a full night's rest. An unfortunate reality for many of us is that it's hard to get any more sleep. Some of us are so stressed that it's hard to fall asleep or stay asleep, others work shifts that make it impossible to get consistent sleep, and still others feel that sacrificing sleep is the only way to get everything done. I'm hoping the research will convince you that if there's any way you can do it, it's worthwhile to find ways to get just a few more minutes every night.

Lack of sleep impacts our ability to recognize and manage our emotions.

Travis Bradberry, who researches emotional intelligence, states that "your self-control, attention, and memory are all reduced when you don't get enough—or the right kind—of sleep. Sleep deprivation raises stress hormone levels on its own, even without a stressor present."[7]

Most of us can relate to this. When I don't get enough sleep, I'm looking at the world through dark and desperate glasses. I am far more emotional; I cry at commercials and snap at my husband and kids much more easily than when I'm well rested. How about you?

What's the difference in your behavior when you've missed out on sleep?

Most of us have similar responses to sleep deprivation: we're more irritable and emotional, we can't think as clearly, and we don't function at our best. It's way more challenging to make good choices when you're sleep deprived. A cookie feels like a much better pick-me-up than a walk. Checking e-mail every few minutes feels more manageable than concentrating on work.

In the first year after my son was born, I scraped our car four times. I can't begin to tell you the number of basic tasks that I screwed up at work during my first year as a sleep-deprived working parent. I was grateful for an understanding manager who'd been through a similar experience.

While working on this book, I had a few nights of being up with my daughter when she was sick. When I tried to write the next day, all that came out was drivel and mush. I was wise enough to focus on less mentally taxing work for those few days until I was better rested. We know we don't operate at our best without sleep, yet so many of us give up sleep in the interest of getting more work done. Giving up sleep is not working. We are just damaging our health and decreasing our productivity.

There are entire books and websites devoted to how to get better sleep, and I'm sure you know most of the tips. Just in case you need a reminder, some common strategies include:

- Turn off electronic devices at least an hour before bed (this includes television).
- Keep the bedroom at a cool temperature.
- Go to sleep at the same time every night and wake up at the same time every morning.
- Spend some time outside during daylight hours.
- Limit caffeine late in the day.
- Limit alcohol.
- Exercise early in the day.
- Meditate.
- Listen to a sleep story or guided meditation (found on the apps Headspace, Calm, or Smiling Mind).

I've found that the more I can calm my mind down, either through meditation or getting some perspective on my stressors, the better I sleep. Please think about small actions you can take to get just a little bit more sleep. Doing so will have an incredibly positive impact on every aspect of your life.

- What are some factors you know have positive impacts on your sleep?
- How can you start implementing them into your routine?
- What are the negative impacts on your work and relationships when you don't get enough sleep?

- What habits have you gotten into that negatively impact your sleep?
- What changes do you need to make in your life so you can get more sleep?

If sleep is difficult to come by, I empathize but you've got to find a way to get more sleep. Sleeping less than seven hours a night compromises our immune system, makes us more vulnerable to obesity, diabetes, heart disease and cancer.[8]

Sleeping more will change your entire outlook on life, improve your health and your ability to handle stress and to get more good-quality work done.

GET MORE EXERCISE

This is definitely a case of do what I say, not what I do. Although I will say that after reading all the research on exercise while writing this book, I've been getting more disciplined. I'm now partaking in some form of gentle exercise (yoga, swimming, or walking) at least twice a week; sometimes, I get to three or four times a week. Research has found that exercise is really good for us. Shocker, I know. Yes—it's hard to believe but studies have found that "besides lifting your mood, regular exercise offers other health benefits, such as lowering blood pressure, protecting against heart disease and cancer, and boosting self-esteem."[9]

Obviously, none of this is news to any of us. Some of us, myself included, might have even been in a good rhythm of regular exercise in the past, and we remember how good we felt. But we're busy. Stupidly busy. And exercise doesn't feel fun. It feels like a lot of work.

I'm trying to find ways to make exercise less painful and to build it more naturally into my life. So, I walk. Everywhere I can. I walk when I'm coaching. I walk with my kids. I walk around the block after dinner. Because I enjoy walking. And going for a walk doesn't really feel like exercising.

How about you?

What are some of the physical activities that you enjoy (or, at the very least, don't hate)?

Can you think of simple ways to build them into your day?

Here's some good news for people like me who don't really enjoy feeling like their lungs might explode: "Plenty of research has also shown that moderate exercise tends to be as good or better for longevity than vigorous activities such as running, which can take a toll on the body over time."[10] Bring on the moderate exercise! That I can get on board with.

What are some ways you can create time and motivation to exercise? Here are a few ideas:

- Arrange to meet a friend so you won't bail.
- Make walking or biking a mode of transportation.
- Hire a personal trainer.
- Replace meeting a friend for dinner and drinks with meeting a friend for a walk.
- Combine exercise with something you enjoy (listening to your favorite podcast as you walk).
- "Game-ify" exercising. (My husband and I got into a fun competition to see who got more steps every day using the Health app on our phones. He won almost every day, which just made me walk longer until I finally won.)
- Choose to do a super easy activity that doesn't hurt, and then work your way up to something that challenges you a bit more.
- Set a goal for yourself and give yourself a reward—if you do some form of exercise three times in a week, you get to (fill in the blank with the best reward you can think of).

Here's another reason to exercise: research has found that "typically, people who exercise start eating better and become more productive at work. They smoke less and show more patience with colleagues and family. They use their credit cards less frequently and say they feel less stressed."[11]

Okay, I've inundated you with enough research that tells you what you already know: exercise is good for you. It will reduce your stress and increase your productivity. So, go for it—find a way to make exercise work for you and start sweating (or just walking more to start with).

TAKE A DEEP BREATH

After all that talk of exercise, let's move on to a nice sedentary way to take care of yourself. No sweat required. We just have to breathe. When we are feeling stressed or anxious, we tend to take short, shallow breaths. This means we aren't getting enough oxygen through our blood stream. When we can spend a couple of minutes noticing our breath and take a few conscious deep breaths, we feel far more relaxed and focused.

When my kids were young, they learned the breathing method of "smell the flowers, blow on the soup" to help them calm down when they were upset. They never used it, but I'd sit there pretending to smell flowers and blow soup while they just ignored me and kept screaming. It worked for me—I was far more calm when dealing with their tantrums.

A very simple breathing technique to help us be grounded and focused is used by both special forces military units and yoga teachers. It's called box breathing or tactical breathing. Using this technique, you inhale for four seconds, hold your breath for four seconds, exhale for four seconds, and hold your breath for four seconds.

My yoga teacher leads us through it by repeating: "**Inhale,** one . . . two . . . three . . . four . . . **hold,** one . . . two . . . three . . . four . . . **exhale,** one . . . two . . . three . . . four . . . **hold,** one . . . two . . . three . . . four . . ." for a few minutes. She encourages us to hold the breath lightly during the holds. Box breathing has magical instant stress-reducing qualities—I've been using it while stuck in traffic, dealing with difficult children, before big presentations, and in moments when I'm highly stressed, and it immediately calms me down.

You might want to try it before you're going into a high-pressure meeting or presentation, in the middle of a difficult conversation, or just make time throughout the day to spend a minute or two doing box breathing. Notice how much calmer and more focused you feel after paying attention to your breathing and taking some deep breaths. We take breathing for granted but if we can lengthen and deepen our breaths, we'll see a significant reduction in our stress instantly. Give box breathing a try—if it works for the special forces in life-threatening situations, surely it will help us mere mortals.

Box breathing is hard to describe, but there's a demonstration of box breathing and a few other breathing techniques in the free *Working Well* companion video on my website.

SET BOUNDARIES

I coach a lot of people who are extremely stressed out by all that work demands of them, not to mention their family responsibilities. We focus our coaching sessions on setting clear boundaries, so they can enjoy both work and life. So many of us, myself included, need to learn to prioritize, to say no, and to set reasonable expectations and clear boundaries. We need to leave work at work at the end of the day. But how do we do that?

A participant in one of my workplace stress talks shared a strategy that she has used to help her set boundaries between work and home. Every day when she leaves the office, she stands by her office door and she says consciously, "I am now leaving this place; when I close this door, I am leaving all of my work behind me and going home to my life there, where I will give my full attention. My work will be waiting for me tomorrow, and I will pick it up when I open the door in the morning. But when I close this door, I am leaving work behind."

I love this intentional way she has created boundaries—far too often we are frantically running from work to home with thoughts and worries from our workday trailing along behind us.

What are the ways that you could consciously set a boundary between work and home?

When we set boundaries and take some time for ourselves, it actually makes us more productive.

Research has shown time and again that the extra hours you are putting in aren't making you more productive. They're making you less productive. According to a study published by John Pencavel of Stanford University, "Research . . . found that employee output falls sharply after a fifty-hour workweek, and falls off a cliff after fifty-five hours—so much so that someone who puts in seventy hours produces nothing more with those extra fifteen hours."[12]

How often are you working more than forty hours per week?

Many people think that if they just work longer hours, they can get a handle on their stress and increase their productivity. The irony is that working more doesn't help. It actually makes us more stressed and less productive.

We have limited capacity and when we push beyond it, the results aren't great. Our productivity decreases because we aren't taking the time to recharge.

Taking time to relax fills our tank, so we can return to work with energy and drive. No one can work on an empty tank forever.

- How do you feel physically when you are working too many hours? Be specific, do you have headaches, trouble sleeping, neck or back pain, or stomach issues?
- How's your stress level after working too many hours? Rate your stress on a scale of one to ten, where one is no stress at all and ten is ready to run screaming down the street.

- How productive are you the day after you've put in a really long day at work? How about the day after that?
- How are your family relationships and friendships impacted when you're working a lot? Be specific: have you missed events with your children, fought with your spouse, felt unable to support friends or aging parents?

Hopefully thinking through the answers to these questions will help you see that working too many extra hours is not the answer.

So, what do we do? The work needs to get done. Our first instinct is to work longer, but what if we just started working smarter? "According to US researcher Alex Soojung-Kim Pang, most modern employees are productive for about four hours a day: the rest is padding and huge amounts of worry."[13]

Four hours a day! That's our capacity for productivity, yet we easily put in ten- and twelve-hour days, thinking that will help us keep up with our unreasonable workloads. We are using the wrong tool to try to solve our problems. It's like bringing a chainsaw to a job that requires a screwdriver. The research indicates that in order to be more productive and less stressed, working more is the exact opposite of what we should be doing. Working smarter means taking breaks to recharge, working with our brains (which you'll learn more about in Chapter Ten), and using tools and systems to be more productive (which you'll learn in Chapter Eleven).

How can you change your mindset and your schedule so you make the best use of those four hours, being as highly productive as possible and using the remainder of the time to recharge? Perhaps you could do a walking meeting with a colleague, spend some time thinking about and planning out your work—rather than going from one thing to the next with no plan in mind—or maybe even take a lunch break.

I know it's hard to set boundaries and work less, but I promise you that working more isn't solving your problem, it's making it worse.

PUT YOUR PHONE DOWN

Have you seen those signs on the highway that say: *Leave Your Phone Alone?* Most of us could use one of those signs in our offices and in our homes. How would it feel to turn your phone off for a few hours (gasp)? And I'm not just talking about when you're at home, but also when you're at work. When we have our phones on and nearby at work, we're less productive and less capable. A 2017 University of Texas study "found that the mere presence of our smartphones, face down on the desk in front of us, undercuts our ability to perform basic cognitive tasks."[14]

Our phones are making us stupid. And we're getting addicted—they're controlling us, rather than the other way around.

According to a recent study published in the *New York Post*, "Americans check their phone on average once every twelve minutes—burying their heads in their phones eighty times a day."[15]

There is a pretty nefarious reason we're picking up our phones so often. We are getting addicted to the chemical hit of dopamine (said to be as addictive as cocaine) that comes from having positive experiences on social media. And that's not random, it's by design.

As David Brooks says in this *New York Times* article, "The critique of the tech industry is that it is causing this addiction on purpose, to make money. Tech companies understand what causes dopamine surges in the brain, and they lace their products with "hijacking techniques" that lure us in and create "compulsion loops."[16] Social media sites are using "algorithms to leverage our dopamine-driven reward circuitry. Smartphones and social media apps stack the cards—and our brains—against us."[17]

I don't know about you, but based on this information, I'm spending a whole lot less time on social media sites. Because they are messing with my brain. To make money.

Instead of seeking that dopamine hit through likes, make some time to connect face-to-face and get an even better dopamine hit. When we're online, our connections tend to be more superficial and surface level. When we connect in person, we're having more deep and meaningful connections.

Let's aim for true connection and intimacy, for reflection and pause, and a deeper level of thinking than social media require of us. I can't think of a better way to do that than putting down our phones and connecting in person.

How are you impacting the quality of your relationships when you're picking up your phone every twelve minutes?

How much work are you getting done with all those interruptions?

I'm sure you're thinking, *Well, other people might do that, but not me.* That's what I thought too. Until I installed an app called Moment on my phone, which tracks how often I pick up my phone and how long I spend on it. Turns out I was below average, but still coming in at forty to fifty pickups a day.

I can't think of anything else I do forty to fifty times a day. I decided I should do a push-up before every time I picked up my phone. It didn't work. It was just a little too awkward in public places. But I did force myself to open up the notes page and write for ten minutes before I let myself check e-mail. Now I'm down to about twenty to thirty pickups a day. Still alarming, but at least I'm heading in the right direction.

Having a constant connection to work without getting a true break isn't helping us be more productive or be fully present in our work or personal lives. We're missing out on connections with the people we care about when our faces are buried in our phones.

It's hard to disconnect, I know. Especially when you see an e-mail or a text pop up that pulls you right back into the world of work. But resist the pull of the phone. Turn it off, or, at least, put it away for a few hours every night. Try to do this at work as well.

We are also missing a lot of opportunities to build and maintain good relationships at work when we are too plugged into our phones.

Focusing on your coworkers, either in a meeting or during a lunch break instead of looking at your phone makes them feel valued. I'm sure we've all felt the frustration of attempting to engage with a coworker (or family member or friend) who is checking their phone in the midst of our conversation. It's not a great feeling, so please leave your phone alone as often as you can.

> **What's one step you can take to reduce your phone time and increase your face time?**

When we disconnect from work, it not only gives us perspective, it helps us recharge. A break from what we are doing energizes us, and when we come back, our productivity skyrockets.

> **What's one small step you can take to cut down on the amount of time you spend connected to work after-hours?**

Please take that step. Not only does your productivity depend on it, your relationships do too.

TAKE BREAKS

How many of you take a nice long lunch break? And how about your morning coffee break? Don't forget the afternoon one. Most of you are probably like I used to be and don't actually know the meaning of the word *break*. Well, it's time to get reacquainted.

Research by Tony Schwartz suggests that for optimal productivity, we should take breaks every ninety minutes.[18] What we do on our breaks will make the difference as to whether we return to work recharged or drained. Research has found that "a good break provides psychological detachment and positive emotions."[19]

Think about what you do most often on your breaks. Most people I know check their social media or personal e-mail, guzzle caffeine, or vent to coworkers. These activities are not giving us a true break! For a break to recharge us, we need to disconnect from screens, do something that makes us happy, and move our bodies. At the risk of sounding like your mother, take a proper break: put your phone down, get outside, talk to a friend, have a drink of water, eat something, do some stretches, or take a moment to think about what you feel grateful for.

Too often we skip lunch—some of us even skip breakfast. We are working all day on an empty tank. How efficient do you think you are when you have no fuel? How pleasant are you to be around when you are hungry? How does this impact your health?

I promise you that stopping to take a lunch break and getting some healthy food is going to make you way more productive in the afternoon.

In order to be *Working Well*, we need to go back to the basics: eat, sleep, drink plenty of water, and exercise.

Here are a few suggestions to encourage you to take breaks:

- Set up a time with a coworker to go for a walk (and commit to each other that you won't talk about work).
- Set yourself a calendar alert for breaks and lunches.
- Tell your coworkers you'll be taking breaks and why you're taking breaks. They'll hold you accountable (or make fun of you. But they'll stop making fun of you when they see that not only are you more relaxed, you're getting more done).
- Have a water bottle on your desk. This will encourage you to drink more and, if nothing else, you'll have to get up from your desk to go to the washroom more often.
- Schedule walking meetings. You'll still be working, but you'll be outside, getting some fresh air and exercise. This activity will help you think more clearly and creatively, and it will feel like more of a break than sitting in an office for your meeting.

We'll talk more about breaks in Chapter Eleven because taking a break isn't just good for your mood and your health, it will also sky-rocket your productivity.

CONCLUSION

Work gives us many things, but not everything. When you find yourself slipping into focusing too much on work, take a step back and remember that no one at your funeral will speak of what a good employee you were. They will speak of what a good parent you were, what a good friend you were, and what a good spouse you were, what a loving family member you were—because you made the time for your cherished relationships.

Steal back your time from work. Go home early. Put the phone away. Get some sleep. Ask the people you love to spend time with you— time when you disconnect from everything but them. Give them your full attention.

Put the time and the effort into having quality relationships. It's the most important thing you can do. Set good boundaries so you can get good work done, and, at the end of the day, you'll have time and energy to live a life that you enjoy.

Focus on creating happiness at work and at home and remember that happiness really is an inside job. When you're happy, you'll be less stressed out, you'll get more done, and you'll have more energy for your life.

Choose one or two strategies to help you take better care of yourself and begin to practice them. Like everything, the challenge is to take action. After you choose a strategy, start using it right away.

The research is very clear. Happiness works. Self-care matters. Make yourself a priority. When you take care of yourself, it will make all the difference to your entire life.

QUESTIONS

1. How happy do you feel on a scale of one to ten, one being the least happy you've ever been and ten being the happiest you've ever been?
2. What could you do to increase your happiness by just one point?
3. How would your life improve if you were happier?
4. What's one strategy from this chapter that you'd like to implement? Write it down and plan it into your schedule.
5. What are the specific steps you will take to implement that strategy (go to sleep earlier, plan a walking date with a friend, turn our phone off for an hour every day, and so on)?

ACTIONS

- Schedule phone-free time every day at work and at home.
- Think about a time in your life when you felt really happy and relaxed. What were some of the things that you were doing?
- Find ways to start doing more of those activities in your life.
- Identify a boundary that you can set so you can disconnect from work.
- Choose one of the proven ways of becoming happier and add it to your daily schedule (exercise, seeing friends, etc.).
- Schedule break times in your calendar for the next week and commit to taking breaks.
- Check out the free *Working Well* companion video on my website to learn box breathing and stretches you could do on your breaks: https://www.managetoengage.com/join-us/.

Chapter Six

Practice Gratitude, Meditation, and Mindfulness

"Gratitude unlocks the fullness of life. It turns what we have into enough, and more. It turns denial into acceptance, chaos to order, confusion to clarity. It can turn a meal into a feast, a house into a home, a stranger into a friend."

—Melody Beattie

I don't know about you, but a lot of my stress comes from a nonstop stream of thoughts, worries, judgements, criticisms, and an endless mental to-do list. Our mind-chatter is exhausting for our brains, and the best way to give them a break is through meditation and mindfulness. In addition to all of the strategies shared in the previous chapter, research has found that practicing gratitude, meditation, and mindfulness can increase our happiness and decrease our stress.

It's worth spending time every day noticing the good things in our lives and feeling grateful because gratitude is an antidote to stress. The same goes with meditation and mindfulness. Even spending just a few minutes a day in a state of mindfulness, particularly in the midst of stress, can help us feel calmer and more able to handle whatever challenges we are faced with. Mindfulness and meditation can help us be more present in the moment, which can reduce our stress. I often feel anxious or worried when I'm thinking about the future. I can't tell you the amount of stress I've caused myself worrying about things that never came to pass. Meditation and mindfulness have helped me spend less time in the future and more time in the present. When I'm actually paying attention to the present moment, I usually feel calm and relaxed (unless I'm at a children's birthday party). I began to practice meditation and mindfulness more regularly during the last few years of my mother's illness, and I was able to find calm and peace in spite of the incredibly stressful circumstances.

PRACTICE GRATITUDE

Gratitude is something that I've come by quite naturally in my life, primarily because I grew up with a younger brother with severe cerebral palsy who had no control over his body. He couldn't walk or talk or hold his own head up. He had serious medical challenges throughout his entire life, and he was one of the happiest, most loving people I've ever known. I learned from him to be grateful for the simplest of things, to love well and to choose happiness in the most challenging of circumstances. I share a lot more of that story in my book *Nine Strategies for Dealing with the Difficult Stuff.*

Because I grew up with an awareness of how fortunate I was to do basic things like walk and run and talk, I've always naturally practiced gratitude.

When we choose a perspective of gratitude, we fight our natural tendency to spend too much time and energy consumed by what's stressing us out.

You can hold only one thought in your mind at a time. When that thought is a grateful one, you feel energized and filled up, rather than drained.

Research has consistently shown how gratitude can have huge mood and health benefits for us. An article by Amy Morin called "7 Scientifically Proven Benefits of Gratitude" in *Psychology Today* shares research about how gratitude is good for us:

- Gratitude opens the door to more relationships. Showing appreciation can help you win new friends.
- Gratitude improves physical health. Grateful people experience fewer aches and pains and report feeling healthier than other people.
- Gratitude improves psychological health. Gratitude reduces a multitude of toxic emotions, from envy and resentment to frustration and regret. Gratitude effectively increases happiness and reduces depression.
- Gratitude enhances empathy and reduces aggression. Grateful people are more likely to behave in a prosocial manner, even when others behave less kindly.
- Grateful people sleep better. Spend just fifteen minutes jotting down a few grateful sentiments before bed, and you may sleep better and longer.
- Gratitude improves self-esteem. A 2014 study published in the *Journal of Applied Sport Psychology* found that gratitude increased athletes' self-esteem, an essential component to optimal performance.
- Gratitude increases mental strength. For years, research has shown gratitude not only reduces stress, but it may also play a major role in overcoming trauma. Vietnam War veterans with higher levels of gratitude experienced lower rates of post-traumatic stress disorder. Recognizing all that you have to be thankful for—even during the worst times—fosters resilience.[1]

Practicing gratitude has helped me come through many challenging times and appreciate the wonderful moments that happen on a daily basis. I've kept a gratitude journal off and on over the years. These days, I feel too busy to actually write anything down, but I do make time during my day to notice and express what I'm grateful for.

When you can take a few deep breaths and concentrate on generating feelings of gratitude in your body, rather than just thinking grateful thoughts, you feel even happier. When we feel gratitude, we change the chemistry in our body. Generating feelings of gratitude rather than just thinking about what you're grateful for is the difference between thinking something is funny and laughing.

Trust me. There is always something to be grateful for. We take so much for granted. If we wanted to, we could spend every moment filled with gratitude.

The fact that you can take a breath without a ventilator, that you can read these words, that you're able to drink your favorite drink, or eat your favorite food, or talk to your favorite person are all reasons to feel grateful in any moment.

What's one simple thing that you feel grateful for?

Take a minute to concentrate on what you're grateful for and fill your body with feelings of gratitude.

I have frequently used gratitude as an antidote to some of those life stresses that I can't control. I was working with a very difficult client for a while, and I could do nothing to influence or change his behavior. So I focused instead on what I felt grateful for.

Every time I came home from seeing this person, I would catch myself beginning to complain to my husband about him, then I would stop and say, "I'm so glad I'm not married to him!" We would both laugh, then I would be filled with gratitude that I was married to my husband. Our focus goes where we allow it to go.

Too often, we choose to focus on what we're stressed or upset about. That will drain you. Gratitude will fill you.

What are the ways that you can become more intentional about being grateful? Here are a few ideas to get you started:

- Think of three things you are grateful for at the start or end of the day or at meals. Every night at dinner, everyone in our family shares three things they are grateful for from the day.
- Find one thing that you genuinely appreciate about someone in your life: a coworker, friend, partner, or family member. Get into the habit of expressing gratitude and appreciation daily.
- Make it a practice to appreciate yourself. Take a moment to notice when you've been a great parent, employee, spouse, son or daughter, or friend.
- Notice the little things that you take for granted—search for opportunities to feel grateful. Hot coffee to start your day, a warm house to return to after work, the littlest things are worth of our gratitude.
- Take a moment before you start eating to feel and express gratitude for your food.
- If you have a meditation practice, end it by thinking of what you feel grateful for, and fill your body with feelings of gratitude.
- Start your morning by noticing everything in your life that you are grateful for. You can write down your thoughts, spend a few minutes generating feelings of gratitude in your body, or just take a moment to notice that you've got a bed to sleep in and a warm shower to start your day with.

Spend a day committed to noticing what you are grateful for and what is going really well in your life. It might just feel so good that you decide to keep doing it.

MEDITATE AND PRACTICE MINDFULNESS

(Don't skip this section. I promise I have some suggestions to make meditation work for you.)

Unlike gratitude, meditation has never come naturally to me. Meditation sounds simple but I find it quite challenging. But it's worth figuring out how to make it work for you because meditation and mindfulness have amazing mental and physical health benefits. Research shows that "regular meditation can permanently rewire the brain to raise levels of happiness, lower stress, even improve immune function."[2]

Just spending five minutes a day meditating and focusing your mind can significantly decrease your stress, enable you to better manage your emotions and relationships, and can help you be more productive. Companies everywhere are embracing the benefits of mindfulness and meditation: Google, Nike, Apple, General Mills, HBO, Deutsche Bank, and Target to name just a few.

Dr. Andrew Newberg, a neuroscientist and author of *Words Can Change Your Brain*, says "the type of focusing involved in meditation activates the brain's frontal lobe, which is involved in concentration, planning, speech and other executive functions like problem solving. Studies have shown meditation can bolster all of these mental tasks. But the greatest benefits may spring from the interplay between your brain's focus centers and its limbic system—a set of structures that manage your emotions and regulate the release of stress and relaxation hormones."[3]

When we can slow down and take some time to focus our minds on a single object, thought, or movement, our minds get a rest from their usual busy brain state. This mental relaxation helps us perform our work better and feel less stress. Not only that, but, over time, we'll get more skilled at handling our emotions and difficult interactions with coworkers, family members, and friends.

Dr. Newberg found that when we meditate, "'There's also a softening effect when it comes to emotional responses.' Just as weightlifting allows your muscles to lift a heavier load over time, working out your brain with meditation seems to fortify its ability to carry life's emotional cargo. That stress-dampening effect has tied meditation to improved mood and lower rates of heart disease, insomnia and depression."[4]

I've never found meditation easy, but it sure sounds a lot easier than weightlifting to me. I tried mindfulness meditation when my mom got sick. I was terrible at it. I couldn't calm my mind, and I felt like I was failing at meditation. I gave up.

Then, after my brother died, I was in such a deep state of grief that I was having trouble functioning. A friend offered to take me to a ten-day loving-kindness meditation retreat. Ten days! Of total silence. But I went because I didn't know what else to do. And for whatever reason, perhaps because I was so broken open and ready to surrender to meditation, or perhaps because it was just the right kind of practice for me, it worked. My meditation practice carried me through the final devastating years of losing my mother and the grief that came after she died. I've practiced loving-kindness meditation off and on for fifteen years (more off than on if I'm completely honest), and it's my favorite kind of meditation.

There are a few different apps you can use to guide you through meditation: Calm, Headspace, and Smiling Mind are some of the more common ones. I've placed those apps and the websites of some of the leaders in the field of meditation in the resources section. I also have a short six-minute video that guides you through my morning meditation and gratitude practice in the *Working Well* companion video on my website, if you'd like to use it. I'd suggest trying out different meditation styles and practicing five to fifteen minutes a day for a week or two to find the right type for you. Keep trying different kinds until you find one that feels like a match for you and your busy brain.

In terms of the more common meditation practices that I have been exposed to, they seem to fall into three different categories:

1. Concentration meditation

A concentration meditation practice enables you to calm down your monkey mind by concentrating on one thing over and over again. In some situations, this focal point might be your breath: every time you notice a thought, you simply bring your attention back to your breath. Box breathing is an example of concentration meditation: we focus on our breathing and can come back to it every time we get distracted by thoughts.

Another way that you can practice concentration meditation is by looking at an object like a candle flame. Every time you notice a thought arise, you bring your attention back to the candle flame.

You can also practice concentration meditation by choosing a word or a phrase to repeat in your mind. You can use a simple word like "peace" or "calm" or "happiness" or "ease." You can also use a phrase like: "May I be peaceful, may I be at ease, may I live with gratitude." When I do my morning meditation, I use a concentration practice called loving kindness, and I send peace and love and ease to people who I love (including myself). I also use this practice as a way to manage the stress I feel when I'm worried about someone. I think of them and repeat the phrases: "May you be peaceful; may you be at ease; may you live with gratitude." Doing this helps me reduce my anxiety and send them some loving energy when I can't do anything else to help them.

2. Insight meditation

This type of meditation is focused on noticing and paying attention to our thoughts and our patterns of thinking. In insight meditation, we notice our thoughts, but we don't identify with them or judge them; we simply observe what's happening. It's called insight meditation because you can get a great deal of insight from slowly and mindfully observing your thoughts. When I first started to meditate, I slowed down enough to see that most of my thoughts were sad, and some were fearful.

Rather than identifying with the sad thoughts and becoming sad, I simply noticed that there was a lot of sadness in me. I didn't judge my thoughts as good or bad; whereas normally, I would think of sadness as a negative feeling. Instead, I let the thoughts roll by and brought my attention to my breath as often as I could. When practicing insight meditation, we observe ourselves with compassion the way we might observe a friend. The goal is not to fix or judge or identify with our thoughts and feelings but simply to notice the patterns we fall into. When we can pay attention to the litany of thoughts running through the mind without judging them, we become more self-aware and compassionate with ourselves.

3. Moving meditation

There are plenty of ways to meditate through movement. Doing yoga, tai chi, or qigong are all forms of moving meditation. You can also just go for a mindful walk, slowing down and noticing your thoughts as well as paying deep attention to everything around you. In a moving meditation, our thoughts will often naturally disappear because we are focused on the physicality of the task at hand. When I'm doing yoga, I'm too focused on not falling over to think about anything. Sometimes, I'm in a particularly painful pose (like pigeon) and I'm pretty sure that I'll die if it doesn't end soon. But when I can slow down and notice the thought, I can remind myself that it's only a sensation. I only feel like my hips will break. They haven't yet. Likewise, when I'm in tree pose and feeling strong and healthy, I can notice that thought and see how it energizes me.

In the companion video to this course, my phenomenal yoga teacher Hillary Keegan shares some quick, easy poses and stretches you can do throughout your workday. I've also included her fifteen-minute video of yoga poses that will put you in a powerful, positive state to start your day.

Yoga is both meditation and exercise, and in my opinion it's magic exercise: you get stronger and calmer and lose weight, all without breaking a sweat! I've included Hillary's online yoga classes in the resource section and I highly recommend you check them out. Her classes are fun, energizing, and powerful, and I always feel like my body, mind and spirit have all been nourished after one of her classes (and I actually have bicep muscles now!).

This year, I've committed to practicing meditation again because I know it's so good for me. I've been practicing fifteen minutes of loving-kindness meditation most mornings and I'm getting to yoga at least twice a week.

Starting to practice again was not easy, and I had to make some different decisions: I chose to allow my children to watch half an hour of TV every morning. It felt like the only way to get that time to myself, and I knew it was worth it for me—for all of us.

I don't meditate every day and sometimes I set the timer for only five minutes, but I'm meditating far more often than I have in many years, and it's having a good impact.

On the days when I meditate, I am so much happier because I start each day in a relaxed and loving place. Sometimes that loving happy state lasts about five minutes, until I check my e-mail or try to get the kids out the door for school. Other days, it carries me through the whole day. I find that when I'm meditating more consistently, I can respond to life's various stressors with ease rather than anxiety.

PRACTICE DAILY MINDFULNESS

Similar to the insight-meditation practice, when we practice being mindful, we don't get caught up in the drama of our thoughts, we simply notice them and don't judge them. We can apply the same approach to all that is happening around us. Rather than getting caught up in our coworker's rant about how awful management is, we simply notice that our coworker is feeling upset, without getting upset ourselves. With mindfulness, when our manager appears frustrated and is difficult to interact with, we simply notice the behavior; we don't judge it, and we don't take it personally. You can see that mindfulness is at the core of many of the concepts I've already shared.

Mindfulness is about how we live moment to moment—it's about slowing down and being more present as we go through our days. Mindfulness gives us the opportunity to take a breath and pause before we react.

As neuroscientist David Rock explains, research has shown that "mindfulness turns out to be very important for workplace effectiveness."[5]

We only have a sliver of an instant to choose our reaction to an event. Being mindful allows us to slow down enough to make a conscious choice about how we react to stressful situations or people rather than slipping into an automatic response.

Going through our days more mindfully helps us be more thoughtful about how we approach our work, our colleagues, and any stressful situations we encounter.

One of my favorite descriptions of how to become more mindful came from an Eckhart Tolle lecture I attended, in which he suggested that to be mindful is to "come to our senses." To slow down and be more present, all we need to do is tune into our senses: what are you seeing, feeling, hearing, smelling, tasting?

A common exercise to help people reduce their anxiety is to ask them to focus on their five senses. When we pay attention to our physical experiences, we become more grounded in the present moment.

In our fast-paced, always-on world, we never give our busy brains a break. Although it feels counterintuitive, slowing down and taking a deep breath can actually help you be more productive (and more pleasant to be around).

A *New York Times* article by David Gelles titled "How to Be More Mindful at Work" suggests:

> When you are experiencing a particularly stressful moment, a popular mindfulness exercise known as S.T.O.P. can be helpful.
>
> **S**top. Just take a momentary pause, no matter what you're doing.
> **T**ake a breath. Feel the sensation of your own breathing, which brings you back to the present moment.
> **O**bserve. Acknowledge what is happening, for good or bad, inside you or out. Just note it.
> **P**roceed. Having briefly checked in with the present moment, continue with whatever it was you were doing.

MEDITATION AND MINDFULNESS YIELD BIG RESULTS

As David Gelles reports in the same article, at Aetna, a large health insurance company, more than ten thousand employees have participated in a mindfulness or yoga class that the company offers, resulting in a healthier and more effective workforce. In a study conducted with Duke University, Aetna found that among those who took part in the classes, there was a 28 percent reduction in their self-reported stress levels, a 20 percent improvement in their sleep quality and a 19 percent reduction in pain recorded in surveys of the participants. They also became more effective, gaining an average of sixty-two minutes per week of added productivity.[6]

CONCLUSION

There are plenty of benefits to slowing down, making some time to meditate, and becoming more mindful on a daily basis. Having attempted various versions of meditation and mindfulness for nearly fifteen years, I'm the first to admit that it's not easy but it *is* worth it. When we can find ways to be more mindful in the moment or to practice meditation on a regular basis, we can significantly reduce our stress. And, can you imagine having an extra hour of productivity every week? Not to mention better sleep.

While it can feel challenging to fit gratitude, meditation, and mindfulness into our daily schedules, if we can find ways to do it, we'll feel better, get more work done and be happier. When we can slow down, we can better manage our emotional reactions, be more thoughtful about our choices and be more present.

Take a few minutes and think of how you can bring more gratitude and mindfulness into your ways of thinking and interacting with others, as it will significantly reduce your stress and improve your relationships.

Let's all take a few deep breaths, appreciate what's good in our lives, and give ourselves a reprieve from all those asteroids that are bombarding us. We'll be calmer, happier, and more capable of whatever challenges come our way.

QUESTIONS

1. What are three things that you are grateful for today? In general?
2. How often do you express your gratitude to others? Can you find ways to express gratitude more frequently?
3. What form of meditation appeals to you the most (concentration, insight, movement)?
4. What's one way you could implement meditation or mindfulness into your day?

ACTIONS

- The next time you find yourself feeling stressed out, practice STOP.
- Tell one person what you feel grateful for today.
- Create a habit of searching for at least three things you're grateful for each day.
- Have a look at the apps Headspace, Calm, and Smiling Mind. They have free meditations as well as paid ones. They have meditations for kids as well.
- Get my free morning gratitude meditation video by joining my newsletter at https://www.managetoengage.com/join-us/.
- Give Hillary's energizing and strengthening yoga sequence a try. You can get it free by joining my newsletter at https://www.managetoengage.com/join-us/.
- Find five minutes in your day to meditate.

Chapter Seven

Notice Your Beliefs and Behaviors

"Whether you believe you can or you can't, you're right."

—Henry Ford

Our beliefs are very powerful. They can dramatically impact the results we get in every area of our lives. What we believe about ourselves and the world leads to our behavior and the experiences we have. Our beliefs form the basis of the stories we tell ourselves to make meaning of our lives and how we interpret our experiences can completely change the course of our lives.

It doesn't matter if a belief is right or wrong. A belief is simply a filter for how we experience the world. For example, I believe that people are fundamentally good. I seek and find evidence of this belief everywhere. I have a friend who believes that people are fundamentally bad. He finds evidence to support that belief on a regular basis (which he loves to share with me, then I counter with my evidence that people are good). We are both right because we've found evidence to support our beliefs. What matters most is what we are choosing to believe and how those beliefs influence us and what we choose to pay attention to. I would argue that I'm happier than my friend because the evidence I've found leads to better life experiences. He would likely agree.

The specific beliefs we have don't matter as much as our awareness of them and how they impact our lives. When we become more aware of our beliefs and the impact they have on our behavior and our experience of life, we can decide if we want to hold on to those beliefs or change them.

Many of our beliefs are unconscious; we aren't even aware of them or how they are driving our behavior.

When we can recognize that many of our choices and reactions stem from specific beliefs that we have, it makes it easier to choose different responses.

For example, let's say that someone doesn't respond to a text or an e-mail we've sent them. We will often automatically go to a *natural response*. That response might be anger because we believe that we are being disrespected. Or that response might be feeling insecure because we believe we aren't important enough for them to bother responding to.

Those responses feel *natural* because we've had those underlying beliefs (people don't respect me, I'm not good enough) for so long that we're hardwired to react based on those beliefs. But there are a million different ways to react to someone who is not responding to our e-mail or text that we might want to choose instead.

Maybe we'll choose to believe that another person's behavior rarely has anything to do with us and think, *Wow, that person must be really overwhelmed.*

We increase or decrease our stress levels based on our beliefs and the behavior that follows from them. Choosing to see someone's lack of response as disrespectful and getting angry creates a lot more stress than sending them a quick follow-up because you think they've forgotten to respond due to being really busy.

The key is to be aware of our beliefs and consciously choose them, rather than just letting our beliefs drive our behavior without any awareness. We're all carrying some long-held, deep-seated beliefs that may or may not serve us. Once we become aware of them, we can decide whether we want to keep those beliefs or trade them in for beliefs that will make our lives easier.

Lately, when our kids are being difficult or scheduling becomes a challenge, my husband will look at me, shake his head, and say, "Nothing's ever easy."

The first few times he said this, I shrugged and laughed. Then I realized that his belief was causing him unnecessary stress. He was focused on finding all kinds of evidence to support his belief that things weren't easy. And then things were less easy.

So, I told him my theory and we had a long and interesting talk—discussing the concept of belief influencing our reality with an engineer is fascinating. He wasn't 100 percent convinced, but he was willing to go along with me. He may be an engineer, but he's a husband first!

I suggested that he look for evidence that sometimes things flow really smoothly and are actually quite easy. (Yes, I'm super fun to be married to—really, I am.)

He hasn't been saying "nothing's ever easy" lately, and I've certainly noticed things running far more smoothly (but, of course, I would because it supports my belief).

It doesn't matter whether I'm right or wrong, it only matters that I believe it. Because when I believe something, it determines how I view the world, how I make sense of my experiences, and how I behave. Our beliefs can cause us a lot of stress, or they can make life easier, which is why it's so important that we become aware of our beliefs.

YOUR BELIEFS ABOUT YOURSELF

The beliefs that have the most powerful influence over our behavior are our beliefs about ourselves. If I believe that I'm pretty smart, I'm going to behave quite differently than if I believe I'm not smart enough. Believing I'm capable gets me different results than believing

I'm incapable. Believing I'm good enough leads to different behavior and outcomes than believing I'll never be good enough.

Our beliefs about ourselves drive the choices we make in life. If you believe you're awesome and can do anything, you'll probably live a very different life than someone who believes they're useless and incompetent. Whatever you believe, you'll easily find evidence to support that belief. I can find plenty of examples from today that I'm totally competent. For example, I had a call with a new client and got a huge contract in less than ten minutes; I designed an excellent new course on self-care that one of my clients was really happy with; I got my kids to school with no one screaming or crying.

I can also find some great examples of incompetence in my day. I forgot to give my daughter breakfast; I am two weeks behind my deadline for completing this book; I can't download a book from the library onto my Kobo to save my life; and I've forgotten my iCloud password yet again. Whether I believe I am competent or incompetent all depends on what I focus on.

Being the positive thinker that I am, I feel like I'm on fire today— did I mention I got the kids to school with no one screaming or crying?

Believing in yourself can have positive impacts on your results. According to research, students with high self-efficacy (belief in their abilities to succeed) display better academic performance than those with low self-efficacy.[1] Our belief in ourselves is more important than our knowledge or abilities. This isn't limited to our experience as students. A recent Melbourne study "found a strong correlation between confidence and occupational success."[2]

Being confident and believing in yourself doesn't always stem from your skills; it comes from your beliefs about yourself. I've met plenty of confident people who don't have all the right skills for their work, but they do have the mindset they need to succeed. If you're confident that you can learn the skills you need and you believe you can resolve whatever challenges come your way, you'll be more successful than if you doubt yourself.

How often are you holding yourself back simply by doubting yourself? Women can be especially guilty of this: "A Hewlett Packard internal report found that men apply for a job or promotion when they meet only 60% of the qualifications, but women apply only if they meet 100%

of them. What doomed them was not their actual ability, but rather the decision not to try."[3]

When we start believing in ourselves, we give ourselves a true chance at success. Our beliefs about ourselves are a far stronger predictor of our success than any of our abilities, so let's focus on building positive and empowering beliefs.

What beliefs do you have about yourself?

Are they serving you or sabotaging you?

I've found the best way to identify your beliefs is to look at your life. It's a direct reflection of what you believe. Have a look at the areas of your life that are working really well and identify the beliefs you want to hold on to because they are serving you. Then have a look at the areas of your life that aren't so great and identify the beliefs that you need to change.

One belief I've had for most of my life is that I have to "hustle for my worthiness," as researcher Brené Brown so aptly puts it. When I first read that concept, it was like a chime went off in my heart—yes, that's me! I used to feel like I had to work hard to prove to myself and others that I was good enough. I thought I had to be doing something worthwhile in order to be worthy of taking up space on the planet, instead of trusting that I'm worthy and good enough just as I am. But that belief is changing, and my life circumstances are changing to reflect it.

Fifteen years ago, I was dating guys with commitment issues, I lived in a four-hundred square foot apartment that I could barely afford, and I worked at a really hard job that consumed all of my mental and emotional resources. I hustled and hustled, and I still didn't feel worthy.

Finally, I realized that hustling wasn't getting me anywhere, and that maybe I should look at some of the beliefs I had that might be causing me some problems. I stopped hustling, and I put a lot of time, effort, and money into counselling, self-help books, and personal development retreats. Slowly but surely, I began to believe that I was worthy.

Now, I'm married to an amazing, loving man, I run my own business, and I earn three times as much as I did then. We live in a great house that we really enjoy, and I've finally got the wild and wonderful little kids I'd dreamt of for so long. I still find myself occasionally hustling and trying too hard, but it's a lot less of an issue than it once was. After all that personal development work, I finally feel worthy just for existing. No hustling required.

My new beliefs are based on some intense personal development work I did almost fifteen years ago. My teachers helped me identify my limiting beliefs, and then we worked together to identify replacement beliefs. A few of my replacement beliefs include: I am absolutely good enough, I am completely perfect, and I am completely lovable. When I first started repeating these statements to myself, I didn't believe them at all. But over time, by searching for evidence to support these beliefs and finding it, I now wholeheartedly believe that I'm absolutely good enough and completely lovable. On some days I even believe I'm completely perfect (I'll probably need another few decades before I lock that one in).

Man, do I love these new beliefs. They're a thousand times more energizing and significantly less stressful than "I need to hustle for my worthiness."

After you've looked at the areas of your life that you want to change, create a new replacement belief and start believing it. The replacement belief is sometimes called an affirmation—we may not believe in it initially but when we affirm it in our minds, we can move towards believing it. An affirmation or replacement belief should be short, present tense, and powerful. A simple example is identifying a belief you might have, like, "I could never be a (insert your dream job here)," and replacing it with the affirmation, "I'm competent and capable. I'm a great (insert your dream job here)." This affirmation won't feel true because it isn't true yet, but when we believe something and seek evidence to support our belief and take steps towards achieving our desired reality, it becomes true.

I spent about three years repeating the affirmation "I'm in a loving, healthy marriage with an amazing man." But I didn't just do the affirmation, I also joined online dating sites, went on dates, and did personal development work. We need to believe in ourselves and take action to achieve our goals.

Dealing with our core beliefs about ourselves is not easy. Exploring our childhood experiences and why we believe certain things about ourselves can be challenging, complicated, and sometimes quite painful. Working with a coach, a counselor, a support group, or attending personal development retreats or workshops can be valuable ways of identifying and questioning our core beliefs. I've also listed some books in the resources section specific to working with your beliefs. Changing our self-limiting beliefs is a challenging and rewarding process that doesn't usually happen overnight. I went to my first personal development retreat over twenty years ago, and I'm still working on changing some of my self-limiting beliefs.

QUESTION YOUR BELIEFS

We all have beliefs that drive our behaviors. Most of the time, we aren't aware of those beliefs, but when we stop and examine them, we will sometimes find that they don't serve us. Some of us might believe that we'll never be good enough to get promoted or that people don't like us or that we're failing miserably in some aspect of our lives.

Those self-limiting beliefs are holding us back. We don't put ourselves out there, or take risks, or be authentic, and then we don't get anywhere. As Canadian hockey legend Wayne Gretzky says, "You miss one hundred percent of the shots you don't take." Once we've identified our self-limiting beliefs, we can choose different beliefs that serve us.

I used to believe that I should only work in not-for-profits because that was where I could do the most meaningful work. And I believed I had to do meaningful work because I wasn't good enough. Doing meaningful work would validate my existence. Hustle, hustle, hustle. Super healthy belief.

I spent nearly two decades doing very meaningful work in not-for-profits. I worked with some incredibly wise and inspiring people who came to their work from a healthy desire to do good in the world. I had some amazing experiences, contributed a great deal, learned a lot, and eventually gave it up. I had to: I was burned out, broke, and done with the belief that I wasn't good enough. I stopped hustling for my worthiness.

I uncovered my belief about why I worked in not-for-profits when I was at a ten-day personal development retreat. That was the same retreat where I replaced my self-limiting beliefs with healthy and empowering beliefs. It was only when I questioned some of my beliefs that I was able to make changes. Without the insights I experienced at the retreat, I might never have made the changes that have allowed me to grow.

Many of the beliefs we have about ourselves aren't even ours. We have adopted them from our parents or our siblings or our teachers. Those people didn't know the whole of us then, and they sure don't know who we are now. I remember my lovely grade eight teacher, Mr. Wills, taking me aside and explaining that if I didn't get over my shyness, I'd never be able to succeed. I was the kind of kid who turned bright red when called on in class and never ever spoke up willingly.

I'm not shy anymore. I'm one of those rare people that loves speaking to large groups—either teaching or giving conference presentations. I'm not the same person I was when I was in grade eight. Neither are you. Thank goodness. Let's let go of the beliefs we might have taken on way back then and question them. Then we can make some conscious choices about what we want to believe about ourselves.

......

Remember, your belief doesn't have to be true. Or right. All that matters is that you believe it.

......

I spent ten years telling myself over and over again, "I'm absolutely good enough. I'm completely lovable." I told myself these things repeatedly in order to build a new belief. Then I looked for evidence to support the new belief. It felt strange and I know it might seem cheesy and weird, but it helped. What have you got to lose by trying it?

The only thing that changed was my belief. I have always been good enough and lovable. The difference is, now I feel lovable and worthy. With this new belief, the circumstances of my life have dramatically improved.

Changing our beliefs about ourselves is no easy feat, but it's a challenge worth taking on because it can change our entire lives.

- What are three inaccurate beliefs you have about yourself?
- What behavior do those beliefs lead to?
- What beliefs would you like to replace?
- How would replacing those beliefs have a positive impact on your life?
- What are your new replacement beliefs?
- What behavior do you think these new beliefs might lead to?

OUR BELIEFS ABOUT WORK

Think about what some of your beliefs about work are. Often, we can identify our beliefs by looking at our parents' beliefs or work ethics. We'll usually be the same or the polar opposite.

I had one client who genuinely believed that he was only doing a good job and showing his commitment when he was super stressed out and overworked. His core belief was: "If it doesn't hurt, you're not giving enough."

It took some time to uncover this core belief, but when we did, he realized it was destroying him and wreaking havoc on his family life. When we further explored his work situation, he realized that he was actually a far better employee when he was relaxed and well rested. He found a way to replace his belief with a new one, "When I take care of myself, I can give more."

As we talked about his belief, he recognized that it wasn't his. He grew up with a father who worked two jobs and was always stressed. That became my client's vision of being a good provider and a good employee even though his circumstances were vastly different than his father's had been.

Are you a workaholic because your mother was? Or are you not living up to your potential and taking on new challenges because you don't want to be like her? Do you get highly stressed about deadlines because that's how your father always reacted? Or maybe you think you'll never be good enough because you had one of those annoying older siblings who always outshone you. Our beliefs lead to our results. When we examine our beliefs about work, we'll often find that we want to replace them.

- What are three beliefs you have about work?
- To get you started, here's a few possibilities:
  » It's hard.
  » You're supposed to love it.
  » It'll make you miserable.
  » It's the most important part of your life.
  » You'll never get ahead.
- How many of these beliefs are yours and not your parents/teachers/siblings?
- What beliefs would you like to replace?
- What new beliefs can you replace them with?

PAY ATTENTION TO YOUR BEHAVIORS

Our behavior stems from our beliefs, and as we become more aware of our beliefs, we can change the behavior that stems from them.

I don't know about you, but I have some behaviors that cause me stress. Some of them are tied to beliefs I have, and others are habits I've fallen into.

For example, when I decided to write and publish this book, I was a bit unrealistic with my timeline and how it would work with the other demands in my life. I decided that I'd write two drafts of the book in September and October and get it to the editor by the end of October. Because that's realistic, right? Just to be clear, I wasn't spending eight hours a day writing. No, over those two months, my husband and I had seven different business trips between us. My daughter had just started kindergarten, so I spent the first two weeks of September in kindergarten transition. My kids had after-school activities; I had two leadership retreats to facilitate, many clients to coach, courses to build and teach; and a deadline for my book—all this, and I was solo-parenting on the weeks that my husband was traveling.

So, I was a bit stressed out while writing a book about reducing workplace stress. Talk about writing the book you need to read.

What really caused me stress was my behaviors. I was unrealistic about what I could accomplish, and I put unnecessary pressure on myself. I didn't say no to work even when my schedule was getting really full. I have a habit of filling my time just a little too full. I like to think it's the optimist in me. Of course, I can do it all and then some. Except I can't. I get it all done, but just barely, and I feel stressed out and overwhelmed, then I dial it back a bit. Three months later, I've forgotten what that felt like, and I take on too much once more. Sometimes I fall into the trap of hustling. It's a cycle I'm working hard to break now that I'm more aware of it. *Working Well* is a practice. We have to live it and learn it over and over again, day in and day out.

The first step to reducing my stress was to recognize the behaviors I engaged in that significantly increased my stress. With awareness, we can make different choices.

I encourage you to pay attention to your behaviors and the beliefs that drive them. Are you hustling for your worthiness? Or operating from beliefs based in fear or lack? When we become more aware of these beliefs and behaviors, we can make different choices. Those choices will ultimately yield different results—hopefully, less stressful and more pleasurable ones. A few of the behaviors I have engaged in in the past that caused me stress include the following:

- Booking back-to-back meetings with no breaks, not even lunch.
- Running late for social commitments.
- Agreeing to help someone even though it's not ideal for me.
- Being unrealistic about the amount of time tasks will take.
- Putting a lot of pressure on myself, setting unreasonable expectations.
- Taking on more work than I can handle, instead of saying no.
- Saying yes to social engagements because I feel like I should go, rather than I want to.
- Skipping exercise and doing something easier like watching TV, drinking wine, or basically anything because everything feels easier than exercise.

- Avoiding tasks that I dislike, like paperwork, for so long that what was a relatively easy task becomes a really big, stressful deal (tax season is not my friend).

Take a minute right now and think about one behavior you have that causes you stress. It likely stems from an unhealthy belief. What is a replacement belief that would serve you better? Give the replacement belief a try and see what happens. Ideally, it'll lead to different behavior.

My unhealthy belief:

My stress-inducing behavior:

My new belief:

My new behavior:

Your new beliefs and behaviors will probably feel awkward and uncomfortable, and it'll be tempting to go back to your lovely, comfortable, childhood beliefs. I still fall into the trap of hustling for my worthiness, but I catch myself fairly quickly. I remind myself there's no need to hustle, *I'm absolutely good enough and completely lovable.* It sounds hokey, but it works because it interrupts the old belief.

I behave differently now that I'm more aware of how I'm causing my own stress. I keep learning as I go. In writing the final few drafts of this book, I've loosened up the tight deadlines and said no to paid consulting work in order to schedule writing time. If I ever write another non-fiction book, I'll know that it takes me six months to do the writing, not two.

I no longer run late. I book lunch breaks and even coffee breaks, and I go for walks during my breaks. I've put way less pressure on myself, and I've been way more productive and relaxed. I'm also using some of the excellent brain-based strategies that you'll learn about in Chapter Ten, which have increased my productivity.

Spend the next few days paying attention to the behaviors you have that contribute to your stress. Every time you feel stressed out, ask yourself the personal responsibility question:

What have I done to create this situation?

If you want to jot down a few notes on what you're noticing, go for it. That's how you'll find out what your stress-inducing behaviors are. After you've identified them, think of what you can do instead. Often, it's the opposite: try to be early instead of late, try saying no instead of yes. Give it a try, and see how it feels, you might just find yourself a little bit calmer. Then, when your body starts craving all those stress hormones that it's so addicted to, you've got to wean it off. Go for a walk or meet a friend for coffee or tea. Remind yourself that being calm and relaxed is actually a much healthier and more productive way to live, even if it feels unfamiliar.

TAKE RESPONSIBILITY FOR YOUR BEHAVIOR

Okay, so now that we've identified some beliefs and behaviors that don't serve us, it's time to make some changes. Simple, right? Sadly, not usually. Change is hard. Really hard. Those old patterns are hardwired and very easy to fall into. So, how do we make the changes we need to? One of the best ways to make a change is to understand the impact of your behavior, not just on yourself but on those around you.

I realized I needed to slow down my crazy schedule because I was snapping at my kids and husband. It wasn't fair to subject them to my inability to handle my stress.

Who do you think is most affected by the stress you have in your life?

Usually it's our family and our coworkers.

Take a minute to think specifically about the impact of your stress on those closest to you. Make a list of the people affected, and identify the ways that you are negatively impacting their lives.

When we see the negative impact of our behavior on others, we're more likely to make changes. When we see the positive impacts of our new behavior, we're inclined to continue it.

TIM'S BEHAVIOR CHALLENGE

Tim has been one of my clients for almost seven years. He was a student in one of my courses, then I started to do facilitation and coaching with his team. And I've coached him individually off and on over the years. Tim works in an operations environment with predominantly men. He's an easygoing, likable guy in his early forties.

When I met him, he was driving a truck and doing general labor, but he knew he had leadership capabilities. He was right. He's been a manager for five years now, and he's a natural. He really cares about people, and it shows. He's always cracking jokes, and he's fun to work with. He's a no BS kind of guy who calls things as they are. He also deeply understands the work he's directing, so his staff respect him. He just has one problem: Tim has a temper. And no filter.

That's a tough combination for a guy who really values relationships and cares a lot about the people he works with.

When Tim asked me to start coaching him, he'd realized that his temper was negatively impacting his relationships at work. People would say or do things that would upset him, and, instead of taking a deep breath and responding calmly, he would make a bitter or sarcastic comment. On bad days, he would even yell at the other person—once, at an entire group of his staff.

When we first started discussing why he lost his temper, Tim explained, "Stephanie, I just can't help it. It's my natural reaction."

I replied, "Fair enough, it feels like your natural reaction because it's what you have always done so it's the easiest response. When we're under pressure, we can feel like our reactions are out of our control, but they aren't."

The moment between what happens and how we react is usually less than a minute, yet it's the only time we have to make a choice about how we respond. Most of us don't even think. We just instinctively respond in the way we always have. This is natural, but it doesn't always serve us. As we discussed in Chapter Six, practicing mindfulness can help us make different choices in that sliver of an instant.

Once Tim realized this, he really wanted to make a different choice. He told me, "I feel terrible when I lose it on people. It's not that they don't deserve it, but I know there's a better way to express my frustrations. I also know it's hurting my relationships; people don't trust me after I blow up. I want to do it differently."

Tim felt motivated to change his response because he fully understood the impact of his behavior.

We decided that taking personal responsibility for his behavior would help him repair his relationships and change his response. We agreed that every time he lost his temper, he would go and apologize to the person he'd gotten angry with. We also talked through some alternative reactions and responses.

Options we came up with included:

- Taking three deep breaths or doing box breathing.
- Thanking the person for their comments.
- Talking through his challenges or frustrations with a trusted colleague or coach before or after a difficult meeting.
- Preparing for potentially difficult meetings. Having all the information, going for a walk before the meeting, and thinking about his strategies for staying calm.
- Focusing on being open-minded and curious (rather that going in with his mind already made up and full of judgment).

- Approaching conversations with a genuine intent to listen and understand the other person, rather than trying to get his point across.
- Saying to himself when he felt angry or upset, "I'm feeling angry right now," because identifying the emotion calmed down the feelings.
- Practicing restraint and not saying what he was thinking.
- Requesting a few minutes to think about his response or getting back to the person the next day.

When we talked through all these options, Tim realized that he had plenty of alternatives to being sarcastic or yelling. Two weeks later, we had our next session. Tim had been working hard to replace his natural response of anger with taking a deep breath or asking for some time to think about his response.

TIM'S RESULTS

"How's it going?" I asked.

"I've had a few wins and one total disaster," he explained. "The first week, I was doing really well. When I was feeling frustrated, I'd just take a deep breath, which really helped. It stopped my natural response of making a snide comment. Other times, I'd thank the person for their thoughts or ask for some time to think about it. Usually afterwards, I'd go into my coworker's office and vent about everything."

"That's fantastic!" I was pleased for him as I knew how hard he was trying.

"But a few days ago, I totally lost it. You know that guy who works for me who really drives me nuts? He was in the office complaining about something, and I told him to get a grip and get over it because it was never going to change. He yelled at me. I yelled at him. I had to walk out of the office before fists started flying."

Part of the reason that this might have happened for Tim is that willpower is a limited resource, as you'll learn more about in Chapter Ten. He'd spent two weeks using a lot of willpower and self-control.

He might just have used it all up before his most difficult staff member walked in, a tough situation for anyone to manage.

"So, what happened next?" I asked.

"Well, like we discussed, I went to him the next day and I apologized."

I nodded, impressed. "It takes courage and humility to do that," I said.

"It did. But I didn't enjoy it. I don't want to have to go around apologizing to people anymore. Particularly guys like him."

"How did it go?"

"Pretty well. I told him I'd been wrong to raise my voice and not listen to his concerns. He said he shouldn't have yelled. It went better than I expected; I thought he might blow up again."

Tim was influencing his staff member's behavior the only way we can ever influence another person, through leading by example.

We worked on Tim's temper for a few months. With time and practice, taking a deep breath and listening became a more natural response for Tim than making a sarcastic comment or yelling. He now knows the meaning of a filter, and he often chooses not to say the first thing that comes to his mind. Instead, he reminds himself that he doesn't know the whole story, asks a question, and listens with genuine curiosity. Tim's temper still sometimes gets the better of him, but it's rare.

Near the end of our coaching, he said, "You've really helped me learn to be a better listener and not always think about a comeback remark. I truly make an effort to listen to other people's opinions, even if they are different than mine."

I'd call that a win, not just for Tim, but for everyone he interacts with.

We all have habits of behavior, and when we fall into them, we forget that we are making a choice. We feel powerless to make a different choice, and we become trapped in the behavior.

What are some of the natural reactions you have that you'd like to change?

What are some other options of different ways to respond?

Choose one and start practicing it now.

When we start taking personal responsibility for our behavior, everything changes. We are energized because we have the power to make changes to find new and healthier behaviors that produce better results in our work and our relationships.

OWN YOUR CHOICES

Take a good long look at your life.

- Do you love your life?
- Do you feel happy and fulfilled?
- Are you contributing your gifts to the world and being the best version of yourself that you can possibly be?

If you honestly answered yes to those questions, that's fantastic!

If not, the solution is to take personal responsibility for the changes you'd like to make because your life is the result of the choices that you've made, the actions that you've taken, and the behavior that you've engaged in.

It's not up to anyone else to make us happy, productive, and engaged at work or at home. It's up to us. Many of us chose our jobs because we love them. Don't let the love get lost. When we can share our passion and work within our areas of strength, we can accomplish great things. Remember how it felt to be excited about your work? I want to help you get back to that place.

If you've never had any passion for your work and you've been settling, maybe it's time to think about what jobs might be a better fit for your natural strengths, interests, and talents. When we own our choices, we take responsibility for our own level of engagement and happiness.

Marshall Goldsmith, a leadership coach and author, encourages us to ask the following questions when we think about our engagement at work:

ENGAGEMENT QUESTIONS

1.   Did I do my best to increase my happiness?
2.   Did I do my best to find meaning?
3.   Did I do my best to be engaged?
4.   Did I do my best to build positive relationships?
5.   Did I do my best to set clear goals?
6.   Did I do my best to make progress toward goal achievement?[4]

I love this approach because too often we think it's our company's responsibility to make us happy, productive, and engaged. While our workplace can do a lot for us, it's ultimately up to us to manage our own engagement. I have worked in many wonderful organizations in which 95 percent of their staff are engaged, productive employees.

The remaining 5 percent of disgruntled employees were treated the same as all the highly engaged employees. They had the same managers, the same work, and the same workplace challenges. The difference was they were failing to take any personal responsibility for how they showed up to work and the impact they had on themselves and others.

What can you do differently to make sure you're answering yes to the questions above? If you ask yourself these questions at the end of every week, you'll be taking personal responsibility for your level of engagement and happiness at work. Just keeping the engagement questions front-of-mind and making choices that enable you to say *yes* will have a huge impact on increasing your productivity and decreasing your stress.

THE POWER OF CHOICE

So many of us forget that we are making choices every day, all day long. It's a good idea to pay attention to this, because when we're conscious of our choices, we recognize that we're in control of our lives. This makes us more motivated and more productive. Charles Duhigg shares in his book *Smarter Faster Better* that research has found that:

> Motivation is triggered by making choices that demonstrate to ourselves that we are in control. . . . When people believe they are in control, they tend to work harder and push themselves more. They are, on average, more confident and overcome setbacks faster. . . . [They] often live longer than their peers.[5]

Do you feel like you are in control of your life (as much as any of us can be)?

What choices can you make that help you feel more in control?

When we ask the personal responsibility question, "What have I done to create this situation?" we recognize that we're in control of our lives and we can make changes. Then, we can follow through on our insights, take action, and ba-boom, we feel a sense of control over the situation.

Some of us think, *But I don't have a choice! I'm stuck. Stuck in this job, stuck with this boss, stuck with this project.* Of course, there are many things you can't control, but you still have plenty of choice within those circumstances.

When you pay attention to the choices you are making, you feel more motivated. One choice we always have is what we focus on, think about, and talk about.

Many of us tend to focus on our challenges and stressors. This is natural, and I too am guilty of it. On the days I haven't slept enough, I start complaining about the kids waking me up at night; in the weeks when work is really busy, my husband and I spend dinnertime talking about how busy and stressed out we are. It's natural to engage in these discussions, but I'm doing my best to catch myself and make different choices. Recently, my husband and I noticed we were discussing all of our problems over dinner; we switched to talking about things we were feeling grateful for. We both came away from the conversation more energized and relaxed than if we'd spent the entire time focusing on what was stressing us out.

Research has found that when our conversations are focused on what's not working for us, it increases our stress: "As sensible as venting at first appears, a new study published in the *European Journal of Work and Organizational Psychology* suggests that verbalizing your anger doesn't dissipate it."[6] In the study, a clear pattern emerged: the more a person vented, the worse they felt their days had gone.

This is contrary to what many of us believe is a good way to relieve our stress. I can't tell you the number of people I know who think venting is their best stress-reduction tool. I have a feeling it might be one of those unhealthy coping mechanisms that feels good in the moment, but the aftereffects aren't great.

Rather than venting, we can make a tweak to our conversations and focus on trying to gain further understanding of the situation and seek solutions.[7] When we shift the focus of our conversation from blaming to taking personal responsibility, it decreases our stress and strengthens our relationships.

Over the next few days, take time to notice the types of conversations you're having and what you are focused on. Recognize when you are making a choice to focus on the negative, rather than the positive aspects of your life. Take a minute right now and practice focusing on the positive:

- What are three things that you like about your job?
- What are three things that you feel grateful for?
- Who are three people that you feel grateful for?
- What aspect of your life is going really well and why?
- What are three good things that happened today?

How do you feel after thinking about all of these positive elements of your life? Generally, we're far more energized when we make a conscious choice to focus on the positive. I'd encourage you to ask yourself those questions every day for a week and see how you feel.

Take every opportunity you can to make choices. The simple act of making a choice will help you feel more motivated and energized.

If nothing else, notice all the choices that you do have and are making on a daily basis: you're choosing to show up at work; you're choosing your thoughts and your topics of conversation; you're choosing your beliefs and your behaviors; you're choosing your friends. If you're not happy with the results you're getting, you can make different choices.

If you hate your stressful job, but you keep choosing to work there, you need to question your choices. We've always got a choice, sometimes we just need to have the courage to exercise it.

If you decide to stay in your job because it's the right choice for you in spite of some of the drawbacks, turn your thoughts to what your job does provide you, seek solutions to your challenges, and choose to focus on what you appreciate about your workplace.

MEETING OUR FUNDAMENTAL NEEDS

We all look for three fundamental needs to be met by work:

- Survival
- Belonging
- Contribution

Work helps us pay the rent and put food on the table (survival); it gives us a sense of community and connection (belonging); and it provides us with the opportunity to use our gifts and strengths towards a larger purpose (contribution). If you don't get these things from your workplace, it can be very stressful. If there is a mismatch of values, the work culture is unhealthy, or you aren't working in an area of your strength, I encourage you to look for a job that meets these fundamental needs—financial stability, a sense of belonging, and the ability to contribute your strengths and natural talents.

I once had a client who realized that he was never going to be happy in the organization he worked in and that he needed to find a job that was a better fit for him. He ended up finding a job that looked great but involved a $20,000 pay cut. He was hesitant to make the move. He had financial pressures, but he was miserable at work. After we had a long discussion, he made a choice that felt good for him. He decided he needed to get out of his job, and it was worth earning less money to have a job he liked. After a few months in the new job, he said he'd taken a $20,000 decrease in pay and a 200 percent increase in happiness. Two years later, he had worked his way up in the new organization and was making more money than he had in his previous role. Why? Because as we now know, our happiness fosters our success.

It takes courage and faith that things will work out to make a big change, but it's worth it to find work that feels right for you.

Often, we stay stuck in bad situations because we're afraid we won't find anything better. I promise you there's a job out there that's a better fit for you. Every time I've left a job, I've ended up in a better situation than the one I left. So, if you're afraid and feeling stuck, find a trusted friend or coach to help you work through your fears and focus on solutions, then go for it.

FOCUS ON THE POSITIVE ASPECTS OF YOUR JOB

Whether you realize you need to find a new job or you've decided to stay in your current job, don't contribute to a negative workplace by focusing on what's not working and complaining about things you can't change. If you're job searching, continue to be professional, and focus on what you appreciate about your job. And if you choose to stay in your job, learn to appreciate what's good about it. Maybe it's not your dream job, but it gives you time for your other passions. Maybe you really love the people you work with, or the benefits are fantastic. Maybe you're learning a lot. Focus on what you can do each day to answer *yes* to Marshall Goldsmith's questions and get the best out of your days.

If you've made the choice to stay at your job, you may as well choose to make it a worthwhile and enjoyable experience.

When we focus on what is good and what works well in our lives, we draw more of that to us. When we focus on what's negative and isn't working, we draw more of that to us.

Even if there is just one little thing that is good about your job, spend your time focusing on it. It makes you feel better; it helps you appreciate what's working well; and focusing on the positive will create more positive energy in your life.

CONCLUSION

What we believe matters. We will generally go about proving ourselves right, so knowing what we believe about ourselves and our work is helpful. If we're going to spend our lives building a solid case to prove our beliefs are true, we want them to be healthy beliefs that enable us to be successful.

The more aware we are of our beliefs, the more we can make conscious choices, not just about what we believe, but about the behavior that stems from those beliefs. When we make different choices, we'll get different results.

The more our beliefs serve and support us, the more likely we are to succeed. If we can find ways to believe in our abilities, we're way ahead of the game. We can also significantly reduce our stress by becoming conscious of our beliefs and behaviors.

If you've realized that you have a belief that work is supposed to be super stressful or that you have to hustle for your worthiness, it's an amazing opportunity to make a change. Find a belief that's going to reduce your stress and liberate you from the pressure you put on yourself. Concentrate on the choices you do have and find ways to focus on what's working well in your life each day.

I believe in you, and I believe in the capacity of each one of us to make real and meaningful change because I've seen so many clients make significant and lasting changes that have led them to healthier, happier, and more fulfilling lives.

QUESTIONS

1. How would your stress decrease if you changed just one of your beliefs about work, about life, or about yourself?
2. What is a replacement belief that would serve you better?
3. What evidence can you find to support this new belief?
4. Who in your life has been most impacted by your stress?
5. What are some of your *natural reactions* and how can you change your mindset so you can respond differently?
6. What's one behavior you have that causes you stress?
7. How can you change that behavior so that you have less stress?

ACTIONS

- Choose three new beliefs that you want to have, and repeat them to yourself as often as possible.
- Seek and record evidence to support those new beliefs. You might want to keep a notebook (or use the notes app on your phone) to jot down evidence that proves your new belief.
- Choose one behavior that you would like to change. Tell one person in your life about it, so they can help you stay accountable to that change. Take note of the positive impacts of your new behavior as that will reinforce it.
- Notice the choices you make every day—what you focus on, what you talk about, how you engage with others.
- If you want to collect some data, keep a notebook or your phone's notes app close by. When you make a choice about anything (how you work on a certain project, or react in a meeting, or interact with a certain individual), make a note. Rate how happy you are with your choice on a scale of one to ten. Look to see if there are particular choices that make you more or less happy.
- When you notice yourself complaining, stop and focus on seeking solutions and identifying what you're grateful for instead. Create a list of at least three things every day.

Chapter Eight

Manage Your Mental and Emotional State

"You are your state of mind. Your state of mind creates your view, or your window, on life."

—Frederick Lenz

Everything we achieve, whether our results are good or bad, flows from us. When we are in a positive mental state, we are able to achieve more and get better results. All of your outcomes at work and in your life are a product of your mental state—this is why happier people have more success. Their energy is higher, and they are able to produce higher-quality work, connect with others more easily, and engage more fully. When you get yourself into a positive state, you can achieve far more. I'm sure if you think about your own life, you'll see evidence of this.

Can you think of a time when you were really productive and having great success?

Usually, you were in a pretty good state of mind, and that was why you were getting such good results.

I'm not suggesting that we should be in a positive mental state all the time. I don't think that is realistic or even desirable. We need to experience our feelings, be authentic, and welcome the darkness as well as the light. That said, sometimes our minds get snagged on thoughts that don't serve us. That's when we would benefit from paying a little bit more attention to our thoughts and discerning if they are repetitive or unhealthy, so we can interrupt the pattern.

We've all experienced that moment when some relatively small and insignificant event has happened, and we can't stop thinking about it. Our minds run circles around themselves, going over and over what was said or done, and we get stuck. We can't move on, but we aren't really resolving anything. We're just running through the scenario over and over again, often torturing ourselves and growing angrier or more stressed by another person's behavior.

The mental train of thought is something along these lines: *Did she really say that? Did I really say that? Did I really show up to my first day of work in a see-through blouse with no camisole?* Yes, yes, I did. Let me tell you, my mind ran rings around that mortifying event for a few painful nights.

Instead of letting our minds run rampant, let's catch and interrupt the negative spiral of thinking. Then we can either find ways to move to action and resolve the situation, or we can let it go. I have had the great fortune of having a young daughter during the time that the movie *Frozen* has been so popular, so I hear the song "Let It Go" on a daily basis. Whenever my mind starts spinning in useless circles, I start singing "Let It Go" in my mind to remind myself that I am in control of my thoughts rather than allowing my thoughts to control me. It's a good way of interrupting the loop and it usually makes me laugh. Once I've noticed and interrupted an unhealthy thought pattern, then I can move on to more productive thoughts and behaviors.

A crucial element of being in a positive state is having positive and empowering beliefs. While we all have down days or times when we doubt ourselves, we aren't doing ourselves any favors by indulging in self-doubt. Give yourself a few minutes for the pity party, then focus on creating a positive state for yourself. Remember that the mind can only hold one thought at a time—let it be a thought that helps you rather than hinders you.

When we really believe in ourselves—when we have our own backs the way we would have a friend's back—we can achieve amazing results.

MANAGE YOUR EMOTIONS

When we are at work, we need to manage our mental and emotional states so we can be positive and productive. That's our unwritten contract with our workplace. They pay us and we do our best to give them our best. In most companies, they also give us benefits like paid sick leave or employee assistance programs, so that when we are struggling, we have the opportunity to look after ourselves and to take care of the issues and the challenges we're experiencing.

After my brother died, I struggled to be at work. It took all of my energy to show up, and when I was there, I wasn't effective. After a few weeks of trying hard and failing to be productive during my workdays, I finally realized that I couldn't function until I took some time to deal with my grief.

I took two weeks off, and I did everything I could to allow myself to feel all my emotions and to move through them. I went to see a grief counsellor. I exercised. I slept. I cried. Then I went back to work because work was also helping me to heal. It was giving me a reprieve from the grief that waited for me at the end of the day.

I managed my emotions as well as I could while I was at work, so I could be present and productive. When I went home, I allowed myself to have the feelings that I needed to feel in order to heal.

If you are really struggling and having a difficult time, please get help. There are plenty of options:

- Contact a local crisis line.
- Ask your manager, union rep or Human Resources rep about any benefits and services you can access through work.
- Use your sick time to take care of yourself.
- Search for a support group that is related to your challenge and start attending it.
- Talk to a trusted friend about your challenges, and ask them to help you find a counsellor, a crisis-line, or a support group to attend.

Whatever the resources you use, it's so important to take care of yourself. Then bring that good version of you to work.

Even if you have no big crisis or challenges going on in your life, it's still easy to get caught up in an upsetting emotion at work. Because being highly emotional can be unprofessional and have negative impacts on our work and our relationships, it's good to find a way to manage these emotions that overtake us.

As I sometimes say to my kids (and a few clients), just because you're feeling an emotion (angry, upset, scared) doesn't mean you need to act on it. How do your coworkers react when you burst into tears at work or when you fly into a rage in a meeting?

But if we don't act on our feelings, how can we handle them? Most often in workplaces, I see people trying to suppress their emotions: when we have feelings, we do everything we can to push them back down. But trying not to feel what we are feeling doesn't work. Not only that, it makes the people around us uncomfortable.

Research has found that when we try to suppress our feelings, our limbic system is still giving off cues that we are upset. People pick up on those subtle cues and sense that we are feeling an emotion. When they look at us and don't find one, their blood pressure increases.[1]

Neither acting on our emotions nor attempting to suppress them is an effective strategy for handling emotions at work. So, what's the solution? Well, according to James Gross, associate professor of psychology at Stanford University, who is at the forefront in the field of emotional regulation, we need to think about the situation differently. There are two options for doing this: We label our emotions, which helps us move into a different part of our brain and calms us down in the moment. Or we change our interpretation of the event or experience.[2]

I've used changing the way I interpret an event to deal with my emotions in the moment with great success and so have my clients. Think about something simple that may cause you stress—perhaps someone cuts you off in traffic or a coworker doesn't say good morning to you. We can choose how we want to interpret that event. We may interpret this rude behavior as a personal affront and get very upset, or we may choose not to take another person's behavior personally. If we don't take it personally, we're unlikely to get stressed out or upset. When we can change our perspective and reinterpret a situation in the moment, we can significantly reduce our stress. It takes practice, but it can be done.

Far easier to do in the moment is simply to label your emotion. Naming our emotions help us move us into a different part of our brains and reduces our emotional reaction.

Remember Tim, who often lost his temper at work? When he noticed his angry feelings, one of his strategies was to say, either to himself or out loud, depending on the situation, "I am feeling frustrated."

When we label the emotion, it's a good idea to relate to it as an emotion we're feeling, rather that identifying with it completely. That's the difference between, *I'm feeling frustrated*, and *I'm frustrated*. In the first one, we recognize the emotion as separate from us and as something that will pass. In the second one, we identify with the emotion to the point where it defines us. Which way do you think makes it easier to let go of the emotion?

The key with labelling is to simply identify the emotion and move on. As Gross says, "Here's the bottom line: describe an emotion in just a word or two, and it helps reduce the emotion. Open up a dialogue about an emotion, though, and you tend to increase it."[3] Just naming the feeling to yourself in your mind is a good way to calm yourself if it's not appropriate to speak the words out loud. You can see how this connects to mindfulness and the STOP exercise. When we slow down and notice what's happening for us, we can choose a different response.

Is there an emotion that sometimes surprises and overtakes you when you're at work?

The next time you find yourself having this emotion at work, try labelling it to reduce the emotion.

You might need to come back to the feelings later to let yourself feel them and understand what was going on for you. The personal responsibility questions can help with this.

ALLISON'S TEARS

Allison was a client of mine many years ago. She was a very passionate young woman who was committed to her job, working as a supervisor in a male-dominated environment. Allison cried frequently at work.

"I just can't seem to stop the tears, they well up, and before I know it, I'm crying," she explained to me.

"And what do you think the impact is when you cry?" I asked her.

"It's terrible. I'm the only woman on the management team, so it's extra embarrassing. I work with three men, and they all just get quiet and awkward."

"How often do you cry at work?"

Her eyes welled up with tears. "Almost every day."

Wow, did we have a problem. Crying every day at work is unprofessional at the best of times. In the environment she was in, it was a serious issue.

"Okay, let's go through this. What makes you cry?"

"Well, if I'm angry, and I don't agree with what's been decided; or if I'm really upset or hurt; or if I'm frustrated." I could see her holding back the tears as she spoke.

"So, when things aren't going smoothly?" I clarified.

"Yes, when I'm upset by anything, I start to cry. I try so hard not to, but I just can't help it." Tears started streaming down her face as if to prove her point.

"So, right now, why are you crying?"

"I don't know. I just feel like I'm not explaining myself very well, and I'm embarrassed. I am feeling frustrated and a bit hopeless, like I'll never get this figured out." As she spoke, the tears stopped flowing.

"Do you see what's happening here?" I asked her.

"I stopped crying." She half-laughed in disbelief.

"Right. Because you are now expressing what you're feeling. Through identifying what you're feeling, you've switched to a different part of your brain. Would I be right in saying that you feel like it's a natural response to cry and that crying is a way to express every emotion you're feeling?"

"Yes." She nodded.

"But you know that crying at work is unprofessional and you want to stop. Not to mention, you're not expressing yourself, you're just emoting."

"Emoting?" she asked.

"Yes, you're allowing the emotion to control you rather than making a conscious choice. What would happen if the next time you felt like you were going to cry, you simply expressed what you were feeling, like you just did with me?"

"That sounds pretty scary. My staff and colleagues might find it weird if I just blurt out what I'm feeling."

"So how do you think everyone feels when you cry rather than expressing your opinions?"

"Annoyed. Irritated. Frustrated. I think they're getting to a point where they're just dismissing me."

"So, do you think it might be worth expressing your opinion and your feelings so you can actually participate in discussions at work?"

I kid you not—she started crying again. After a few more rounds of practicing expressing her emotions instead of crying, she began to get the hang of it. She promised that when she went back to work, she was going to work on identifying her feelings rather than crying.

ALLISON'S RESULTS

Two weeks later when we met, she'd had limited success. Allison found that she could stop herself from crying in some situations by simply naming the emotion and moving on in the conversation. She'd identified that when she felt frustrated, she could simply say, *I'm feeling frustrated,* in her mind and that would eliminate the crying. She could then have a healthy conversation from that point on. When she was feeling hurt, she still cried. When she was feeling stressed out, she spent her days on the edge of tears, and it was much harder for her to manage her emotions.

We worked together for a few more months; Alison learned and used some stress-reduction strategies, and we focused on labelling her emotions and changing her interpretation of situations to help her manage her emotions at work. Allison turned from an every-day crier to a once-a-month crier. For many people, it would be mortifying to cry at work once a month; for Allison, it was a serious win.

When we can control our emotions rather than letting them control us, everything changes. When we're feeling negative, upset, worried, anxious, or overwhelmed, we're going to cause more stress for ourselves just by the way we perceive events and approach life. When we consciously create a positive state and we are able to operate from that positive state, we'll naturally be more relaxed and productive. Knowing what we now know about how happiness impacts us, creating a positive and happy state is the best way to improve every outcome in our lives, from relationships to school to work.

Tony Robbins, coach, author, and motivational speaker, suggests that to get into a positive state, we must master the three forces that control our emotions: our physiology, our focus, and our language.[4]

USE YOUR PHYSIOLOGY TO CREATE
A POSITIVE STATE

In 2012, Amy Cuddy shared the results of her research on how we can use our physiology or body language to dramatically alter our mental state, using what she calls "power poses." She suggested that our body language governs how we think and feel about ourselves, which means that how we hold our bodies can have an impact on our thoughts and feelings. In other words, by commanding a powerful stance, we can make ourselves actually feel more powerful:

> The evidence of power posing came from a study that Cuddy completed while at Harvard University, where participants sat in either a high-power pose (expansive posture) or a low-power pose (leaning inward, legs crossed) for two minutes. Cuddy found that those who sat in the high-power pose felt more powerful and performed better in mock interviews than those who had not.
>
> Cuddy's research had two major findings. The first was that people who sat in high-power positions felt more powerful than their low-power-pose counterparts. The second was that the power posing actually changed their body chemistry. Cuddy's study suggested that those who adopted high-power poses demonstrated an increase in testosterone and a decrease in cortisol (commonly known as the stress hormone).[5]

Most of us aren't even aware of our posture and how we use our bodies. By becoming more aware and doing power poses, we can increase our energy and create a more positive mental state. I've included the link to Cuddy's TED Talk and examples of power poses in the resource section at the end of the book and on my website. A simple example of a power pose is to stand like Wonder Woman, with your legs shoulder width apart, your feet firmly planted, and your hands on your hips or with your arms held up high and strong, taking up as much space as possible. See if you can spend a few minutes every morning to do a power pose (I like to do mine in the shower) or find a private space to do one during the day at work before a big meeting or potentially challenging interaction.

We make conscious choices to change our physiological state frequently. Maybe we've come from a difficult meeting and we're really upset by a coworker or a project, but when we walk into our next meeting with a client, we immediately put on a fake happy smile and change our tone of voice. We're making a choice with our facial expression, tone of voice, and body language to show up differently than we were doing just seconds before. That's using your physiology to change your state.

This isn't just faking it, changing our body language actually makes us feel better. What are the ways that you use your physiology to adapt your mental state?

Sometimes we feel inauthentic when we change our state, but what I've noticed is that when I've been in that "fake state" for a while—even just a few minutes—it's hard to return to my previous upset state. In other words, it's possible to fake it until you feel it.

I find music a very powerful way to use my body to generate an energetic, positive, happy state. If I have time in the mornings, the kids and I will dance around. If you love dancing as much as I do, give it a go. If dancing around the living room sounds like torture to you, spend five minutes listening to an energizing, happy song on your way to work and see how your mood and body language change. I've shared my playlist full of happy, upbeat music on my website. Just listening to upbeat music or spending two minutes in a power pose can significantly positively impact our state.

WATCH YOUR LANGUAGE

When we become aware of the language that we use, we can see how it shapes our reality. How often do you talk about your limitations and weaknesses rather than your strengths and desires? Usually, we're spending too much time talking ourselves down instead of talking ourselves up. Our language is very powerful: it can shape our experiences as it reflects our beliefs about ourselves and the world.

Start paying attention to the language you use—not only when you are speaking with others, but to yourself. We speak to ourselves more than we speak to any other person.

What language does your inner voice use when commenting on events, people, or your own actions?

Too often, we use judgmental, critical language with ourselves. We speak to ourselves far more unkindly than we would ever speak to another person. Start paying attention to your inner voice and thoughts and see if you can find ways to be more gentle and less judgmental, of yourself and others. Treat yourself the way you'd treat your best friend: have your own back, go easy on yourself, and notice what you're doing well. Try to be kinder to yourself over the next few days and notice how it changes your state.

Twenty years ago, I was fortunate enough to study with some very wise teachers and counsellors. I spent a year in Australia, taking a program that trained stress-reduction facilitators. One of my teachers explained to me that the subconscious mind doesn't distinguish between what's true and what's false. Its only goal is to deliver on what I say, so my language is key to shaping my reality. If I go into an interview telling myself, *I'll never get this job*, the subconscious mind will find ways to deliver on that belief, and I will unconsciously sabotage the interview.

We act in ways that demonstrate what we believe to be true, even if we aren't consciously aware of it. This is why it's so important to pay attention to your beliefs. One of the ways that you can develop a deeper understanding and awareness of your beliefs is to pay attention to the language you use.

One suggestion to better use the power of language: when making a statement of lack, add the word *yet* on to it. When I was single and every person in my life would ask me if I had met someone, I would say "not yet." Or when I met new people and they asked if I was married or had kids, I'd always say "not yet." It sent a very different message to my subconscious than if I'd simply said no. This addition of "yet" cues the subconscious mind that you're working on changing the situation. It also cues well-meaning friends to set you up on blind dates.

Take a few minutes to write down three negative things that you often say about yourself. Some examples might be: I'm no good with people; I'm too shy to be a good leader; I'm not creative enough; I'm lazy. After you've identified what your top three consistently repeated negative statements are, take some time to reframe them.

For example:

Negative statement you make about yourself: I'm not good with people.

Reframed statement about yourself: I'm growing my interpersonal skills.

Your turn:

Negative statement you make about yourself:

Reframed statement about yourself:

When we start to pay attention to our language, we learn a lot more about ourselves. I think of myself as fairly easygoing, and I've done a lot of work to be more loving towards myself, but it's still a work in progress. The other day, I was explaining to a colleague why I couldn't fix a basic glitch in my PowerPoint presentation and I said, "Because I'm an idiot."

I may be a lot of things, but I'm fairly confident that I'm not an idiot. I'm an intelligent woman who is not technologically adept (yet).

We need to be gentler with ourselves, and our language can be a good way to start. The more thoughtful and positive our language is, the more positive our state is.

USE YOUR FOCUS

I bet there are some people reading this right now thinking: *Well, all of this research on how to create a positive state and all the good outcomes I'll get are nice in theory, but I can't possibly be in a good state. I have too much work to do, and I'm totally overwhelmed. My kids are being nightmares, and I have serious health issues. I'm worried about my sister, and I'm pretty sure I'm going to miss that big deadline, and . . .*

We go on and on, talking ourselves into being miserable. Stop doing that. There are always things to be stressed out and upset about. And there are always things to feel happy about and grateful for. This is where we get to use our powers of focus.

We have a choice about what we can focus on. Choose to focus on the good stuff. At least for the first fifteen minutes at the beginning of your day.

We have to take control of what we focus on because our minds will often worry over things that we have no control over. It's our mind's way of feeling like it is doing something to solve the unsolvable. But the reality is, all we are doing is putting our energy into thoughts that drain and upset us.

Our mind is hardwired to look for risks and seek out the negative, so we need to train it to seek out and focus on the positive. Remember that I mentioned each person in our family shares three things they are grateful for at dinner every night? It's based on this research shared in Shawn Achor's book *The Happiness Advantage*:

> One study found that participants who wrote down three things each day for a week were happier and less depressed at the one month, three months, and six-month follow-ups. More amazing: even after stopping the exercise, they remain significantly happier and showed higher levels of optimism.[6]

What are some of the well-traveled pathways that your mind often goes down?

How can you interrupt that negative thinking and switch your focus to something more productive?

What are three good things that happened today?

When we choose our focus, we have significantly more control over our own state.

The mind should not run us. We should run the mind.

START YOUR DAY OFF RIGHT

I'm not talking about breakfast here; I'm talking about what we feed our minds. When you start your day off right, it can set you up for a much better day. You know what I mean—think about a time when you "got up on the wrong side of bed." You wake up feeling cranky. Nothing feels good or right in the world. You listen to the news and feel fairly certain the world is falling apart. Then you realize you are out of milk, and you get toothpaste on your last clean shirt. How does the rest of the day go? Do you get lots of work done and have really good positive interactions? Are you anxious and overwhelmed or relaxed and happy? Usually the rest of the day goes terribly when we start out in a bad state.

How many of us start every day in that bad state? Way too many of us. If you can change the state that you start in, you can change your whole day. If you pay attention and notice your language, stories, and body language, you can consciously create a positive state. When we get intentional about our state of mind, we can make our days and our lives far more positive.

When you go out into the world with a positive frame of mind, you seek out and focus on the positive. You notice what's working well: the coworker who was kind to you, the success you had on a project, or the efficiency with which you dealt with a situation. The stories that you tell yourself are positive. You experience and notice what's working well, and you begin to expect more good things, and by some magic, they come. Your days get better and better because you're choosing your state, rather than letting your mind run amok.

What's one small step you can take to start training your brain to help you start your day right?

Here are a few ideas:

- Start each morning listing three things you feel grateful for.
- Listen to music you love at home in the morning or on the way to work.
- Do a quick loving-kindness meditation to generate feelings of love and happiness in your body. Please watch my morning meditation video if you need guidance.
- Tell someone one thing you appreciate about them.
- Remind yourself of something that you've done really well in the past week.
- Give your kids (or your dog or your cat or your friend) a hug. A six second hug generates oxytocin (the happy chemical).

Choose one small and achievable step, give it a try, and watch how much happier and more productive you become.

BE AWARE OF THE INFLUENCE OF YOUR FRIENDS

Who are your closest friends at work? What is their normal mental or emotional state? What's their outlook on life? We don't often think about how the people we spend time with influence our state, but we should.

I consider most workplaces a slightly more sophisticated version of high school; your peer group has a huge influence over how you perform each day. Are you hanging out with the slackers or the keeners? The complainers or the problem solvers?

Many of you may have heard renowned businessman Jim Rohn's famous quote, "You are the average of the five people you spend the most time with."[7]

That in itself is powerful food for thought.

Take a minute right now and think of the five people you spend the most time with.

What are the first three qualities that come to mind when you think of those people?

Research has found that the influence of your peer group goes far beyond the five people you're closest to. The first major study on the breadth of social influence was conducted by Nicholas Christakis and James Fowler, and they discovered that not only do your closest friends influence you, but their friends also influence you (even if you've never met them):

> According to their results, if a friend of yours becomes obese, you yourself are 45 percent more likely . . . to gain weight over the next two to four years. More surprisingly . . . if a friend of your friend becomes obese, your likelihood of gaining weight increases by about 20 percent—even if you don't know that friend of a friend. The effect continues one more person out.

Christakis and Fowler also found that "happy friends make you happier—no surprise there. But if your friend of a friend of a friend is happy with their life, then you have a 6 percent greater likelihood of being happy yourself."[8]

It seems pretty simple: if you want to be relaxed, happy and productive, hang out with people who are relaxed, happy, and productive. Think about your friends and coworkers, is there anyone you might want to start spending a little less time with? How about people you want to seek out or spend more time with?

We want to choose our peers wisely because research has found that our emotional states are contagious. In a new study in *Nature Neuroscience*, Jaideep Bains, PhD, and his team at the University of Calgary have discovered that stress transmitted from others can change the brain in the same way as a real stress does: "Recent studies have found that stress and emotions can be 'contagious.'"[9]

Keeping the contagion factor in mind, we want to be around people who infect us with their positivity and productivity. You also want to be someone who infects people with your positive state rather than your negative state.

REMEMBER THAT YOU CHOOSE YOUR RESPONSE

Too often we react to external events and give them power over us, whether it's a screaming child, a difficult coworker, or a project going sideways. Often, we will choose to get upset and stressed out by these events, but that's a choice. We can make a different choice and choose not to get upset by these events. We can control our own state regardless of the external events we are experiencing. That's how we reduce our stress.

When you realize you can control your response to external events and not lose your positive state, your entire life changes. You are no longer at the mercy of what happens to you. You have a choice in how you respond, and you're in complete control of your internal state, no matter what happens.

One of my clients is highly disorganized and seems to think that they are my only client, assuming that I can switch my teaching dates around at any time. They are always changing dates of classes without asking me and mixing up the locations on invitations, so I end up in the wrong place. There's no better feeling than standing in a room with your presentation all set up and ready to go, your white board full of notes, and wondering where everyone is when you realize they are all in another room, waiting for you.

In the past, every time I saw this client's name in my inbox, my heart rate would increase, and I'd be upset before I even opened the e-mail. Then I'd read the e-mail and get irate about whatever frustrating situation the client was creating for me to deal with. The rest of my day, I was usually a little bit annoyed, composing a response and dealing with the fallout of their disorganization.

Then I caught myself giving all my power away, choosing to get stressed out by something really minimal, and I committed to choosing a different reaction. Now when I see an e-mail from this client, I take a deep breath and remind myself I can choose my response. I read through the e-mail and smile when I see that there's been another mix-up of dates or locations. I expect it now—I've accepted reality. I try to be compassionate towards a person who is likely overwhelmed, and I send back a quick e-mail to deal with the issue. Then, I let it go. I don't spend any more time thinking about it. I choose not to get stressed out.

What are some events in your life that cause you stress?

How can you reframe them and choose a different response?

For those of you who are thinking, *But really terrible things happen to me, and I can't possibly react any differently than I do*, think about people you know who have thrived in spite of their challenges. Here are a few examples to inspire you: Wayne Dyer, bestselling author and motivational speaker, grew up bouncing between foster homes. Media mogul Oprah Winfrey was sexually abused as a child. Nobel Peace Prize laureate Malala Yousafzai was shot in the head for her advocacy and desire to go to school. She survived and is even more of an advocate today, speaking internationally and running the Malala Fund.

Who do you know who has had really difficult life experiences and has managed to overcome them? The reason they've been successful is because of their mindset and what they've chosen to focus on.

It's not about what happens to you; it's about what you do in response to the events in your life.

The Wayne Dyers, Malala Yousafzais, and Oprah Winfreys of the world have taken the difficult events in their lives and used them to spur themselves to greatness.

Each one of us has the capacity to persevere in the face of obstacles and make our lives even better. We all make meaning out of the events in our lives and how we respond to them. Let's tell ourselves stories that serve us. Let's choose to focus on our strength, our resilience, our creativity, and our abilities. We've all got the capacity to survive and even thrive in the most challenging of circumstances.

There's a strength within each of us that is greater than we could ever imagine, and when we tap into it, we become more than we realized was possible.

We can use our resiliency and grit to keep going through the most challenging of times, and we emerge strengthened, flourishing in spite of the difficulties we've experienced.

CELEBRATE SMALL WINS AND HAVE FUN

According to an article in *Psychology Today*, "The average four-year-old laughs three hundred times a day. The average forty-year-old? Only four."[10] Can you imagine laughing three hundred times a day? How good would that feel? Rather than being filled with joy and laughter, most of us adults are running around, feeling the weight of the world, overwhelmed and stressed out, wondering what our life's purpose is.

Well, it would appear that our life's purpose is to love people, to share our unique talents with the world, to be present, laugh often, and enjoy the sweet moments.

We know it when we are young children, but we forget.

It's time to start remembering.

We think it's our job to teach children how to be in the world, and, for sure, there are things they need to learn—not to hit, not to swallow marbles, not to lose their minds just because they have to wear socks. But if we're smart, we'll pay attention to some of the amazing things we can learn from kids. They can teach us to slow down, to delight in the simple things, to laugh, to enjoy the moment, to love fully, and to feel all our feelings deeply. Children are amazing teachers (until they start screaming about those damn socks. But even then, they can teach us to be calm and choose our response to their ludicrous behavior).

My friend's two-year-old daughter came running out of her room the other morning, screaming with delight, "I got my pants on, I got my pants on!" She was running around laughing, full of wonder that she got her pants on that morning.

Do you know how much we have to learn from that little girl? What would happen to our mental state if we started delighting in our ability to do both the simplest things and the hardest things? Imagine having a moment of celebration every day: "I made that tough phone call. I'm amazing!"; "I filed my taxes. I'm incredible!"; "I was so nice to that person who was being rude to me. I am awesome!"

Do you know what we did when that two-year-old came out absolutely thrilled with herself that she got her pants on? Did we say, "No big deal kid, everyone does that every day."? No, we cheered and clapped and delighted along with her! That's what we need to do for ourselves and for each other.

We all have a battle to fight, we all have a hill to climb, we all are struggling in one way or another, and we are lifted up and connected and supported by the people who clap when we put our pants on.

What are three things that you feel delighted that you've accomplished this week?

Clap, cheer, express delight and amazement and appreciation. Take a moment to appreciate someone else, to help them celebrate their own wins. Not only will you feel good, you'll build your relationship and increase productivity.

If you put your pants on this morning, do a little dance of delight because you got something awesome done today.

How different would your state be every day if you could take a moment to celebrate the little wins? Those little wins would snowball and lead to more wins. We underestimate the power of the small win, but as Charles Duhigg shares in his book *Smarter, Better, Faster*:

> A huge body of research has shown that small wins
> have enormous power, an influence disproportionate

to the accomplishments of the victories themselves. . . .
Once a small win has been accomplished, forces are set
in motion that favor another small win.[11]

When we celebrate our small wins, we begin to believe big wins are possible. That is one powerful belief. My seven-year-old son has been playing flag football this spring. So I've been watching a lot of football lately, and I see this phenomenon play out on the field regularly. When the team gets a small win—an interception or a turnover—it changes the entire momentum of the game. Because that little win made them feel like winners, they believed in themselves, and the entire game turned around. They won when before they'd been losing.

Can you think of experiences in your life where small wins have propelled you forward to bigger wins?

How can you find ways to celebrate the smallest of wins?

It could be as simple as taking a moment at the end of each day to reflect back on what you did accomplish (rather than worrying about everything you still have to do) or sharing your wins in a conversation with colleagues.

Our moments of celebration can be big or small. You might want to take yourself out for a nice dinner or treat yourself to a movie or a massage, set up a night to see a comedy show, or go for a walk with a friend. When I finished draft number six of this book, my husband and kids clapped for me and even though it was a bit silly, it felt good. I treated myself to a delicious chocolate bar with caramel and sea salt. That small celebration of a small win spurred me on to writing the seventh and final draft of the book. When I submitted the final draft, it was a big win, so my husband and I went to my favourite sushi restaurant and celebrated with a glass of prosecco. When I start my coaching sessions, we discuss what small wins people have had since we last met and take a moment to appreciate them.

Before I had children and I had time to do such things, I used to write my accomplishments on little Post-it notes and put them in a jar. When a month had passed, I'd open the jar and read them over and feel pretty great about myself. I'd celebrate by buying myself flowers and taking myself out for sushi. Find a fun way to celebrate your small wins because when you do, you'll set yourself up to have bigger and bigger wins.

CONCLUSION

Everything in your life is a result of your mental and emotional state. A positive mental and emotional state generates fantastic outcomes.

Do whatever you can to create a good state at the beginning of your day and watch your days flow with more ease. Find ways to have fun. Pay attention to the thoughts, reactions, and feelings you are choosing throughout the day, and make sure that they are serving you. Use your powers of language and focus to help you maintain a positive and productive state.

You can take simple actions like starting the day with happy music or spending your commute thinking of what you feel grateful for. When you start your day off in a good state, you'll usually have a great day, and a lot of great days equal a great life. That's what I call *Working Well*.

QUESTIONS

1. What words do you use most often and how do they reflect your beliefs?
2. What's the focus of most of your conversations? What's working well or what's stressing you out? How can you change that?
3. What kind of people are you spending your time with, and how do they influence you?
4. What are the actions you take every day, and what state do they put you in (a positive and energetic state or a drained and stressed out state)?

ACTIONS

- Determine what state you are naturally in most often: positive or negative. It might be helpful to ask someone you trust for their perspective. If you'd like to take this on as an assignment, ask three people who are close to you from a mix of your personal and work life how they perceive you: Do they see you as more naturally positive or negative? Choose people that you trust will be honest with you.
- Identify one action you can take first thing tomorrow morning to start the day in a positive state.
- Pay attention to your inner voice—the language you use and the stories you tell yourself and others throughout the day. Identify the language and stories that negatively affect you. Try reframing them towards the positive.
- Spend a few minutes in a power pose and notice how it changes your energy.
- If you put your pants on this morning, do a little dance of joy.
- Find a small win to celebrate every day.
- Check out my morning meditation video and positive music playlist: www.managetoengage.com/working-well/.

Chapter Nine

Build Positive Working Relationships

"People will forget what you said, they'll forget what you did but they'll never forget how you made them feel."

—Maya Angelou

Most of us spend eight hours a day, every day, at work. That's usually more time than we spend with the person we've chosen to marry, let alone our friends or our family. Wouldn't it be nice to enjoy good relationships with the people that we spend most of our waking hours with? Not only does having positive working relationships make life more pleasant, research has proven repeatedly that good working relationships lead to higher productivity and more workplace satisfaction. In a recent study of workplace dynamics reported in the *Harvard Business Review*, researchers found that "having a lot of coworkers who eventually developed into friends significantly increased employees' performance, as judged by their supervisor."[1]

Too often at work we are only focused on getting our work completed. Ideally, we want to balance our time between our tasks and the relationships that help us get our work done.

Many people don't see the value in building positive relationships at work, but let me ask you this: If someone who is a bit of a jerk asks you to do something for them, how quickly are you going to do it? If someone you dislike asks you for advice or help, how likely are you to give it? How much do you want to help this person succeed?

Now switch that around. If someone you really like asks you to perform a task, help out, or offer advice, how likely are you to do it? How much do you want to help *this* person succeed?

Most of us will agree that we're far more interested in helping people we like and respect. If you can build positive relationships at work, you're going to get more work done.

If you don't want to become friends with everyone you work with, that's fair, but at the bare minimum, it's in your best interest to be professional and respectful. Professionalism is demonstrated by talking to your colleagues in a respectful tone, engaging in discussions with an open mind, and working effectively together. When you can do this, you get work done more easily, and you reduce your stress.

I work with a lot of teams that are stressed beyond belief. Most have high workloads and big demands, but their number one stressor is usually interpersonal relationships.

How often do you find relationships with people at work stressing you out?

It's tough dealing with other people all day long, especially when they aren't people you would have chosen to spend a significant amount of time with. But we've got to find a way to make it work; otherwise, we are spending too much of our lives feeling stressed out. Think about the people who you work with; there are likely some who make you feel positive and energized and others that fill you with a deep desire to drink.

How can you spend more time with the people who have a positive impact on you?

How can you use the strategies you've already learned to help reduce the impact of those more difficult people?

BRING YOUR SOCIAL SKILLS TO WORK

I've been very social and friendly all my life, but I never brought my social side fully into work because I thought it was unprofessional. Then I did a master's degree in leadership and discovered all the research that shows the value of building positive relationships with people at work. I was encouraged by my professors to be as social and friendly in my workplace as I was in the rest of my life.

I started asking about people's weekends, learning more about their lives and making connections. I shared more about myself and my life, and this invited others to open up too. I developed close friends. Work didn't suffer for those ten minutes that were spent chatting in the morning or the extra fifteen minutes taken on a lunch break as we laughed about a meeting that went sideways. No, we connected in that time, and as a result, our work flourished.

We are social beings. We have a biological need to connect with other people. As Paul Zak explains, "The brain network that oxytocin activates is evolutionarily old. This means that the trust and sociality that oxytocin enables are deeply embedded in our nature. Yet at work we often get the message that we should focus on completing tasks, not on making friends."[2]

Not only is friendship a biological need, it helps us get our work done more efficiently. Gallup, a company that conducts research on employee engagement and organizational effectiveness, has designed twelve questions to help assess employee engagement. Gallup defines high engagement as "having a strong connection with one's work and colleagues, feeling like a real contributor, and enjoying ample chances to learn."[3] Their research has found that high engagement at work "consistently leads to positive outcomes for both individuals and organizations. The rewards include higher productivity, better-quality products, and increased profitability."[4]

Three of the twelve questions that Gallup asks on its survey centered around our relationships at work:

- Does your supervisor, or someone at work, seem to care about you as a person?
- Is there someone at work who encourages your development?
- Do you have a best friend at work?

Our working relationships form 25 percent of what Gallup ranks on how engaged we are. A strong connection with work colleagues has a huge impact on productivity and engagement—research has shown that we will stay at a workplace longer and work harder when we have friends at work. Think about the people you look forward to spending your days with; they make it easier to get up on a cold and rainy Monday morning and make your way into work. In short, friends make everything more enjoyable, even the crappiest day at work.

REPLACE JUDGMENT WITH CURIOSITY AND COMPASSION

You know that story about the two wolves that each of us has on our shoulders? It goes something along these lines:

A grandfather is talking with his grandson. The grandfather explains that we have one wolf living on our left shoulder and another living on our right shoulder and they are always battling for our attention.

One is a good wolf, which represents kindness, bravery, compassion, and love. The other is a bad wolf, which represents judgement, greed, hatred, and fear.

The grandson stops and thinks about this, then he looks up at his grandfather and asks, "Grandfather, which one wins?"

The grandfather quietly replies, "The one you feed."

When it comes to how we treat others, one of our wolves is kind and compassionate and wants to connect with others; the other is judgmental and mean and values feeling superior over having meaningful relationships.

Which wolf are you feeding?

We all have our good days and our bad days, but let's hope that we're feeding the good wolf more often than the bad one. I don't know about you, but I usually feel much better when I choose to be compassionate and kind rather than judgmental.

Sometimes we have to fight against our natural tendencies in order to feed the kind and compassionate wolf. It's usually our first reaction to judge others, rather than to give them the benefit of the doubt. As Stephen M.R. Covey writes in his book *The Speed of Trust*: "We judge ourselves by our intentions and others by their behavior."[5] When a coworker is late on a deadline, you judge them harshly for the result. When you are late on a deadline, you know that you were late because you had a number of other pressures on your time. What would it feel like to extend the same level of understanding to one another as we do to ourselves? That good wolf might just get a little stronger, making it easier for us to keep feeding it.

We tend to make quick judgments about one another, and we filter all of our interpretations and interactions through those judgments. This doesn't help us work more effectively with others. It's one of the reasons that building friendships at work helps us to be more productive—we are less likely to judge people who we know and trust.

In all your relationships at work, whether with friends or your most difficult colleagues, I suggest you take the approach of replacing judgment with curiosity. Every time you notice that you're having a judgmental thought, remind yourself that you don't know what's really going on for that person and replace your judgmental thoughts with curiosity. Everyone has circumstances that we know nothing about.

Approaching a person with curiosity rather than judgment makes our relationships stronger.

Over a decade ago, I worked with someone who was incredibly difficult to deal with. I was not getting my work done because I was avoiding him. I found him unfriendly and unreasonably abrupt and irritable. Then I found out that his son was dying of cancer. That changed my story about him completely. I had new compassion for him, and I understood the source of his behavior more.

We all have things going on in our lives that stress us out, break our hearts, and make life difficult. Many times, our coworkers have no idea. It's entirely possible that you don't know what is happening in the lives of those people that you find difficult.

When we have made up our minds about people, we are filled with judgment and frustration every time we deal with them. But if we can remind ourselves that we don't know the whole story of what's going on for another person, we can be more open and engage with them from a place of curiosity rather than judgment.

When we make assumptions about others, we can really damage our relationships.

When I'm at work, I'm quite good at noticing when I'm making an assumption and reminding myself to be curious. In my personal life, I occasionally fall down on catching my assumptions. For some reason, I often assume my seven-year-old son is up to trouble of one type or another—usually by trying to get around his limit of sixty minutes of screen time per day (I know, I'm sure all the research shows that I'm destroying his brain, but that screen time is keeping me sane). My assumptions are correct 80 percent of the time, and he's snuck onto a phone or an iPad to play a game, but the 20 percent of the time that I'm wrong—wow, do I ever damage our relationship.

He blows up, asks why I don't trust him, and gets quite justifiably angry. I think a lot of adults probably feel this way when they've been unfairly judged; we just don't express it as clearly as my son does. I'm getting much better at using the skills of open-mindedness and curiosity that I bring to my work relationships in my personal relationships as well.

The other day I came downstairs and saw my son on the phone. Rather than jumping to the conclusion that he was playing a video game, I asked him what he was up to. "Just checking the weathercast, Mommy." He held the phone up to show me. I smiled because I hope he never stops saying weathercast. We both had a much better morning than if I'd jumped to assumptions.

Are there people in your life that you tend to judge more quickly or make more assumptions about?

If so, what can you do to change your approach to one of genuine curiosity?

UNDERSTANDING BREEDS COMPASSION

Last year, I was called into work with a highly dysfunctional team that was having a lot of conflict and not functioning effectively. They weren't getting their most basic tasks done, let alone working as a team.

We did an exercise in which each person shared one story from their childhood in an effort to help the team members understand one another better. After people got some insight into their peers, it changed the dynamics of the group for the better. Knowing a bit about each person's childhood helped the team members see why some people were more emotional than others, why some people struggled with authority, and why others were unusually critical.

This is not to say that childhood experiences can excuse behavior.

We aren't responsible for what happens to us as children, but we are responsible for how we behave as adults.

Doing this exercise helped team members have more compassion and less judgement of one another. They also took each other's behavior less personally and worked harder to reduce their impact on each other.

When we endeavor to understand others, we recognize that they are human, just like us—and that their behavior is about them, not us.

It's unlikely that you will know the reasons why someone is being difficult, but if you can cut them some slack and remind yourself that you don't know the whole story, you can be more open and less frustrated with them, which can make your life easier. When we stop judging one another, we build stronger working relationships, which decreases our stress and increases our productivity.

Is there someone you work with that you might need to learn a bit more about or just stop judging so harshly?

YOU NEVER KNOW HOW FAR SOMEONE ELSE HAS RUN

Nearly two decades ago, I was training for a mini-triathlon. I've always been a good swimmer, but I bike more slowly than most people run, and running just about kills me. It was quite the feat I was trying to pull off. I'd signed up for it thinking that it would force me to exercise which would help me manage my stress. Unfortunately, it didn't inspire me to exercise and I just became more stressed out by the training I wasn't doing, until a few weeks before the mini-triathlon when I kicked it into gear because I didn't want to make a complete fool of myself.

I did primarily run-walks for my training, working my way up to the five kilometers I would need to be able to run. One day I was jogging my first five hundred metres and feeling pretty good. I could tell that I'd improved (because I could actually jog five hundred metres), and I was faster than I'd ever been, which was still really slow.

I saw someone running slowly towards me and I thought with jubilation, *I'm running faster than her!* As we grew closer to one another, I saw that she was an acquaintance. I knew she was pretty fit, so I felt extra good that I'd been running faster. We jogged slowly in place and had a quick chat. She was training for a marathon and was at the end of a thirty-kilometer run!

A very profound insight hit me then. We never know how far another person has run. We only see them at a particular point in their lives, and we make all kinds of judgements based on what we see. We don't know what their childhood was like or what griefs and challenges they've encountered along the way.

Is there anyone you work with who just might be at the end of a thirty-kilometer run?

One thing that I have learned over many years as a consultant is that people are complicated. The employee who stays for an extra hour to help you out might be the same employee who is stealing from the company. The coworker who is always ready with a joke and makes everyone happy cries himself to sleep every night and fights depression, so he can come to work every day.

We are all complicated and imperfect. Be compassionate with yourself and with your coworkers. Let go of the stories and judgments you have about the people you work with, recognize there are many things about them you don't know, and keep on open mind and a compassionate heart.

When you are compassionate, not only will you be happier, your relationships and interactions will be much easier. That will reduce your stress and increase your productivity.

ACCEPT PEOPLE AS THEY ARE

Do you want a simple way to significantly reduce your stress? Just start accepting people as they are. Forget wishing they'd be more communicative (or less) or more organized (or less) or more friendly (or less). Just accept everyone in your life—coworkers, managers, friends, family members, children, your accountant—exactly as they are without wanting them to change. You can't change people, so stop dreaming about it and watch your stress plummet.

Plus, they'll like you more. Who doesn't want to spend time with people who accept them? You don't even need to express your acceptance to the other person. You just need to feel acceptance, and it will change the way you interact with that person. Can you imagine what it would feel like to stop hoping another person will change and being disappointed when they don't?

I've been practicing accepting people as they are, and I tell you, it's liberating. I've stopped hoping my highly disorganized client is going to magically become better at organizing courses. Instead, I've started sending her super-specific details and double-checking our event plans. I'm doing it with grace and ease because I've accepted her as she is. I've stopped trying to rush my five-year-old daughter in the mornings and then getting upset when she digs her heels in and moves at the pace of a sloth, screaming, "I don't like to be rushed." She doesn't like to be rushed. I've accepted that. Now I just wake her up fifteen minutes earlier.

Accept people as they are. Seriously. It will bring you and them so much happiness.

Maybe you know this already, and I'm the only one who finds this revolutionary. But wow, has it ever reduced my stress levels!

ELLEN'S ACCEPTANCE

I recently worked with a client who had a very demanding manager who never offered praise or positive feedback. Ellen was a very competent project manager in her midforties who worked for a large organization. She'd had great career success, and she knew she was good at her job. Ellen felt valued and appreciated when she received acknowledgement, positive feedback, and kudos. Her manager didn't meet this need at all.

Ellen explained to me, "Whenever I've finished a particularly challenging project or gone above and beyond, my manager doesn't even mention it—not even a thank-you, let alone acknowledging what good work I've done. She just starts talking about the next project."

"And how does that make you feel?"

"So frustrated. I mean, how hard is it to point out a few good things before moving on? I gave my manager the feedback that I felt more engaged when receiving positive feedback a few months ago. She smiled and said she knew she was bad at giving positive feedback, but she was working on it. Nothing has changed since then."

"Do you think it will change?"

"No." Ellen shook her head. "It's clearly just the way she is. I've told her what I need, and she's not able to do it. I'm not going to bring it up again."

"Yet you feel frustrated every time she doesn't offer you positive feedback?" I asked.

"Yes! It really bothers me," Ellen said.

"What would it feel like to just accept the reality that your manager is bad at giving positive feedback?"

"Umm . . . good, I guess?" Ellen didn't sound convinced.

"Here's the thing. Your manager doesn't naturally offer praise. It clearly has nothing to do with you since she's indicated that she's bad at it. You've asked her for what you need, and you're not getting it. You can either go back to her and explain the negative impacts of her not responding to your feedback, start looking around for a manager who is going to give you the positive feedback you need, or accept the reality of who your manager is, without expecting her to be any different."

Ellen laughed, "Well, I know I'm not comfortable having another conversation with her about my need for positive feedback, and I generally like working for her. And I love my job, so finding another manager isn't appealing. I guess that leaves accepting her as she is."

She agreed to try it, and the next time we met, she was far less frustrated and irritated. She was able to focus on her manager's strengths and what she appreciated about working for her, rather than feeling irritated that she wasn't getting any positive praise. We also talked about ways for her to meet her need for positive feedback, and she made more time to connect with her clients as they often provided appreciation for and positive feedback about Ellen's work.

Through adjusting expectations, accepting her manager for who she was, and getting her need for feedback met in other ways, Ellen was able to respond differently to her manager.

This helped reduce her stress and increase her productivity because instead of working for praise that would never come, she was working for her own satisfaction.

When we accept others as they are, we significantly reduce our own stress and we probably reduce their stress as well. When people don't feel accepted or included at work, it can be very painful. In fact, research has found that "exclusion or rejection is physiologically painful. A feeling of being less than other people activates the same brain regions as physical pain."[6]

What a gift we can give to our coworkers if we can accept them as they are, if we can let them be themselves and feel a true sense of belonging. Accepting others for who they are helps us build better working relationships and significantly decreases our stress because, whether we accept them or not, people are unlikely to change. Who do you need to start accepting just as they are? Try it for a few days and see how it changes your relationship with them.

LET GO OF STRANGER DANGER

Who do you hang out with at work? It's often the same people all the time. Having vast and varied social connections at work improves our performance and reduces our stress, but many of us don't venture past the comfortable cliques we've fallen into.

According to neuroscientist David Rock: "That's because collaborating with people you don't know well is a threat for the brain. The brain determines, subconsciously, whether each person you meet is a friend or a foe. People you don't know tend to be classified as foe until proven otherwise."[7]

This explains why we stick to our cliques, but what can we do about it? If we want to grow, we need to find ways to break out of our safe, comfortable social circles and engage with potential foes. Stranger danger is a biological phenomenon. Viewing people that we don't know as threats is how we've survived as a species for so long. But it's not usually that helpful, especially at work. If we decide every stranger is a foe, not only do we miss out on important social connections, we may misinterpret their intentions.

Have you ever done that? I sure have. I've also seen plenty of people get into really messy situations because they misread intent and discarded other people's ideas just because they perceived those people as the enemy. Just because we're hardwired to see strangers as threats doesn't mean it's good for us. When we can catch ourselves making judgments or feeling negative towards someone, it's a great opportunity to replace our judgment with curiosity.

Get out of the stranger danger mindset! Push yourself to get to know new people at work and make connections with them. Remember that someone who doesn't know you also thinks of you as a potential foe, so if you can take the initiative, everyone's going to relax. A really easy way to build connections is to spend a few minutes at the beginning of each meeting connecting on a personal level. Take some time to chat about the weekend, the weather, or local sports.

Remember that research on how our social circles influence us? That's another really good reason to break out of your cliques and build relationships with different people at work. If you can choose the right people, they'll have a good influence on you.

GIVE POSITIVE FEEDBACK

Want to win friends and influence people? Tell them what you appreciate about them. I know we've already talked about the value of positive feedback, but I'm bringing it up again because it can have powerful impacts on our working relationships. You've probably lived this—don't you have just a little more love in your heart for those people who share genuine and meaningful positive feedback with you?

IBM's WorkTrends survey of over nineteen thousand workers in twenty-six countries, across industries and thousands of organizations:

> revealed that the engagement level of employees who
> receive recognition is almost three times higher than
> the engagement level of those who do not. Recognition

has been shown to increase happiness at work in general and is tied to cultural and business results, such as job satisfaction and retention.

High performers offer more positive feedback to peers; in fact, high-performing teams share nearly six times more positive feedback than average teams. Meanwhile, low-performing teams share nearly twice as much negative feedback than average teams.[8]

Many of my clients think that only managers should give feedback, but anyone can offer specific and deliberate positive feedback. Feedback from our peers often feels more meaningful, because they've been working alongside us and they see our daily challenges and successes. Taking a few minutes to share what you appreciate about someone, the positive impact they've had on some aspect of your work or life is a great way to build relationships, create a positive workplace culture, and improve productivity. If you haven't already done so, why not try using the AIID model we talked about in Chapter Three and share some positive feedback with your coworkers? Remember to share not just the action, but also the impact.

Framework for Feedback - AIID

A	**Action** – identify the specific action you are giving the person feedback on
I	**Impact** – share the impact that their action had on you
I	**Input** – ask for their input
D	**Desired outcome** – together, come up with a desired outcome to be able to take action on the feedback

When I was teaching a class on feedback, one of my students said, "I go around and give out 'attaboys' at the end of every day." When I suggested he try to change his "attaboys" to very specific feedback that was unique to each individual, he tried it and got tremendous results. He was amazed at how much harder his staff were working. One tweak in how he delivered feedback made a big difference in how it impacted people.

PAY ATTENTION TO HOW STATUS INFLUENCES YOUR RELATIONSHIPS AT WORK

Remember the research that showed that our brains perceive every possibility as either a potential threat or a potential reward? It turns out that our sense of status strongly triggers the threat or reward response. Although we aren't always conscious of it, we're more concerned with our status than we realize. Black and Blake's research, shared in David Rock's book *Your Brain at Work* found that "maintaining high status is something that the brain seems to work on all the time subconsciously."[9]

What are the ways you unconsciously try to improve your status? Do you mention the high-level project you're working on or the fact that you had lunch with the boss last week? Do you drive a fancy car or wear brand name clothes or display other status symbols? Is your job a way you define your status, so you talk about it nonstop? Do you tell everyone about how much your fancy vacations cost? Do you name-drop? There's nothing wrong with any of these things but it's fascinating to notice all the ways we subtly (and sometimes not so subtly) try to improve our status. The problem with our desire to improve our status is that we are often focused on being better than other people, which activates their threat response.

In workplaces, our status can be determined by hierarchy, but it can also be determined by the subtle politics of each workplace. Who is close friends with the boss? Who has worked here the longest? Who is the informal leader or most popular person? Who gets the window office or the first choice of the baked goods in the break room? All kinds of factors influence our status and the perceived status of others.

Most of us don't consider how much our threat-and-reward response to status influences our interactions with others at work, yet it can have far-reaching and long-lasting impacts. I've worked with some teams where people haven't spoken to each other for years because of some seemingly small disagreement. I've always been confused by that, but now I see how being perceived as "wrong," "less than," or "losing" activates our status threat response. We generally avoid people or situations that may activate our threat response. Status is the root cause of so many of the workplace conflicts that I'm asked to facilitate. It's way more important than I realized.

> **When you think about your workplace, where do you consider your status level in relation to those you work with?**
>
> **Can you think of any workplace challenges you've had that are influenced by status?**
>
> **What are some of the everyday ways that status influences your workplace interactions?**

When we are paying attention and aware of how status threats influence us, we can respond differently. When we notice that a status threat is influencing our interactions, we can calm ourselves down and approach the situation differently. The next time you find yourself in a difficult interaction, take a minute to consider how status might be influencing the situation. With that perspective, you may choose to respond to the situation differently.

Neuroscience has found one strategy to enable us to calm down another person's threat status when they are engaging with us. It may sound familiar to you: "giving people positive feedback, pointing out what they do well, gives others a sense of increasing status, especially when done publicly."[10]

When you're dealing with someone who you sense may feel threatened by your status, try giving them some positive feedback and see if that influences your interactions.

In addition to reassuring others and reducing their threat response, we want to be able to calm down our own status-threat response as much as possible. When we are operating in a relaxed state rather than feeling threatened, we usually make different choices.

We can create a lot of stress for ourselves by trying to increase our status. Whether it's putting way too much pressure on ourselves to impress those with higher status in the company or spending more money than we have on expensive clothing, purses, or cars, our need for high status can cause us high stress. Think of ways you strive to increase your status and how you could make different choices now that you're aware of them.

There are a few ways we can increase our sense of status without creating a threat response in others: we can work to grow, learn, or get better in some aspect of our lives. And we can also acknowledge our accomplishments and growth to ourselves and celebrate our wins.

Being aware of how our behavior is shaped by our threat-and-reward responses to status can help us make different choices about how we engage in relationships at work. Instead of racing into a fight when we feel our status is threatened, we can identify what we're feeling, then respond more thoughtfully. When you think about people you've had difficulties with at work and you consider the element of status, do you see the situation differently? Even just being aware that status might be influencing the way we interact with another person can enable us to make different choices.

BUILD TRUST

Within a culture of trust, everyone is happier and more productive. If you think about different places you've worked, you'll notice there's a huge difference between working in a high-trust environment and a low-trust environment. Low-trust environments are generally fear-based; everyone's running around trying to cover their butts. High-trust environments are safe places where people can make mistakes, be vulnerable, and learn at work.

Trust is a big concept, but researcher Brené Brown has made it pretty simple. She makes the analogy of trust being a jar, finding that acts of trust are marbles that you either fill the jar up with or empty out of the jar. Through her research, Brown found, "the feeling [of trust] is actually the sum of small gestures, kind words, secrets kept, and other everyday actions. If you want to build trusting relationships, you need to do small, good deeds every day—and avoid equally small slip-ups that lead to an empty jar of trust."[11]

So how do we build trust? One marble at a time.

What are some of the things that you do that put marbles in other people's trust jars?

What are some of the things you do that might be emptying the jar of trust?

I love the idea that trust is built (or destroyed) one marble at a time because it helps us become aware of the actions that we take every day and how we normally interact with others. Even something as simple as pulling out your phone to check a text or an e-mail in the middle of a conversation can reduce trust in your relationships. People are less likely to open up when they feel your attention isn't focused on them. When we're more conscious of the impact of our behaviour, we can choose small daily actions that help build trust and avoid the ones that destroy trust.

Stephen Covey, the author of *The Speed of Trust*, has identified thirteen behaviors of high-trust leaders that we could all benefit from, whether we are in an official position of leadership or not. The thirteen behaviors are:

1. Talk Straight
2. Demonstrate Respect
3. Create Transparency
4. Right Wrongs
5. Show Loyalty
6. Deliver Results
7. Get Better

8. Confront Reality
9. Clarify Expectations
10. Practice Accountability
11. Listen First
12. Keep Commitments
13. Extend Trust[12]

When you look at the behaviors that lead to trust, are there ones that you do really well? How about ones that you could get stronger at?

Take a minute to think of one or two things that you could do differently in order for you to become stronger in the behavior that you identified.

One common workplace challenge I've noticed with building trust is people don't practice accountability or deliver results. They commit to doing a task by a particular deadline, but they don't complete it. I'm guilty of this too. Did I mention I'm two weeks behind on my deadline for this book? How about you?

What are the behaviors you could pay more attention to that would help you build more trust in your relationships?

In addition to the behaviors of high-trust leaders that I just shared, a few actions that can build trust include:

- Follow through and deliver on your commitments
- Don't gossip
- Be a straightforward communicator: address issues when there are challenges
- Don't spread rumors
- Do good-quality work

- Help others when you can
- Admit when you've made mistakes
- Admit when you don't know something
- Give credit to others when credit is due
- Take personal responsibility rather than blaming others for challenges
- Be transparent and a clear communicator: let people know your thought process and the decisions behind your actions

LISTEN WELL

One of the best ways to build great relationships is to listen well. You'll recall we spoke about this in the tools for having difficult conversations. If we're really listening well, we're building stronger relationships and often dealing with issues before they turn into difficult conversations. So many of us enter into conversations to make our own point, not to listen or to understand where the other person is coming from. If you can go into a conversation with the intent to truly listen to the other person and let go of your own agenda, you will dramatically improve your listening skills and your relationships.

When we can concentrate on the person we're listening to, give them all of our attention, and listen well, we build stronger relationships. When we add the element of replacing our judgment with curiosity, we can listen even more effectively. When the person we are interacting with feels listened to and understood, our relationship improves.

What can you do to help you listen well? A few reminders include:

- Turn your phone off and put it out of sight
- Remove any other distractions—including internal distractions
- Go into the conversation with curiosity and an open mind
- Ask questions or paraphrase to clarify that you've understood the person

When you're fully engaged in a conversation and genuinely interested, you won't need to force yourself to use any listening tools like leaning in, nodding, asking questions, paraphrasing, pausing, and not interrupting. You will naturally do these things because you genuinely care about the person and the content of the conversation.

Often my children talk about things I'm totally uninterested in. My son is currently obsessed with *Star Wars*, and because I love him, I now know a lot more than I ever wanted to about *Star Wars*. I listen to him, not because I'm interested in General Grievous or Senator Palpatine or the Inquisitor, but because I'm interested in him, and I want him to feel loved, listened to, understood, and cared for.

What are the little things that you can do in every conversation you have to make sure that whoever you're talking to feels like you care and you're listening well?

CONCLUSION

Building positive relationships at work can be really easy or really hard, depending on the people that you work with and your own style. Whether you're working with difficult people or wonderful people, whether you're naturally extroverted or naturally introverted, I encourage you to draw on what's already been discussed in previous chapters and to use the strategies from this chapter to build trusting and positive relationships at work.

When we let go of our judgements and approach people with new-found curiosity and compassion, we can be completely surprised by the results we get. We'll often find common ground, new respect, and a deeper connection with our coworkers by getting to know people on a personal level. On those days that it feels particularly challenging, let's remember to feed the good wolf and choose compassion and curiosity over judgement because it will make our life easier.

Take small actions every day to build trust with your coworkers and watch your relationships flourish. When we can accept others as they are, listen well, and build trust at work, we're going to build stronger working relationships. We all know, both from the research and our own personal experience, that having better relationships makes work more pleasant, less stressful, and enables us to get more done. Work is more fun with friends, so use some of the strategies you've just learned to build stronger working relationships and enjoy the people that you work with.

QUESTIONS

1. What three potential rewards would you experience by having more positive working relationships?
2. What judgements have you made about your coworkers (and maybe even friends and family members)? How can you replace those judgments with curiosity or acceptance?
3. Is there one person that you need to be more compassionate and less judgmental with?
4. What is one small change you can make in how you interact with that person?
5. In the past, what has helped you build strong working relationships? How can you do more of that now?
6. What insights have you had about how status influences your workplace relationships?

ACTIONS

- Identify one action that you can take today to start building more trust in the marble jars of your colleagues.
- Choose one of the thirteen trust-building behaviors and commit to doing more of it. If you want to monitor yourself, at the end of the week, write down what actions you have taken and the impact they've had.
- Identify one way that you can disengage from workplace drama and still maintain your professional working relationships.
- Choose one person that you can be more accepting of and practice acceptance.
- Identify one colleague you'd like to get to know better. Invite them out for coffee.

Chapter Ten

Work with Your Brain

"Everything we do, every thought we've ever had, is produced by the human brain. But exactly how it operates remains one of the biggest unsolved mysteries, and it seems the more we probe its secrets, the more surprises we find."

—Neil deGrasse Tyson

If you're anything like me, the workings of your brain are a mystery. For me, it's a bit like the engine of our car: I'm thrilled that it works, but I have no idea how. Neuroscience is a complicated subject, which is why you'll see that this chapter relies on the work of neuroscientist David Rock. If having a deeper understanding of your brain and the various neuropathways and chemical reactions going on is your happy place, grab David Rock's excellent book, *Your Brain at Work,* and give it a read.

Our brains are incredibly complex and sophisticated. They can deliver tremendous results if we work with them. Unfortunately, most of the time we are working against our brains without even realizing it. This chapter will give you some ideas about how to create the conditions for optimal functioning of our brains. If we use these strategies, we can work with flow and ease, accomplishing far more than if we simply work harder and put in longer hours.

More and more in our fast-paced world, we tax our brains. Our brains need quiet time to process and reflect, but how many of us give ourselves even a few minutes a day of mental stillness? I'm sure I'm not alone in finding it very challenging to quiet my inner voice and to create that critical calm that my brain needs to be most effective. As you know, I'm turning more and more to yoga and meditation as they force me into quiet time. When I take the time to do meditation or yoga, something wonderful happens. I get far more work done with far more ease. If you haven't tried it yet, please give meditation a shot. It doesn't have to be complicated. You can lie in the bath and do box breathing for three minutes or go for a walk at lunch and notice your five senses. The more we slow down, the better our brains work.

ATTENTION IS A LIMITED RESOURCE

We can't concentrate for eight hours a day. We can't even concentrate for five hours a day. Think of yourself as a kid in school: you need recess, lunch break, and a whole lot of school holidays.

Our capacity for focus and attention is limited. We run out of attention. We can't keep focusing. But we try anyway. All of a sudden, it's eight at night; we're still working, but we're not getting much done.

Let's start to recognize that we've only got so much capacity to pay attention. Then we can use our powers of focus wisely. David Rock explains, "Every time you focus your attention you use a measurable amount of glucose and other metabolic resources. . . . Each task you do tends to make you less effective at the next task, and this is especially true for high energy tasks like self-control or decision making."[1]

Decision making and self-control consume our limited resources. They wear us out. In today's high-pressure, multitasking, filled-with-distractions-and-demands world of work, we often use up our self-control and decision-making powers on tasks that don't warrant them. If you spend the first hour of your day going through e-mail and making decisions about how to respond, you've used up critical decision-making powers. Your decision-making ability might be done for the day, but you have a whole lot more you need to get done.

When we can be more thoughtful about how we use our mental energy and recognize it as a limited resource, similar to our physical energy, we can be much more productive. Just as you would never expect to be able to run without a break for eight hours a day, you shouldn't expect uninterrupted activity from your brain either.

With this understanding of how our brains work, we can make better choices about what we give our focus and attention to. When we think of our mental energy (ability to concentrate, make decisions, and think clearly) as limited, we can be more thoughtful about how we use it.

MAKE LISTS TO SAVE YOUR BRAINPOWER

While it was once commonly believed that the number of items we can hold in our mind was seven, a survey of by Nelson Cowan at the University of Missouri found that it's "more like four, and even then this depends on the complexity of the four items."[2]

I don't know about you, but I feel like I'm holding eighteen things in my mind at any given time—not just work-related items, but also school events, childcare scheduling, and social plans. I'm learning to make better use of my calendar and to do giant brain dumps of my mental to-do lists to free up more space for those precious four items that I need to hold in my mind.

I'm also trying to stop taxing my brain by remembering thoughts that occur to me in the moment. I don't know if this happens to you, but I often have an idea come to mind or a thought about something that I need to do. Typically, I will hold on to that idea or thought for hours, consuming precious mental energy and space. Now, as soon as I'm able to, I pull out my phone and jot down a note, so I'm no longer putting the strain of remembering the idea on my brain. That means I'm conserving precious mental energy for other tasks.

Are you someone who holds way too many details in your brain?

If so, how can you capture those details another way and give your brain a break?

STOP MULTITASKING

How many of you are doing two or more things at once, multiple times a day? It's frying your poor brain. I know that we're all maxed out and trying to get everything done, but multitasking is making us dumb. In fact, one scientist, Harold Pashler, "showed that when people do two cognitive tasks at once, their cognitive capacity can drop from that of a Harvard MBA to that of an eight-year-old."[3]

That's alarming. Not that there aren't some brilliant eight-year-olds out there, but I'm pretty sure the Harvard MBAs would give them a run for their money.

So, how do we stop multitasking in a world that holds it as the height of productivity? We go back to focusing on doing one thing at a time, because intuitively we know that we're actually going to be more productive, thoughtful, and present when we're maintaining a single focus.

Many of us have gotten into the habit of multitasking, usually because we are moving at a frantic pace and we think it's the best way to get work done. Now that we know it's not, we need to break ourselves of the multitasking habit. When you notice that you're trying to do two (or more) things at once, stop and retrain yourself to perform one task at a time.

TURN OFF YOUR PHONE

I know I've already mentioned this in the context of having better relationships and taking care of yourself but guess what? Turning off your phone will also significantly increase your productivity. Our phones pull our focus, and we often multitask when we are on them.

A study done at the University of London "found that constant emailing and text messaging reduces mental capability by an average of ten points on an IQ test. It was five points for women, and fifteen points for men. This effect is similar to missing a night's sleep. For men, it's around three times more than the effect of smoking cannabis."[4]

I know there are some of you who are reading this and thinking that you're an excellent multitasker, and this research doesn't really apply to you.

You may be the exception to the rule, but let me ask you this: what is multitasking doing to your relationships, to your ability to concentrate, and to think deeply?

We need to slow down before we lose these important skills.

In a nutshell, if we want to be more productive, we need to quiet our inboxes, turn off our phones, and pay attention to one thing at a time.

These actions will also decrease our stress and improve our health because:

> when the brain is forced to be on "alert" far too much, it increases your allostatic load: a reading of stress hormones and other factors that relate to a sense of threat. The wear and tear from this threat has an impact. Neuroscientists have found that this always on, anywhere, anytime, anyplace era has created an artificial sense of constant crisis. What happens to mammals in a state of constant crisis is the adrenalized fight-or-flight mechanism kicks in.[5]

So many of us live lives where we are "always on," and we feel that we're in a state of constant crisis. We're often in fight or flight mode and that's taxing on our bodies. It's no way to live! It's no wonder that so many people are dealing with physical and mental health issues.

Let's find ways to turn off, to disconnect from work and the hundreds of e-mails bombarding us, so that we can become less stressed and more productive.

What strategies have you learned so far that could help you disconnect? Have you been using them?

If so, what have the results been?

If you haven't already, please find a way to turn your phone off just for a few hours a day, for the sake of your productivity, your health, and your relationships.

PRIORITIZE MORE DEMANDING MENTAL TASKS

Our brains are like our muscles. They get tired. Most of us start our days dealing with e-mails, which consumes our precious mental energy and limited decision-making power. Checking e-mails first thing in the morning also releases the stress hormones cortisol and adrenaline, so we aren't necessarily starting our day in a great state.

It may be wiser to schedule our days differently. Rock suggests that we "schedule the most attention-rich tasks when you have a fresh start and an alert mind. Prioritize first, before any attention-rich activity such as emailing, because prioritizing is one of the brain's most energy-hungry processes. After even just a few mental activities, you may not have the resources left to prioritize."[6]

When we start our days dealing with e-mail (as I certainly used to before I read David Rock's book), we've already worn out our brains before we get to our true work. I found it a difficult habit to break, and I still sometimes check my e-mail before I start work. But on the days that I start with writing or meditating (or on a good day, both), I'm on fire. Give it a try for a couple of weeks, and see what happens. Even one hour (or if that sounds too overwhelming, just start with fifteen minutes) of prioritizing, planning, thinking, or working on your most important tasks before you deal with your e-mail can have a huge impact on your productivity.

MANAGE DISTRACTIONS

I don't know about you, but I find myself very easily distracted these days. I can be pulled from a task or a conversation by the sound of the phone buzzing. (I turn the ringer to silent, but there are times when I can't turn the phone completely off, in spite of all the research that suggests I'd be happier and more productive if I just threw the damn thing away.) Even though I don't look at or respond to the text or e-mail, my concentration is broken.

I'm also often interrupted from conversations or work by one of my kids or my husband asking me a question—there are upsides and downsides to working from home. Other distractions I experience regularly include my own internal distractions: trying to keep track of too many details, my mental to-do list and random thoughts popping into my mind, the urgent need to clean out the closet when I should be writing, a sudden desire to know when and where the next Garth Brooks concert will be, and other similar Internet rabbit holes.

I know I'm not alone, and I'm negatively impacting my productivity with all these distractions.

How about you?

Do you get distracted easily and frequently?

What are some of your more common distractions?

We don't necessarily notice it, but those distractions cost us a lot of time.

A study conducted by Gloria Mark, professor in the Department of Informatics at the University of California, Irvine, "found people switched activities on average of every three minutes and five seconds. Roughly half of them are self-interruptions."[7]

How many of you do this to yourself? You're working on one task but then something pops into your brain and you rush to deal with that instead. This seems like it's not that big a deal, right? You're working on a presentation, but you remember you need to send an e-mail, so you switch tasks. You send the e-mail in two minutes then you get right back to the presentation. Except you don't. Mark's research found that "it takes an average of 23 minutes and 15 seconds to get back to the [initial] task."[8]

Distractions are costing us a lot of time. And they're causing us a lot of stress. Mark's study "used a NASA workload scale, which measures various dimensions of stress, and we found that people scored significantly higher when interrupted. They had higher levels of stress, frustration, mental effort, feeling of time pressure and mental workload."[9]

How often are you distracted when you're working on a task?

Make a list of your most common distractions and ways to avoid them (turning off the phone, the notifications on our computer, turning off the Internet while working, closing your office door, forcing your children to play outside).

When we are aware of what distracts us, we can make different choices and not get caught up in the distraction. When we reduce or eliminate some of our more common distractions, we can gain back up to two hours of productive working time every day.

HAVE A CLOSED-DOOR POLICY

I've coached many people who have an open-door policy, and I've worked hard to get them to spend at least one hour a day with a closed door. They have to train their coworkers and staff to give them this uninterrupted time, but it enables them to have focused time to work on their most important projects.

Otherwise, they spend all day responding to the needs of everyone else, being distracted, and switching tasks frequently, sometimes staying late to get their own work done. Sound familiar? It can be difficult to close our doors, but if we choose a time that is the least disruptive to the people who need us, and if we explain to people that we are closing the door to get focused time to increase our productivity, they will understand, and they might even follow suit.

How many of you go in extra early or stay extra late just to get that time free of distractions?

As we discussed earlier, working extra hours decreases our productivity, so if we can build some focused work time into our days, we'll be better off.

What would be the best time to schedule your closed-door hour?

What else can you do to reduce the distractions during your workday?

TAME THAT MONKEY MIND

While some distractions come from external sources, many come from our own busy brains. We all have many internal distractions that can keep us from being productive. Not only do we jump from thought to thought, but if we're not in a positive mental state, we may be bringing ourselves down with our thoughts.

Many of us get easily distracted when we are working on something we don't want to do or find challenging. At that point, it can seem really important that we go ask Bob how his weekend was or check with Jasmine about the lunch we'd discussed setting up. Or, we'll just take a few minutes to check social media or look up tickets for that game or concert we were interested in, because, after all, taking a break is really good for productivity, right?

Our minds run around like monkeys, flitting from one thing to another, particularly when faced with work we don't want to engage with. It's up to us to take control back. As with everything else, the key is in self-awareness and noticing when we're distracting ourselves. When we can notice our monkey mind at play, we can wrest control back from the little wriggler.

When I practice mindfulness and notice my internal thoughts, I often hear things like: *This is boring, I'll just check my e-mail*, or, *I'll never get this done, maybe I should eat some chocolate instead.* When I'm paying close attention, I can catch myself in the act of getting distracted and make the choice to stay focused, rather than give in to the distraction.

What I'll often do is turn the desired distraction into a reward for myself. I tell myself, *If you do another fifteen minutes of writing, you can take a break and check e-mail or eat a square (or three) of chocolate*—whatever my little monkey mind desires.

Next time you notice yourself getting distracted, either from an internal or external source, bring your focus back to the task at hand while promising yourself a reward for completing that task.

When you reward yourself, choose a treat that's *really* a treat for you—maybe a fancy coffee, a cookie, or a quick walk. Whatever it is, make sure you link it to your ability to stay focused, so you reinforce the new behavior with a real reward. Sounds a bit like training the monkey, doesn't it?! We'll talk more about why this works in Chapter Twelve about habits.

CHANGE YOUR RELATIONSHIP WITH YOUR E-MAIL

E-mails deserve their very own category of distraction as they consume so much of our working lives. Some work relationships are also happening through texts or social media: "According to the Radicati Group, a technology research firm, in 2018, there will [have been] 'about 124.5 billion business emails sent and received each day.' . . . The average office worker receives 121 emails a day."[10] No wonder e-mail is such a workplace stressor!

Based on what we now know about distractions and the mental energy that processing e-mails consumes, what can you do differently in your relationship with your e-mail?

Some of the changes I've made regarding my e-mail are to turn off all notifications, check it only after I've spent at least half an hour doing my thinking and creative work, to check it less frequently, and to respond to e-mails as soon as I check them. I used to just check e-mails to get the rush of dopamine associated with receiving a message and then not deal with them . . . not a great strategy.

If you're looking for some more strategies, here's how some of the world's CEOs are handling their relationships with e-mail as reported by Rachel Gillett in *Business Insider*:

Jeff Weiner

The golden rule for e-mail management, according to LinkedIn CEO Jeff Weiner, is, if you want less e-mail, send less e-mail.

He says: "I decided to conduct an experiment where I wouldn't write an email unless absolutely necessary. End result: Materially fewer emails and a far more navigable inbox."

Arianna Huffington

Media mogul and author of *Thrive*, Arianna Huffington, has three simple rules for e-mail:

- No e-mails for half an hour before bed
- No rushing to e-mails as soon as she wakes
- No e-mails while she is with her children

"The last time my mother got angry with me before she died was when she saw me reading my email and talking to my children at the same time," Huffington writes in her book. "Being connected in a shallow way to the entire world can prevent us from being deeply connected to those closest to us—including ourselves."

Jason Dooris

Jason Dooris, CEO of Australian media agency Atomic 212, never e-mails his employees—and he won't let his employees e-mail each other either.

"We've totally cut out all internal emails," Dooris previously told *Business Insider.*

Dooris was tired of people relying on e-mail as the primary means of communication with their coworkers. "In the office I don't see it as a necessity, when the people you're emailing are only a few [steps] away and you can chat with them," he said.

Instead, Dooris and his employees use Wunderlist to track tasks, Dropbox to share files, and face-to-face contact for anything else. The only exception is calendar invites, which may be e-mailed.[11]

Hopefully, this has given you a few ideas for how you can change your relationship with your e-mail. Obviously, you're limited by what works for your company culture—not everyone is keen on the idea of eliminating e-mail altogether. That said, if your company culture produces so much e-mail that you start each day feeling buried in it, you might want to suggest some changes.

What are three things you can do to better manage your own e-mail?

DON'T BE A KEYBOARD WARRIOR

I've worked with a few people who are self-confessed "keyboard warriors." They save all their difficult communication for e-mail so they can avoid conflict. Sometimes at work, we forget that there is another person on the receiving end of our e-mails, someone who will be impacted by our words or uncertain about our tone. If you have to deliver difficult feedback or have a challenging conversation, please have the courage to do it in person, or at the very least on the telephone. This goes for our personal lives too. It will prevent a great deal of stress and confusion for all involved.

When I teach my communication courses, I emphasize that face-to-face is always our best option for communication. If that's not an option, pick up the phone. Only if there are no other options is e-mail an acceptable last resort. If you do need to use e-mail, keep it fact-based and to the point, and clarify for the receiver exactly what you need from them. Starting our e-mails with an indication of what we need can save a great deal of time for those who receive them. FYI, Action Required, and Urgent, Response Needed are examples of ways to clarify the purpose of your e-mails.

Keeping your e-mails succinct (five sentences or less) will also help you be more productive and save you time in the long run. Keeping your e-mails clear and kind will keep your working relationships strong, which will help you be work more efficiently and effectively.

WORK WITH YOUR NATURAL STRENGTHS

We all have strengths and talents that come naturally to us. We have developed or inherited these strengths, and we take these abilities for granted. Just last week a client asked me how I listen and paraphrase so well. It wasn't an easy answer as it's something I've always done—a natural strength. When our brains are active in an area of strength, we are at ease.

The research company Gallup found if we work in our areas of natural strength and focus on leveraging those strengths and managing our weaknesses, we can be highly productive and successful. Gallup identified three important principles of how to work with our strengths: "For an activity to be a strength, you must be able to do it consistently. You do not have to have strength in every aspect of your role to excel. You will excel only by maximizing your strengths, never by fixing your weaknesses."[12]

For those of us who have been trying way too hard to fix every little imperfection we have, this is totally liberating research. All you have to do is focus on your strengths because trying to fix your weaknesses won't help you excel. Hallelujah! I never have to figure out math.

When I completed Gallup's online test that helps you identify your strengths, the Clifton StrengthsFinder Assessment,[13] it became clear to me why I lasted less than a month in a job as a grocery store clerk but happily spent nearly a decade working with youth. It also gave me insight into why I'm so happy as a coach, facilitator, and consultant. I have natural strengths in relating to people, connecting big ideas, and simplifying them for others, and I love change.

I am not detail-oriented, nor do I move at a particularly fast pace, both strengths that would have served me well in my role as a grocery store clerk. The Clifton StrengthsFinder tool is a quick and affordable way to discover your natural talents and provide some insight about yourself. I've used it with many teams and clients. I've included the link in the resource section.

We also have an intuitive sense of our own strengths and areas of comfort. I've always enjoyed working with people, so it wasn't a surprise when my StrengthsFinder results showed that relating was a top strength of mine.

Think about what people frequently tell you that you're good at.

What is so easy for you to do that you take it for granted?

What makes you lose track of time?

The answers to these questions will help you identify some of your natural strengths and talents.

DOES YOUR JOB FIT YOUR STRENGTHS?

We often feel stressed and unproductive when we're working in jobs that require strengths that we don't have. When I worked as a receptionist at a high school in my late twenties, I went home every day feeling drained. I wasn't skilled at dealing with multiple requests at the same time, filing and organizing paperwork, trying to keep track of details, all while being constantly interrupted by parents, teachers, and ringing phones. Some people thrive in this fast-paced environment with a lot of distractions. I did not.

The complete lack of fit in this job convinced me to quit working and go back to school at the age of twenty-seven to complete my education degree. I was really nervous about returning to school because I knew that I was going to come out with thousands of dollars of debt. But I pushed myself past the discomfort. It was the best decision I ever made.

While I didn't enjoy teaching high school, I love teaching leadership to people in the workforce. In my role as a consultant and coach, I've been able to branch out and do all kinds of work related to my strengths that I would never have been able to access if I hadn't continued to seek opportunities to learn more and find jobs in my areas of strength.

If we are working in an area of natural strength, chances are we will be highly productive and engaged. If we are working in an area of natural weakness, often identified as "skills gaps," or "areas for growth," chances are we will be more stressed and less productive.

This is not to say that skills can't be learned, but you want to capitalize on your natural strengths at work. You'll be more productive and happier.

Think about your strengths and how often you are using those strengths on a day-to-day basis.

How much time are you spending working in areas that aren't your strength?

It's unlikely that any of us are working 100 percent of the time in our areas of strength, but the more time we spend there, the more productive and less stressed out we will be.

Gallup suggests that we need to manage around our weaknesses rather than ignoring them altogether. As I've mentioned, an area of weakness for me is math. My grade twelve math teacher passed me so I could graduate, as long as I promised to never take another math class. I've happily stayed true to that promise.

When I have to do proposals and invoices, I ask my engineer husband to review them. I also have a very good accountant whom I rely on heavily. We can find ways to manage around our weaknesses but if we are constantly working in an area of weakness, it can be quite demoralizing and draining.

When you've identified your natural strengths, either through your own discovery process or with the help of the Clifton StrengthsFinder, think of ways you can use your strengths more at work—or find work that's a better fit for you and your natural strengths. Not only will you be happier and more productive when you're working in an area of strength, but your strengths will flourish.

CONCLUSION

When we understand how our brains work, we can make better choices. Like everything in this book, the key is to take action based on what you've learned. Think of ways that you can stop multitasking and turn distractions off. Schedule your days differently, so you're doing your thinking, planning, and prioritizing work early in the day when your brain is fresh. Think about what your natural strengths are, and find more opportunities to use them, at home and at work.

Our brains are incredible, but they aren't invincible. Let's find ways to slow down, give our brains a rest, and create good conditions that enable our brains to operate at their best. When our brains are functioning well, so are we—we're far more productive, happier, and more relaxed.

QUESTIONS

1. How can you schedule your day differently to make better use of your limited mental energy for focusing and making decisions?
2. How often do you multitask? What can you do to switch to a single focus?
3. How would your productivity and your relationships improve if you did only one thing at a time?
4. What is one action you can take to minimize distractions?
5. What natural strengths have you identified? If you need help, ask five people you trust what they see as your natural strengths.
6. Can you estimate how much of your day you spend working in an area of strength? What can you do to leverage your strengths more?

ACTIONS

- Turn off your phone and all of your computer notifications while you are doing work that requires focus—even just for one hour a day.
- Pay attention to your thoughts, catch your urges for distraction in the moment, and choose to maintain your focus.
- Cut the number of times you check your e-mail and texts in half. Install a time-tracking app like Moment to help you be more aware of how often you pick up your phone.
- Commit to turning your phone off for at least one hour each evening, so you can focus on the people you're spending time with.
- Pay attention to how much productive time you're losing to distractions (like checking your e-mail, texts, and phone) every day. If you want to collect some data, keep track of every time you get distracted (either on a piece of paper or on your phone) and count how many times you were distracted at the end of the day.

Chapter Eleven

Use Productivity Hacks

"Productivity is never an accident. It is always the result of a commitment to excellence, intelligent planning, and focused effort."

—Paul J. Meyer

Now that we have a good understanding of how our brain works and the conditions it needs in order to be highly productive, we can be far more effective. In addition to working with our brain, there are a number of productivity hacks that will help us work more efficiently.

I don't use all of the tools I'll share with you in this chapter on a consistent basis. I suggest you don't try to use them all either or you'll be stressing yourself out all over again. Like every strategy I've shared so far, choose the ones that will work for you and leave the rest.

Sometimes, I naturally use some of these tools; other times, I naturally do things that destroy my productivity. Usually, there's a correlation with how stressed out I am. The more stressed I feel, the less productive I am because I end up doing the opposite of many of the strategies that help us be more productive. *Take a break? I can't take a break! I have so much work to get done and not enough time!*

Remember that reducing your stress, taking care of yourself, and being happy are all excellent tools for productivity. Just doing those things alone will significantly increase your output.

When we add in using productivity tools and start working smarter, not harder, we can create more time for ourselves and our lives. Then we arrive at work recharged and happy, and we get even more accomplished with ease. It becomes a wonderful cycle of productivity and feeling relaxed. That's when we are truly *Working Well.*

JUST DO IT

If a task is going to take you fewer than five minutes and you have the time available, do it immediately. That way, you aren't straining your brain trying to keep track of everything you need to do and you're not adding one more thing to your to-do list. In a lifetime before computers, the suggestion was that we only touch a piece of paper once. This meant that the minute we opened a letter or a bill, we dealt with the contents immediately rather than adding the paper to a pile and dealing with it later. While we can't apply this rule to every task on our to-do list, we can take the spirit of it and apply it to much of our work.

When you open an e-mail, you can sometimes deal with the contents right away and then delete the e-mail. When I'm running from one meeting to the next and I remember that I need to send a client an e-mail, I pull out my phone and send the e-mail in the moment rather than using up valuable brain power trying to remember to send the e-mail after my next meeting.

What are the little things that you carry around in your brain that you could do when you have a few free minutes? We can reduce our feelings of overwhelm by not carrying all those details around in our brains and we can get more done if we act immediately.

CHOOSE COMPLETION OVER PERFECTION

A few years ago, I spent months coaching an executive team that shared with me their motto: 80 percent is good enough. Their goal is to get their work done and delivered to their workforce as quickly as possible without working towards perfection. Then, they adapt and evolve as they go. Done is better than perfect. This was mind-blowing for my little perfectionist brain. Their approach made me realize all the ideas that I wasn't developing and all the writing I wasn't doing because I was trying to make everything perfect before I put it out into the world. I decided to give this concept a try—and I tripled my productivity within the first month.

This executive team has over five hundred people working for them and huge financial pressures. There is a lot at stake if they mess up. Frankly, it is way more important for them to get it right than it is for me. If they can produce at 80 percent, surely, I can too.

Yes, it would be ideal to have all the time and resources need. But I don't. And neither do you. We have to work within the circumstances and limitations that we have. Otherwise, we'll be waiting for the right conditions, which may never come. If we don't follow through on meeting our goals and following our passions, we'll miss sharing something valuable that will add to our lives and the lives of others—all for the sake of the elusive perfection, which in itself is impossible to achieve.

Perfect doesn't exist. When we don't share our work because it's not perfect, it's often a way of protecting ourselves. By seeking perfection, we avoid being vulnerable and putting ourselves out there. That's understandable because vulnerability can feel terrifying. But doing the work you're meant to do and sharing your gifts and talents with the world is worth it. It won't be perfect (because nothing is) but it will be in the world and it will be good enough.

Before becoming aware of the 80 percent is good enough concept, I was far too focused on perfection—half of my projects never got completed—or worse yet, never got started. After seeing how the team worked and the amazing quantity and quality of work they produced, I took a completely different approach. I started aiming for production over perfection. Everything that I produce these days is my commitment to delivering my work at 80 percent, because 80 percent is better than not at all. In most classes, that's an A.

In working on this book, I reminded myself to aim for 80 percent. I'd like to think I made it to 90 percent. If my goal had been 100 percent, I'd never get the book done. It would take another year or two or even three. I'd get so frustrated with the pressure I'd put on myself and the challenge of getting the book perfect that I'd throw the manuscript out. I know this would happen because I've done it to a few other manuscripts. But with this one, I'm stepping into vulnerability and choosing completion over the elusive and unattainable perfection.

I'd rather get it to you in this imperfect, but good-enough form, so you can start using the strategies *today*, rather than waiting another year or two to have the book be just a little bit better.

With every cell in my body, I'm fighting a long-ingrained habit of perfectionism in writing and editing this book. I can't tell you the number of times I've decided to put the manuscript on a shelf and walk away because it's not perfect. Then I talk myself back into working on it, so I can put it out into the world and fulfill a goal I've had for many years. Good enough is my new goal. Perfection is the enemy of completion, and these days, I'm aiming for completion.

FOCUS ON THE IMPORTANT, NOT THE URGENT

Stephen Covey made the Eisenhower Quadrant well known in *The 7 Habits of Highly Effective People*. It's designed to help you become a more effective self-manager. Many of us have heard of this tool, often called the Urgent-Important Matrix, but how often are we using it?

	URGENT	**NOT URGENT**
IMPORTANT	• crises • pressing problems • deadline-driven projects, meetings, preparations	• preparation • prevention • values clarification • planning • relationship building • true recreation • empowerment
NOT IMPORTANT	• interruptions, some phone calls • some mail, some reports • some meetings • many proximate, pressing matters	• trivia, busy work • some phone calls • time wasters • "escape" activities • irrelevant mail • excessive TV

Eisenhower/Covey

When we use this matrix, we want to evaluate our tasks based on their level of urgency and importance. Urgent tasks require your immediate attention: a phone ringing, a meeting you're scheduled to attend, a deadline you need to meet. But we want to evaluate those tasks to see how many of them are important. Maybe you don't need to be at that meeting after all, maybe you could ignore the ringing phone to focus on meeting the deadline because the deadline is the only important task in all of those urgent ones.

In a perfect world, we'd focus on our important tasks, and we'd proactively plan time to work on them, which would minimize the urgent tasks that often cause us so much stress and distract us from our most important work. It sounds simple enough, but the problem is that we're far more likely to deal with urgent activities, regardless of importance, because they're right in front of our faces, screaming for attention.

I've decided to make my important tasks feel more urgent because that pushes me to accomplish them. Writing this book is an example of an important but non-urgent task. I managed to get it done by creating circumstances that made it feel more urgent. I contacted publishers and identified my targeted publication date, which pushed me to get the writing of various drafts done by specific deadlines.

If you take even five minutes at the beginning of your day and put your to-do list through the Urgent-Important Matrix, that will help you prioritize your work and ensure that you are putting your limited time, focus, and attention on the work that is most important.

I also evaluate my personal commitments through the Urgent-Important Matrix. It helps me prioritize what is really important to me and ensures that family time is scheduled into my calendar.

When was the last time you put one of your own personal goals on your list of things to accomplish?

How about spending time with your family? Does that land in the important quadrant?

Take some time and think through the elements of your life that feel really important to you. Slide those suckers to the urgent and important side of the quadrant. Schedule time into your calendar to pursue your passions and spend time with your favorite people.

We generally follow through with tasks we schedule. When we start scheduling the very important but less urgent tasks of taking care of ourselves and connecting with the people that we care about, our stress goes down and our productivity increases.

After you've identified your important tasks, it's a great idea to schedule one hour in your day of closed-door office time to work on them.

Take the time to focus on what's important, and refuse to engage with those seemingly urgent but not important distractions.

Turn off your phone and your computer notifications, so you can accomplish your most important work.

CHOOSE YOUR TOP THREE

Productivity experts have identified that many successful people choose their top three tasks to accomplish each day. I've used this principle to identify what my three most important tasks are to accomplish every month, then I use those as the guide for what my top three tasks each day should be.

Those three tasks are the first things that I tackle, knowing that I have limited mental energy. They are not the most urgent, but they are important. I try to schedule fifteen minutes to write every day, and I prioritize spending time with my kids in the mornings and evenings. It doesn't always happen, but just having an awareness of these important tasks makes me far more likely to do them. Because as Covey says, "If the important is left at the mercy of the urgent, it never gets done."[1]

Do I do identify and work on my top three tasks every day? Not every day—sometimes I get busy or I forget, but on the days that I identify my top three most important tasks, even just mentally, I am far more productive. I also spend at least a few hours each month planning and scheduling my priorities, so my calendar is doing the work for me.

Recently my business coach gave me an assignment to track my time for a week, so I could see where I was spending my time and how much time I was dedicating to my identified priorities. Just knowing that I had to track the time and report back on how I was using my time made me better at devoting time to working on my top three priorities.

How can you make the principle of the top three work for you?

Maybe you want to spend some time every morning choosing tasks you will prioritize each day. Or maybe you'd prefer to spend your Friday afternoons planning your next week, or maybe the monthly approach works better for you. Whatever approach you take, if you spend a bit of time thinking about what your top three daily priorities are and schedule the time to work on them each day, you're going to get much more done.

SET SMARTER GOALS

Most of us have heard of setting goals that are SMART: Specific, Measurable, Achievable, Realistic, and Time-Sensitive. I'm going to encourage you to set SMARTER goals which are:

S—Specific
M—Measurable
A—Achievable
R—Realistic
T—Time-Sensitive
E—Engaging
R—Rewarding

Based on what we now know from the research, adding *Engaging* and *Rewarding* will motivate us further. When I set goals for myself or with clients, we make those goals SMARTER. We frame goals in ways that feel Engaging. A client of mine had a goal of "complete safety policy review," and we turned it into "create the best possible policy to keep all our staff safe." When we frame our goals so that we can see the benefits to ourselves or others, we feel much more engaged in completing them.

Then once a goal is accomplished, no matter how small it is, I encourage clients to reward themselves and celebrate that win. We discuss what would feel like a meaningful reward to each person—some of the ideas have included buying themselves chocolate, sharing their accomplishment with a group of supportive friends, planning a night out, or booking a massage to treat themselves. Remember, when we reward ourselves and celebrate our small wins, we build momentum and set ourselves up for bigger wins.

SET STRETCH GOALS

SMART goals have the word Realistic built right into them. SMART goals are meant to be obtainable. This idea is counter to what research has found—that when our goals require us to stretch, they are far more inspiring and motivating than easily achievable goals. On his podcast, *Lead to Win*, Michael Hyatt shares research has found that "when goals are set too low people often achieve them, but subsequent motivation and energy levels typically flag, and the goals are usually not exceeded by very much . . . difficult goals are far more likely to generate sustained enthusiasm and higher levels of performance."[2]

Often called stretch goals, challenging goals can be really inspiring and motivating, as long as we don't put too much pressure on ourselves. A stretch goal is motivating because it's fun to work towards meeting a significant and difficult-to-achieve goal. One caveat with setting stretch goals is that if you're setting them at work, you need to be very aware of the past performance of the company as well as the resources that are available to you to achieve your stretch goals.[3]

I suggest to my clients that they make the Realistic part of their SMARTER goal a very challenging Realistic target—that way they are clear on the goal and motivated to achieve it by stretching themselves.

BREAK GOALS DOWN INTO ACHIEVABLE TASKS

Whatever our goals are—stretch, SMARTER, or some combination of the two—it's good to break them into small, achievable steps. We often don't even start working towards our goals because we are overwhelmed by the magnitude of completing them. But when we break things down into achievable bites, we are much more likely to start working on them—and to feel the reward of accomplishing these more attainable tasks.

I break down my big goals into daily tasks. Writing a book is a big goal. Writing two pages today is manageable. Creating a twelve-week leadership course is daunting. Building week one is doable. Making my kids feel loved and connected is an enormous and lifelong goal.

Giving them a cuddle or making time to read three stories to them is an achievable daily task.

When we see one big task, our minds want to run. We see pain. When we see five achievable tasks, we see possibility and pleasure in their accomplishment. We see the reward. Our minds will run towards that. When we check off one of those tasks at the end of the day, we get a rush of satisfaction, and our reward response is strong. We feel energized about tackling the next achievable task the next day.

While writing this book, I did not have "Write *Working Well*" on my to-do list. That would have been way too daunting. Instead, I had "Research for chapter one" on Monday's to-do list and "Write chapter one draft" on Tuesday's and Wednesday's to-do list.

I also worked with my coach to ensure that I could have a positive, energized mindset while writing the book and focus on the engaging vision of having the book published. This approach helped me enjoy the process rather than stress about the tight deadlines I'd set for myself. Working with my coach also helped me manage my fear that I'd be exhausted and drained and kept me focused on how to stay energized and motivated. As you know, I've had some stress while writing the book. It's been hard work. But, overall, this has been a positive experience that I've enjoyed because I've been working with my brain and using the strategies that I'm sharing with you.

GO SLOW TO GO FAST

I learned the concept of "go slow to go fast" while doing group work for my master's degree. I hated it. I like to go fast. Really fast. But, for two years, my master's program forced me to go slow to go fast, and I came to see the value in it. Now it's one of my best strategies for being productive. When I slow down and take the time to plan and prioritize all my work at the beginning of a project, I move through the project far more quickly than if I rush in and start work without a plan. Even though it seems counterproductive, going slow at the beginning of a project or task is actually one of the best ways we can increase our productivity and build positive relationships.

When we take time to think through every step of a project and plan it out at the beginning it goes far more smoothly than if we race ahead with no planning at all. The same goes for the people that you are working with. Remember the research that found that we treat all strangers as a threat? Our biology reminds us that it's extra important to take the time to get to know any new people we are working with.

When we take time to get to know one another and clarify roles and expectations for each person on the team, we can move forward with clarity and achieve far more than if we didn't have those discussions. This approach can feel painfully slow, but I promise it will save you time later on.

I see so many teams start working on a big project without discussing roles and responsibilities, how they will work together, deal with disagreements, and manage deadlines. Two weeks down the road, everyone is incredibly frustrated, people are behind on their tasks, and no one has any idea of how to solve the problems that are arising. They started out fast but ended up going very slowly because they didn't take the time to lay the groundwork for a smooth, planned way forward.

As a result, more often than not, these teams have to call in a consultant to help them untangle all of the frustrations, failures, and relationship damage that's occurred. When I go to work with teams in this situation, we have to back up and clarify the roles, the tasks and responsibilities, and the processes. While I'm grateful for the work, I'd be even more grateful to be able to do that same work at the beginning of the project when people are energized and hopeful, and we could set everyone up for success.

In different presentations and courses that I deliver, I do a few fun team-building exercises to illustrate how teams work. I give the group a problem to solve in a fifteen-minute time frame. Each group always has one participant who's an observer. The observer pays attention to how much time the team spends planning versus doing, how often the team tries to include everyone, gets input from one another, and keeps the working relationships strong.

The reason that I ask the observer to watch for these things is that these are the elements that fall apart in teamwork the most often. In most of those groups, teams get right into doing. They spend no time planning. They rush into work, and they don't think about how they're including the people on the team. And this lands them in trouble time and time again.

If you put the time in to go slow at the beginning of whatever work you're doing, either in a team or on your own, you will be one thousand times more efficient as you work through the project. That's scientifically verified research, affirmed by my years of watching people go fast and then have to do all the work over again. Just imagine, going one thousand times faster.

How often do you spend your days running from one meeting to the next, not having had any time to prepare, let alone determine whether you should even be there?

Make some time to look at your workload, priorities, and goals. Then slow down enough to do some planning. It might just make you way more energized and productive (possibly one thousand times more).

KNOW HOW YOU WORK BEST

You know yourself better than any productivity expert out there. Think about times when you've been highly productive in the past. What conditions were in place? What time of day was your best time? Many people suggest getting up early so we can work while our brains are freshest. For me, this is a recipe for disaster. I'm a night person; I'm barely coherent in the mornings. I tried getting up an hour earlier to write. And I wrote five pages every morning. Five pages of utter crap. So now, I just wake up at my regular time and write before dealing with e-mail. Do you do your best thinking work early in the day or right after lunch or towards the end of the day? Think about what has worked really well for you in the past and how you can incorporate it into your routine.

What conditions do you need to be highly productive?

Are you one of those morning people who can get up at five and leap right into work? If so, I'm jealous. Or do you need three cups of coffee before you can put a thought together? I feel your pain. Do you need total silence to work, or do you thrive in a busy, noise-filled environment? Do you like to plan out your work and then get into it, or is it easier for you to start on your work and then do the planning once you can see the pieces come together?

When you get clear on creating the right conditions for yourself, the work flows far more easily. You can get so much more work done in half an hour of optimal conditions (for me, that's late morning/early afternoon and complete silence) than you can get done in three hours of terrible conditions (for me, that's early or late in the day and any noise at all). Think about what conditions help you be the most productive, and find a way to build in at least half an hour a day of working in your perfect conditions.

CONSIDER WHAT KIND OF ENERGY YOUR DIFFERENT TASKS TAKE

I can schedule three hours to design a course in my day. And that's it. Because that takes up all my thinking power. I can't schedule teaching in the morning and writing in the afternoon. It doesn't work. I've tried it. By the time I hit the afternoon, I've got nothing left. I can write for about three hours in a day, then my mind goes a little soft. But I can easily schedule a coaching session after writing because it requires a totally different type of energy.

Now that I understand how to manage my tasks by energy, focus, and attention required, I schedule my days differently. On the days that I'm designing a course in the morning, the rest of the afternoon is spent on scheduling, invoicing, or responding to e-mails—or, if I'm really *Working Well*, going for a swim or to a yoga class.

What are the tasks that make up most of your workdays?

How can you start designing your days so that you're scheduling your tasks according to the type of energy and attention they require from you?

When we plan our workdays around focusing on our most important work, creating optimal working conditions for ourselves, and scheduling our tasks to manage our energy and attention, we dramatically increase our productivity.

LET TECHNOLOGY HELP YOU

We've talked a lot about how distracting technology can be, but, if we use it wisely, it can help us be way more productive. I know many people who use technology to great advantage. I am not one of these people (yet).

Even with my limited abilities, a few things that I've been able to use technology to help me with have included:

- Setting a timer on my phone to remind me to take breaks (because breaks make me more productive).
- Using the talk-to-text feature on my phone to send texts, and e-mails, and to write notes on my phone.
- Scheduling meetings and plans into my calendar the minute they're planned.
- Using apps and reminders to help me stay on track with accomplishing goals and taking care of myself. My meditation app sends me a friendly "time to meditate" notification every morning at seven.

These are just a few examples. Many people who are more technologically adept than I am will have plenty suggestions for you—go and ask them. I have one client who has set a reminder on her calendar every day at three p.m. that tells her to go find someone to provide positive feedback to.

We need to start using technology for what it was designed for: to make us more efficient. Let's stop watching cat videos (unless they make you deeply happy) and start using a project-management app to help us complete the activities that will make us more productive. Remember that those activities include taking a break, walking with a friend, or enjoying a few moments to sit quietly and breathe.

STOP EQUATING BEING BUSY WITH BEING SUCCESSFUL

It seems like our culture has put busy people on a pedestal. We view people who have high demands and plenty of responsibilities as the picture of success. The more I force myself to slow down, the more I'm able to question this equation of "busy equals successful."

Feeling busy increases our sense of status. After all, if we're busy, we must be important, right? Or maybe not. Being insanely busy is not what success looks like. The most successful people in the world are not running around like chickens with their heads cut off. They own their calendars, not the other way around. They are in control of their time, and they use their time wisely.

When we can stop thinking of being busy as a badge of honor and see it instead as a symptom of insanity that's infected our whole culture, we can step away from it.

We can recognize busy for what it is: a result of having too much on our plates, not prioritizing our most important work, or having poor boundaries.

Imagine if when someone asked you how you're doing, you could answer, *I'm great. I have lots on the go, and I'm accomplishing everything I need to. I've got lots of time and energy left for my life and I'm really enjoying myself. How about you?*

You'd be modelling a new and far more desirable vision of success.

What's one small shift you could make in your mindset that would help you see that being busy doesn't mean being successful?

When we experience how slowing down and taking care of ourselves enables us to get more work done, we're less inclined to fall into the busy trap.

USE THE POMODORO TECHNIQUE

I love the Pomodoro Technique because it can make work into a game. It was invented by developer, entrepreneur, and author Francesco Cirillo in the early nineties. He named it after the tomato-shaped timer that he used to track his work as a university student. It's a very simple approach to getting work done by concentrating for short periods of time.

Cirillo's book, *The Pomodoro Technique*, is a helpful read, but Cirillo himself shares his method freely.

Here's how to get started with the Pomodoro Technique, in five steps:

1. Choose a task to be accomplished
2. Set the pomodoro (timer) to twenty-five minutes
3. Work on the task until the pomodoro rings
4. Take a short break (five minutes is typical)
5. Every four pomodoros, take a longer break[4]

I find the Pomodoro Technique incredibly useful for creative work. I used it when writing this book. It's easier for me to commit to a twenty-five-minute sprint than a two-hour writing session, but once I'm into it, I'll often do the full set of pomodoros and complete two hours of writing. I also love this method because it has breaks built right into it—remember to give yourself a true break rather than checking your phone. Grab a glass of water, do a few stretches, or go for a quick walk, then go on to your next pomodoro. If you can create some time in your day to do even just one twenty-five-minute sprint, you'll get so much more done than you would expect.

LISTEN TO BAROQUE MUSIC WHILE YOU WORK

Baroque music is a form of classical music (think Bach and Handel) that has been touted as an excellent tool to enhance students' learning and focus. The theory behind this is because baroque music is around 60 beats per minute, the same as our resting heart rate, the music puts us in a deeply relaxed state. Research has found that "baroque music creates an atmosphere of focus that leads students into deep concentration in the alpha brain wave state."[5] Couldn't we all use a bit more deep concentration and focus? I've listened to Vivaldi's *Four Seasons* about three hundred times while writing this book. I've also played classical music on headphones in the past when I've worked in cubicles or open office spaces to cut out the distraction of coworkers talking.

BUILD ACCOUNTABILITY INTO YOUR WORK

We need other people to help us stay accountable. A manager or coworker can sometimes do that for us. The need for accountability is the reason that I work with a business coach and the reason that so many of my clients work with me: they want not only insights and growth, but also accountability, to themselves and to their work. Our coaching allows them to bring the best of themselves to work and to their lives every day.

Who helps you stay accountable, not just to your work goals but to your priorities and life goals? If you don't have someone, find someone. Ask a coworker, hire a coach, partner up with a friend. When we have accountability built into our lives and our work, we're much more likely to succeed. I recommend setting very clear SMARTER goals and having weekly or biweekly check-ins to see how you're progressing. If you're on track, take a moment to celebrate. If you're not on track, it's a great opportunity to explore the reasons why not and find ways to get back on track or to adapt your goals as needed.

If you can't think of anyone who would be a good accountability partner for you, you can check out my *Working Well* online course, where you'll be paired with accountability partners who will keep you on track. The course helps you create a positive mindset, take personal responsibility, and take daily action to reduce your stress and increase your focus and productivity.

DO WHAT THE MOST PRODUCTIVE PEOPLE DO

You probably work with some highly productive people. Go and ask them what they do and how they manage to be so highly productive. Remember to adapt their methods to ones that work for you. If they say that they always do their best work after midnight and you know you're an early bird, take the intent of what they are doing—creating a focused time for working at their highest productivity point—and apply it to your own situation by creating that time for yourself in the morning.

An MIT study conducted by Robert Pozen found that the most productive people had three habits. Pozen shared these habits and their associated behavior in an article in the *Harvard Business Review,* which can be found in the resources section. Here's what his research found:

> **First, plan your work based on your top priorities, and then act with a definite objective.**

- Revise your daily schedule the night before to emphasize your priorities. Next to each appointment on your calendar, jot down your objectives for it.
- Send out a detailed agenda to all participants in advance of any meeting.
- When embarking on large projects, sketch out preliminary conclusions as soon as possible.

- Before reading any lengthy material, identify your specific purpose for it.
- Before writing anything of length, compose an outline with a logical order to help you stay on track.

Second, develop effective techniques for managing the overload of information and tasks.

- Make daily processes, like getting dressed or eating breakfast, into routines so you don't spend time thinking about them.
- Leave time in your daily schedule to deal with emergencies and unplanned events.
- Check the screens on your devices once per hour, instead of every few minutes.
- Skip over the majority of your messages by looking at the subject and sender.
- Break large projects into pieces and reward yourself for completing each piece.
- Delegate to others, if feasible, tasks that do not further your top priorities.

Third, understand the needs of your colleagues for short meetings, responsive communications, and clear directions.

- Limit the time for any meeting to ninety minutes at most, but preferably less. End every meeting by delineating the next steps and responsibility for those steps.
- Respond right away to messages from people who are important to you.
- To capture an audience's attention, speak from a few notes, rather than reading a prepared text.
- Establish clear objectives and success metrics for any team efforts.

- To improve your team's performance, institute procedures to prevent future mistakes, instead of playing the blame game.[6]

How can you learn from the research on what the most productive people do? Which of these habits could you adopt? Think of one or two that you could use over the next week or two and see how taking this action impacts your productivity.

TAKE BREAKS

We talked about taking breaks in Chapter Five as an important tool for self-care, but taking breaks is also an amazing productivity tool. Our brains aren't capable of working endlessly, and when we give them true breaks, we're way more productive.

Tony Schwartz, CEO of the Energy Project and author of *The Way We're Working Isn't Working,* has led studies that indicate our energy rhythm cycles every ninety minutes; those people who take a break every ninety minutes are the most productive. His entire life's work is dedicated to helping people manage their work by energy rather than by time because energy is a renewable resource. He says, "Like time, energy is finite; but unlike time, it is renewable. . . . A new and growing body of multidisciplinary research shows that strategic renewal—including daytime workouts, short afternoon naps, longer sleep hours, more time away from the office and longer, more frequent vacations—boosts productivity, job performance and, of course, health."[7]

Taking breaks is the one productivity tool I can proudly say that I've started using frequently and effectively since learning about it. I never used to take breaks. I'd always work through lunch, and the idea of taking a break during the workday seemed insane—how could I take a break when I had so much to do?

Since experiencing how much more productive I can be by taking a break, the days of "powering through" are over. Mainly because it doesn't work as well as taking a break.

Let's get out of the habit of pushing ourselves to work even when we are past capacity. When we recognize that taking time to recharge and replenish our energy will make us more effective, we can make different choices about how we spend our time and energy. We could take some of our less productive working time to build good working relationships, read a book, exercise, or go for a walking meeting. This approach will make you so much more productive than sitting at your desk and trying to push past your brain's capacity for productivity.

How often do you take breaks?

When can you start scheduling them into your day?

I've worked with a lot of clients who have been very skeptical about the value of taking breaks but after just a few days of scheduling regular breaks, they are complete converts. Commit to scheduling at least two to three breaks a day for the next three days and watch your productivity skyrocket. Remember that a true break requires you to get away from screens and stop thinking about work—try to get outside for a bit of fresh air or do some stretches. If you work in an archaic workplace, you might want to take in some of Tony Schwartz's research to help management understand just how effective taking a break can make you.

LET YOUR SUBCONSCIOUS DO THE WORK

When we take breaks, we are working smarter—not just for our bodies and our energy, but for our brains. I took many breaks while working on this book when I normally would have just powered through. Those breaks allowed my subconscious to work on the problems I was having with the writing, and, more often than not, when I returned from yoga or my swim, I had the solution I needed.

David Rock shares in his book *Your Brain at Work* that Mark Beeman, one of the world's experts on the neuroscience of insights, found that "about 40% of the time people solve problems logically, trying one idea after another until something clicks. The other 60% of the time an insight experience occurs. In insight, the solution comes to you suddenly and is surprising, and yet when it comes, you have a great deal of confidence in it. The answer seems obvious once you see it."[8]

We've all experienced this. On your morning drive to work, the perfect solution to the problem you've been working on all week pops into your mind. Or, when you're in the shower, you suddenly know exactly how to solve the issue you've been struggling with for weeks.

If we can just stop trying so hard to solve problems logically and give our brains a break, our subconscious will kick in and help out.

I know so many people who won't stop working, even to go to the bathroom. I used to be one of them. Go take a pee, for crying out loud! It just might generate the best insight ever—and if it doesn't, at least you won't pee your pants.

CONCLUSION

Hopefully, these productivity hacks have given you some insight into how to work smarter, not harder.

When we're going slow to go fast and taking plenty of breaks, we're going to be far more productive than if we consistently push ourselves past our mental and physical capacity to get work done. By setting SMARTER goals, identifying and working on our top three priorities, knowing how we work best, and focusing on our most important work, we can accomplish more with ease.

When we're intentional about creating a life that fulfills us, we'll be more satisfied than if we fall into the overachiever's trap of doing, doing, doing. Let's not fall into the trap of getting so busy with the urgent but unimportant tasks in life that we miss out on what really matters.

Take a few minutes to think about what is most important to you and how you can be more productive, so you're able to make time for the people and activities you care about. We can use productivity tools to help us live fulfilling lives that allow us both the time and energy for every aspect of our lives.

QUESTIONS

1. In what ways does a drive for perfection decrease your productivity?
2. What changes do you need to make to ensure you're focused on what's most important to you?
3. How could slowing down increase your productivity?
4. Have you equated being busy with being successful? What can you do to change this mindset?
5. When can you schedule your breaks? What will you do on your breaks?

ACTIONS

- Identify what quadrant of the Eisenhower Quadrant system you're spending most of your time in. If you'd like to collect data on your focus, at the end of each day, look through the tasks you accomplished and what you were spending your time on. Chart where those tasks and your time fit in the Urgent-Important Matrix. Do this research for a week to get a sense of where you spend most of your time and what changes you might need to make.
- Choose one project you've been avoiding, and break it down into small tasks.
- Look for opportunities to go slow in a current or upcoming project.
- Make one of your goals SMARTER. Make sure it also stretches you.
- Identify one way that you know you work really effectively (or one strategy you've learned that you'd like to try) and start using it now. Schedule it into your calendar.
- Find an accountability partner to hold you responsible for a specific project, task, or goal. Set up weekly meetings so that you can each hold each other accountable.

- If you want to join my *Working Well* online course, you'll be paired up with accountability partners. https://www.manage toengage.com/working-well/.
- Check out the stretches designed for office workers in the free *Working Well* companion video and make time to do them throughout your day: https://www.managetoengage.com/working-well/.
- Schedule those damn breaks!

Chapter Twelve

Create Positive Habits

"We are what we repeatedly do. Excellence, then, is not an act, but a habit."

—Aristotle

I don't know about you, but I have a lot of habits that I'm not even aware of that guide me through my days and weeks. Some of them are good (getting to yoga every Tuesday), and some of them are bad (checking my phone frequently), and some of them I don't even know I'm engaging in. How much of what you do on a daily basis is a habit? Think about your morning routine—from what you have for breakfast, to how you get to work, and the way you speak to your coworkers, so much of what we do every day relies on our habits. And most of those habits are unconscious—we're not even aware of them. Most mornings, I'm half asleep and relying on my habits to get me dressed and out the door. Other than the day of the see-through blouse, my morning habits have generally come through for me.

If we can get into the right habits to start our days, we can begin every day in a positive mindset which sets us up to have excellent days.

I used to have a habit of listening to the news in the morning. Then I realized how depressing it was. Now I listen to upbeat music instead. It's a small tweak to my morning but it's made a huge difference in my mood and my days.

When we can improve our habits, we can drastically improve our lives. For example, I used to have a habit of sleeping until the last possible moment and racing out the door, flustered and stressed, which didn't make for a great start to the day. Now I have children, so sleeping late is not an option. Ever. As much as I miss my sleep, I do have a way better morning habit now—meditation and stretching.

In this chapter, we'll look at how to build a new habit, how to replace a negative habit, and some of the most effective habits that we can create for ourselves. Think about all the actions you have committed to over the course of this book. You might want to choose a few of those actions that you see as key to reducing your stress or increasing your productivity and turn them into habits.

Habits are the brain's way of saving energy. When we've done something often enough, the brain simply begins to do it automatically. Our habits can be incredibly helpful. Unless they aren't. Some of us have habits of staying up too late, watching too much TV, opening up social media sites every time we pick up our phones, or raging at our coworkers (or family members) when we're stressed out.

What are some of the habits that you have that you know are increasing your stress and decreasing your productivity?

Think about how you might replace those habits with healthier ones as we look at how habits are created and changed.

THE HABIT LOOP

The reason most of us struggle with creating good habits for ourselves is that we don't really understand the way habits are created. In his book, *The Power of Habit*, Charles Duhigg makes it very clear how habits are formed:

> This process within our brains is a three-step loop. First, there is a cue, a trigger that tells your brain to go into automatic mode and which habit to use. Then there is the routine, which can be physical or mental or emotional. Finally, there is a reward, which helps your brain figure out if this particular loop is worth remembering for the future.
>
> Over time, this loop—cue, routine, reward; cue, routine, reward—becomes more and more automatic. The cue and reward become intertwined until a powerful sense of anticipation and craving emerges. Eventually . . . a habit is born.[1]

Knowing how our brains create habits is really helpful. I now realize that every time I've tried to change a negative habit, I've either tried to quit cold turkey or I've been focused on the wrong part of the loop: the routine, or what I would consider the actual habit—like checking my e-mail as soon as I opened my computer. As Duhigg explains:

> [M]ost people, when they think about habits, they focus on the behavior or the routine. But what we've learned is that it's the cue and the reward that really determine why a habit unfolds. . . . [The first thing we need to do is] to diagnose the cue and the reward."[2]

Once I understood the need to focus on the cue and the reward, not just the routine, I had a better sense of how to change my habits. It became easier to recognize the cue (opening up my computer) and choosing a different routine (opening up my manuscript and writing for fifteen minutes instead of opening up my e-mail). Think about the cues that Duhigg lists. What elements cue some of your habits? Is it:

1. A time of day
2. A certain place

3. The presence of certain other people
4. A particular emotion
5. Or a set of behaviors that's become ritualized[3]

Once we understand what's causing a cue for a habit, we can make different choices in response to the cue. Maybe the habit you want to break is picking up your phone eighty-seven times a day. Look for the cues that happen throughout your day. Times to watch for might be:

- When you wake up
- When you arrive at work
- When you're in an elevator, on the bus, in any kind of line-up
- When you sit down at your desk
- When you need a break from work
- When you sit down in a meeting and are waiting for it to start
- When people around you check their phones
- When you're eating
- When you feel bored
- When you're anxious or stressed out

When we can identify not just the cues, but also the rewards we are seeking, we can make different choices about the routine habits we engage in. Once we understand what the craving we have is, we can find a healthier way to meet that particular need. As always, our power lies in self-awareness. It gives us the ability to understand our motivations and make different, healthier choices.

Often the reward of checking our phones is that we look busy, we don't have to engage in awkward social situations, we get a bit of a break or distraction from what we've been doing, or we get the dopamine hit of having positive social interactions online.

What is the reward you're seeking when you're checking your phone?

When we can identify the reward that we are seeking, we can find a different routine to help us achieve that reward. If we're looking for a positive social interaction through checking Facebook or Instagram to see how many likes we have, we could replace that with interacting with a coworker or friend or simply by smiling and saying hello to someone we pass in the hall or on the street. If we're feeling stressed out and we need a break, instead of checking our phone, we could spend a few minutes box breathing. Now that you've thought about what reward you're searching for when you pick up your phone, consider what different routine could get you the same reward.

I had a habit of picking up my phone every morning and checking e-mail first thing, often before I even got out of bed. I knew it was bad for me, I knew it didn't increase my productivity or set me up well for my day, but I couldn't seem to break the habit.

My cue was the time of day, and picking up my phone first thing in the morning quickly became a behavior that had become ritualized. I slept with the phone right next to my bed, so, when I woke up, it was an immediate reflex to check it. The reward I got from checking my e-mail was feeling like I was prepared for the day.

Logically, I knew the downsides: my brain was buzzing with work demands and already full before I'd properly woken up; I didn't have full attention to give to my kids; and I was tiring my brain out first thing in the morning by filling it with e-mails and their associated decisions.

I couldn't break the habit—until I dealt with the cue and the reward. The cue was relatively easy. I no longer sleep with my phone on the bedside table. It stays downstairs, so I don't even see it until after I've fully woken up and engaged with my kids. I also needed to change the ritualized behavior, so instead of reaching for my phone first thing in the morning, I now reach for my water bottle.

The reward felt a bit more challenging. How could I start my day feeling prepared and ready for whatever would come at me? That's where my morning meditation came in.

I knew from experience that when I meditated, I started my days in a relaxed, positive state. Morning meditation never feels as easy as checking my phone, but when I meditate, I feel way more calm and prepared for my day than on the mornings when I dive right into my phone and start reading my e-mails. I'm able to be more present and connected to my kids and to my clients; my thinking is clearer, and my ideas flow more easily. That's a really good reward, and it motivates me to build a different habit.

Take a few minutes now and think about how you can make the habit loop work for you:

1. Choose one habit that you would like to change.
2. Think through the current routine that you engage in.
3. Identify what the cue is.
4. How can you can change the cue or change your response to the cue?
5. What is the reward you are seeking?
6. What might be a healthier routine that would actually get you the same or an even better reward?

REPLACE YOUR NEGATIVE HABITS (RATHER THAN TRYING TO STOP COLD TURKEY)

Duhigg's Golden Rule of Habit Change says that the most effective way to shift a habit is to diagnose and retain the old cue and reward and try to change only the routine.[4] Too often, we naively believe that we can just stop a negative habit, forgetting the power of the cue and the reward. Think of a habit that you'd like to stop and what you might replace it with. Maybe you could replace the habit of grabbing a chocolate bar with the habit of grabbing an apple. Or you could replace the habit of thinking angry, stressful thoughts with the habit of thinking calm, peaceful ones. If you pick up your phone first thing in the morning, maybe you could replace the habit of checking e-mail with the habit of opening up a meditation app and meditating for five minutes. When we replace a habit, there's still a familiar routine but the action is different.

THE MULTITASKING HABIT

In Chapter Ten we learned about how detrimental multitasking can be to our productivity. I used to multitask whenever I was on the phone with friends or family. This is embarrassing to admit because I realize how damaging it can be to a relationship to not give your full attention to it. But I'm human and flawed and super busy, so I thought multitasking would help. My habit loop started as soon as the phone rang. I would immediately put the person on speaker so I could also check my e-mail while I was having the conversation. The reward was that I felt like I was able to get more done, which is of course completely untrue. Not only was I less productive, I was far less attentive to my phone calls than I should have been.

Now when my phone rings, I still put it on speaker but any time I feel the urge to open my e-mail, I stop myself. The only multitasking I allow myself to do while I'm on the phone is walking or stretching, as they are good for my body and don't distract my mind from the conversation. This way, I still get a reward and feel like I've done something good for myself, but I'm able to give my full attention to the person I'm speaking with.

How about you?

What are the situations in which you commonly multitask?

Is there a cue that's leading you to multitasking?

When we notice what the cues are, we can consciously stop the urge to respond to them and find a different routine to replace the multitasking, one that still has a reward associated with it.

It's only by paying careful attention and catching ourselves that we are able to change our habits. This initially takes some mental effort and focus because we are changing a behavior, which requires far more work from the brain than just following an established habit. But once we replace the bad habit (like multitasking) with a good one (like having a single focus and achieving more), we recreate that habit loop, and it becomes just as easy for our brain to follow the healthy habit loop.

THE POWER OF OUR HABITS

When we can get our habits working for us, rather than against us, we can change our lives. The difference between whether we choose to go for a run or go for drinks when we're stressed out often comes down to our habits. And the more often we choose one behavior over another, the more it becomes an ingrained habit that we naturally go to. Think about an unhealthy habit you may have had in the past that you replaced with a healthy one. How did changing that habit improve the quality of your life?

People who have changed their lives for the better often credit changing their habits with helping them improve their lives. We all have habits of thinking, feeling, and responding to stress that we aren't even aware of.

Imagine what would happen to our stress and productivity levels if we created new and healthier habits.

What is one habit that you could change that would have a positive impact on your stress levels?

USE SELF-AWARENESS TO CHANGE YOUR HABITS

One of the first steps to creating change is awareness. Remember I told you how I installed the app Moment on my phone, which showed me how many times I picked it up and how many minutes I spent on it per day? The realization that I was picking up my phone forty times a day and spending upwards of two to three hours a day on it was a serious wake-up call. Becoming aware of my behavior gave me incentive to make a change.

Often, I'd pick up the phone for only a minute or two, seeking the reward of some mental stimulation and distraction. I was working, so some of that time was justified, but I was well aware that at least half of my screen time was a total waste. I was losing approximately an hour a day of productivity because of a bad habit.

I maintained this habit even when I knew it was interfering with my productivity. I had to identify the cue and the reward, so I could make different choices. The cue was usually that I was tired of working or parenting, and the reward I wanted was a break. Once I identified those elements, it was easier to make different choices.

When I felt like I needed a break (the cue), instead of picking up my phone (the routine), I'd walk around the house, get a glass of water, or do some stretches. It helped me feel more relaxed (the reward), but stretching or drinking a glass of water offered a much healthier break than mindlessly checking my e-mails or scrolling through Facebook. The reward was the same; I wasn't wrestling with PowerPoint for at least five minutes.

When we become more self-aware, it's a lot easier to change our habits. Our power lies in identifying our cues and rewards and doing the hard work of changing our routines. If you know you have a habit that isn't serving you, you have the power to change it.

Yes, it will be hard work, but it will be worth it. Once you've accomplished the difficult task of replacing a negative habit with a healthy one, your brain will naturally take the healthy route because it's become a habit. Changing your habits can literally change your life.

How much better would your life be if you had better habits?

1. What is a habit that you know has a negative impact on your productivity?

2. What is a habit you have that increases your stress?
3. How would your life improve if you changed these habits?
4. For each of the habits that you'd like to change, identify the cue, the routine, and the reward.
5. Identify cues that you can eliminate or respond to differently.
6. Come up with a few ideas for a routine you could substitute instead of the routine you currently have.

Think about one habit you could experiment with changing and give it a try. See what the positive impacts are. Usually, when we're getting good results, we're motivated to keep forming the new habit.

PAY ATTENTION TO YOUR HABITS OF THINKING

We've talked in previous chapters about noticing our beliefs and paying attention to our inner voice, the language we use, and the thoughts we have. Often our habits of thinking can become habits we aren't even aware of: "According to the research of Dr. Fred Luskin of Stanford University, a human being has approximately 60,000 thoughts *per day*—and 90 percent of these are repetitive!"[5]

That's a lot of thoughts we have—and a whole lot of echo. We want our habits of thought to be ones that help, not hinder us. Our brains are lazy; they go down our most well-developed pathways of thinking. If your well-developed pathways of thinking are focused on stress, negativity, and drama, your habits of thinking aren't serving you. We've already discussed the value of paying attention to your thoughts—this can be particularly helpful in noticing negative habits of thinking and replacing them with more positive habits of thinking.

I remember discussing with a client once how hard he was on himself. He gave me some examples of the things his harsh inner voice would say to him. His mind was filled with thoughts like: *You suck, You totally blew that, You'll never get this right, You'll never be smart enough, I can't believe how badly you messed up, That guy doesn't really like you, he's just being nice,* and *You'll never be good enough.* He asked me, "Doesn't everyone have this harsh inner voice?"

It was a moment of great insight for him and a burst of happiness for me as I explained, "I used to have that voice. It was cruel and judgmental and put a lot of pressure on me. Then I started paying attention to the thoughts that weren't serving me and replaced them. Now my inner voice is loving and kind and encouraging. Occasionally I'll slip, and my dragon voice will return, but it's rare."

I've created a different habit of thinking and now my brain naturally goes down more compassionate and positive pathways of thinking. My client spent the next few weeks paying attention to his thoughts. He was astounded to find how many of the same themes emerged—all of them negative, none of them serving him. He was even more amazed to realize that he didn't *have* to listen to them.

When we fall into mean, judgmental thinking, we are doing ourselves and everyone we engage with an incredible disservice. Instead of taking that path, let's bring the best of who we are to our work, to our relationships, to our lives.

Whatever thoughts we think and behaviors we engage in most regularly build up neuropathways in our brains and make it easier for our brains to follow that route. The more often we do something, the more likely we are to create a smooth, fast highway for our thoughts and behaviors to travel down. That's why some thoughts and behaviors feel "natural."

It's up to us to create new pathways for our brains and to create new habits of thinking, ensuring that we are operating at our best. If we can create the habit of positive and optimistic thinking, our lives will dramatically improve.

This new pathway will initially feel like driving down a pitted, bumpy country road. But the more you practice thinking positively, the stronger that pathway becomes, until that highway of negative thinking has crumbled into a dirt road and the bumpy country road of positive thinking has become the highway. With practice, your thoughts will automatically go down the positive and optimistic route.

So, how do we change our habits of thinking from negative to positive? We start with self-awareness and begin paying attention to our thoughts. This is where mindfulness and slowing down enough to notice our thoughts can be really helpful. Once we notice our negative thoughts, then we interrupt the unhealthy thought patterns. Every time you notice a negative, mean, or judgmental thought about yourself or another person, interrupt it—I sing a little skipping song from childhood that goes "fudge, fudge, call the judge." This helps me interrupt the negative thought and allows me to change it. After I've sung the song and interrupted my pattern of negative thinking, I replace it with something more positive and compassionate.

Positive habits of thinking and responding to stress are going to lead to good results in our lives just as negative habits in how we think and respond to stress are going to lead to more stress.

Many of us have an all-or-nothing way of thinking, and that includes how we see the process of building habits. We start off with great intentions and momentum. Then, we falter. We miss a day or two, and instead of being compassionate with ourselves and recognizing that it's hard to make a change, we completely give up on whatever habit we were trying to build. As far as I can tell, no good habits are ever built easily. Negative habits seem to form very easily; they have a quick reward response (like a sugar hit after a bite of chocolate), but good habits don't often give us that quick hit. Instead, they give us a more lasting and satisfying reward.

I've got a habit of reaching for chocolate every time I feel stressed or hungry or tired. That was one easy habit to create. The habit of meditating in the morning is still a work in progress after fifteen years.

Few habits are built one day at a time in perfect succession. You will mess up and fall back into old patterns. That's normal and natural, so please, don't give up. To make it easier to build new habits, rely on what the research tells us:

If you believe you can change, surround yourself with supportive people, and reinforce a positive vision of where you want your life to go, you're going to build some really positive habits.

Who are the supportive people in your life?

What are the goals and dreams that inspire you?

What are the thoughts and beliefs that flit through your mind every ten seconds?

Are they helpful thoughts and beliefs? If not, it's time to find some new ones.

What are the stories that you tell about yourself?

Are they stories that serve and strengthen you or are they stories that deplete and drain you?

Let's say you didn't get a job you applied for. Does the story that you tell yourself become, *I'm useless, and I'm not good enough,* or, *I guess that job wasn't meant for me,* or, *It seems I have a few more things I need to learn before I'm ready. What can I do to gain the skills?*

Our habits of thinking influence absolutely everything in our lives. Our beliefs drive our behavior; our behavior produces results that reflect our beliefs. Remember the research that found that confidence in our abilities was a greater predictor of success than our actual abilities?

When we believe that we are capable—of doing a great job, of making change, of being highly productive—we can create habits of thinking and behaving to ensure that we become capable and highly productive.

If we believe that we are stuck, that we can't change, that our habits drive us and we have no power over them, our habits of thinking will reinforce those beliefs.

1. What are some habits of thinking that aren't helpful to you?
2. How can you start to replace them with healthier habits of thinking?

3. What are the cues that trigger your unhealthy thinking habits? For example, you make a mistake and your habit is to think, *I'm such an idiot, why did I do that?*

4. When you experience a cue (you make a mistake), what's a more positive replacement thought you can use? For example, the next time you make a mistake, you could think, *Nobody's perfect. It's not the end of the world. What can I learn from this?*

5. What are the rewards of those unhealthy thinking habits? Often the rewards are that we're reinforcing a negative belief we have about ourselves (*I knew I was stupid! Dad was right, I'll never amount to anything,* et cetera).

6. How can you create better rewards? While it's comfortable to reinforce our old beliefs, we'll feel much better if we're kind and compassionate to ourselves.

USE KEYSTONE HABITS TO INCREASE YOUR PRODUCTIVITY

Keystone habits are habits that have a far-reaching impact on your life. As Charles Duhigg explains, *keystone* habits are central, core habits that have a domino effect and create more healthy habits. Exercise has been identified as a keystone habit, one that positively impacts many other aspects of your life. Remember the research that found that people who exercise eat better, are more productive at work, are more patient and less stressed? That's because research has identified that "exercise is a keystone habit that triggers widespread change."[6]

It was when I read this research that I committed to exercising more regularly. Doesn't it just make you want to go for a run because that's going to make everything in your life better? They even found that people who exercise more have less credit card debt! I mean, come on, that makes it worth getting up off the couch, right?

Keystone habits work because when we do something that makes us feel good (like exercise), that makes us want to keep doing things that make us feel good (like drinking water instead of wine).

We have all experienced this. You replace an old habit with a more productive one, or you start a new habit altogether. You have a small win that generates momentum, so you not only keep doing what you've been doing, you add in other positive behaviors. For example, a friend and I went to yoga the other night, then we went for dinner. Although we usually have a glass of wine or two with dinner, we both felt far too healthy after yoga to indulge in the wine.

SURROUND YOURSELF WITH BELIEVERS

Academics studying the effectiveness of Alcoholics Anonymous found that there were two crucial elements that enabled people to make successful and long-lasting change in their lives after addiction: belief and a supportive community.[7] Duhigg tells us that "belief was the ingredient that made a reworked habit loop into a permanent behavior. For habits to permanently change, people must believe that change is feasible."[8]

When we believe we can change, we begin to find evidence of our ability to change. We think of ways we have changed in the past or find examples of little changes we are making in order to grow right now.

What are some changes that you've made in the past?

What helped you believe that those changes were possible?

The other element that the researchers identified as a crucial part of our ability to create long-lasting habit change was community.[9] Sometimes belief is hard to hold onto all on our own. It's why I work with a business coach and have been involved in mastermind groups in the past. In a mastermind group, people come together with the aim of growing, learning, and supporting one another. The people I met while participating in mastermind groups were highly motivated, and they not only believed they would succeed, they believed their fellow group members would as well. Their support, belief, and similar experiences were very valuable to me when I was starting up my business.

Duhigg shares that researchers have found that "belief is easier when it occurs within a community. For most people who overhaul their lives, there are no seminal moments or life-altering disasters. There are simply communities—sometimes of just one other person— who make change believable."[10]

Thinking back to the research on how our friends and their social circles influence us, it's even more important that we surround ourselves with people who believe in us and in our capacity to change and grow. Take a minute now to think about who those people are in your life; commit to building stronger relationships and spending more time with them, and to support them with their goals and beliefs as they support you with yours.

MAKE A HABIT OF IT

If we can create some good habits, we'll be more relaxed, more productive, and our lives will be way better. And once we've done the hard work of creating a good habit, it becomes easy to do because we don't have to think. The highway in our brain has been built, and we naturally travel down it. Our good habits become automatic (kind of like reaching for that chocolate when we're stressed, only better!).

1. What are some of the actions that you have chosen to take while reading this book?
2. Which ones can you turn into habits?
3. Choose at least one action that you want to turn into a habit and create a cue for it (like putting your running shoes by the side of your bed, so you stumble over them in the morning). Seeing those running shoes will cue you to get out for a run before starting your day.

Here are a few examples of strategies we've discussed that could be turned into habits:

- Scheduling your thinking work for first thing in the morning when your brain isn't tired out.

- Taking breaks during your workday.
- Checking your phone less during the day.
- Not checking work e-mails after work hours.
- Asking yourself the personal responsibility questions in response to stressful events.
- Meditating, using power poses, or music to start your day in a positive state.
- Scheduling self-care into your week.
- Finding three things to be grateful for every day.
- Sharing positive feedback.
- Exercising.
- Getting more sleep.
- Concentrating on one thing, rather than multitasking.
- Doing fifteen to sixty minutes of work before checking your e-mail.

If you haven't already done so, I'd suggest you look back through the questions at the end of each chapter and choose at least one action you can turn into a habit. If you choose only two habits, why not choose exercise and creating a positive state of mind? If we can master those, we'll end up with a whole lot of additional benefits as well.

After you've determined what you're going to make a habit of, I strongly encourage you to find someone who can support you and hold you accountable. Maybe you can pair up with a coworker or friend, start working with a coach, or join a group. An easy option is to ask someone else to read this book and join you by becoming your accountability partner in creating new positive habits.

Whatever you want to become stronger at, start making a habit of it and watch your life transform. Build on the momentum you have now and take the actions to build the habits that will help you create the life you want and deserve.

CONCLUSION

If we can create positive, healthy habits, we'll be *Working Well* without even trying. If you make a habit of taking actions that put you in a positive state, reduce your stress, and enable you to be highly productive, your life will be so much better than if you have habits that put you in a negative, stressed-out state.

With healthy, high-performing habits, you'll be learning, growing, and giving the best of yourself to your work, your family, your friends, and yourself every day. Yes, it's going to be hard work and uncomfortable to replace negative habits with positive ones. I mean, who doesn't want to reach for chocolate instead of an apple? But, as someone who has switched that habit, I have more energy after the apple and a happier relationship with my pants, so the reward has come through and reinforced the new habit.

I encourage you to find one action that you know will help you reduce your stress or increase your productivity, and make a habit of it. It might be something as simple as leaving work on time every day, getting to sleep earlier every night, or closing your door for an hour a day to work on your most important priorities. I realize how hard it can be to change our habits, but it's worth the investment—so go for it!

If you want to make *Working Well* a habit and join a supportive community that will enable you to make lasting change, please check out my online *Working Well* course packages at https://www.manage toengage.com/working-well/. I'd love to help you create habits that will lead you to a life of feeling positive, healthy, relaxed, and productive, no matter what challenges you may be experiencing.

QUESTIONS

1. What's a negative habit that you could replace with a more positive one?
2. What are the negative impacts of this current habit on you? On the people in your life?
3. What's one positive change that would result from replacing this negative habit?
4. What's a realistic way for you to integrate exercise as a keystone habit?

ACTIONS

- Choose one action that you'd like to make a habit.
- Identify the negative habit that you'll be replacing with your new positive habit.
- Identify your cues.
- Identify your routines.
- Identify the rewards you get.
- Find different routines that will get you the same rewards.
- Find an accountability partner, coach, or a group to help you stay accountable to the habit you've chosen to create.

Conclusion

"The greatest weapon against stress is our ability to choose one thought over another."

—William James

As I said a few hundred pages ago, stress is a natural and growing part of our lives. I've given you every strategy I can think of to help you reduce and manage your stress and to increase your productivity, so you can live a life of *Working Well.*

You've got plenty of options, from asking yourself the personal responsibility questions to focusing on creating more happiness in your life; from identifying your top three daily priorities to using power poses or trying the Pomodoro Technique. Not to mention taking breaks.

Now you just have to use the tools.

Are you still going to get stressed out? Probably. I still do. We're all figuring out how to live a life of *Working Well*—finding balance and managing our stress is a challenge that doesn't go away.

None of the strategies I've shared here are rocket science (neuroscience maybe, but not rocket science). It's likely that you knew about some of them before reading this book. But now that you've been reminded of what you already knew and have learned a few new strategies, it's time to put them into action.

Often, when we think about making a change, we see pain. We see a threat, and we decide that we'd rather just buy another book than actually use any of the tools we've learned.

I've done exactly that (which is why I have a huge pile of books on my bedside table). But let's reframe the situation and view not taking action as the threat that will ultimately cause us pain. If we don't take action, our stress will get worse and it will ruin our productivity, our health, and our relationships. Let's reframe making changes so we can see possible pleasure, so we're more likely to move towards the rewards we can see associated with taking action.

That reward is a really good life, where we're happy and productive and we have great relationships at work and at home. Yes, there will still be stress, but we'll have control over how we respond to it.

Our stressors may get more or less intense as our life circumstances push and challenge us in ways we'd never expected. Great things are going to happen in our lives, and terrible things may happen too. But now we've got a few more tools to be able to roll with the tough stuff.

We will falter and stumble as we try to manage everything that comes at us. But let's give it our best shot and celebrate our small wins as we go.

Start right now. Because knowledge that is not turned to action falls out of our brains. Simply knowing what you should be doing yet not doing it, as I did so many years ago during my high-stress years, is not enough. Start with small, achievable actions, turn them into habits and celebrate your wins. Before you know it, you'll be *Working Well.*

Please let me know how it goes—hearing your stories is the most inspiring and motivational part of my writing and teaching. You can e-mail me at: stephanie@managetoengage.com, or leave a review of the book on the site where you purchased the book or audiobook.

If you're interested in having me come speak to your company, joining my super-fun online *Working Well* course and community, or working with me, check out my website at: www.managetoengage .com/working-well/, or e-mail me at: stephanie@managetoengage .com. I'd love to stay connected and carry on the journey of *Working Well* together.

Acknowledgments

I'm so grateful to my husband, Andrew Berryman. Thank you for all that you are and all that you do to make my work and writing possible. I'm also beyond grateful for my kids, Colin and Kate, who definitely delayed the writing of this book, but I wouldn't have it any other way. Thank you to my clients, who trust me with the tough stuff and teach me so much. I'm very grateful to my good friend (who I met through work) Taryn Scollard, who consistently offers her condo for writing retreats. This book was made so much stronger by my first readers and amazing editors who offered excellent edits, suggestions, and advice: Maggie Knowlan, Eileen Cook, David Innes, Shasta Martinuk, and Christina Nikiforuk. Thanks also to my fantastic business coach, Angela Grosvenor, who kept me on track and inspired during the writing of this book. My endless gratitude to my teachers and friends, Graeme and Gayle O'Brien, who taught me so much of what I share in this book. Your love lives on. Thank you to all the fine people at Girl Friday for all that you did to help me bring this book into the world: Christina, Dave, Paul, Georgie, and Josh. And to countless others, including but not limited to Bryana Russell, Gerhard Maynard, Marwan Taliani, Sonja Larsen, Joan Flood, Kristi Fairholm-Mader, Lauri Thompson, Larisa Saunders, Janice Weigel, Hillary Keegan, Bob Bell, Tom Madigan, and Dave Kidd for their support, patience, time, and encouragement. Thank you.

I'm also incredibly grateful to all of the people whose books and research I have quoted. I've been inspired and motivated by you and excited to share your work with my readers. Any and all mistakes are completely my own and all trademarks are the property of their respective owners.

Recommended Resources

BOOKS

You Are a Badass®: How to Stop Doubting Your Greatness and Start Living an Awesome Life by Jen Sincero

Mind Power Into the 21st Century by John Kehoe

The Gifts of Imperfection: Let Go of Who You Think You're Supposed to Be and Embrace Who You Are by Brené Brown

Daring Greatly How the Courage to Be Vulnerable Transforms the Way We Live, Love, Parent, and Lead by Brené Brown

The Happiness Project by Gretchen Rubin

The Ultimate Secret to Getting Absolutely Everything You Want by Mike Hernacki

Think and Grow Rich by Napoleon Hill (this isn't just about making money but about changing your beliefs)

Quantum Learning: Unleashing the Genius in You by Bobbi DePorter and Mike Hernacki

The Subtle Art of Not Giving a Bleep: A Counterintuitive Approach to Living a Good Life by Mark Manson

The Art of Happiness at Work by the Dalai Lama

StrengthsFinder 2.0—Gallup

Now, Discover Your Strengths—Gallup

WEB SITES FOR PODCASTS, ARTICLES, VIDEOS, AND BOOKS

www.brenebrown.com
www.jensincero.com
www.tonyrobbins.com
https://brendon.com/
https://www.speedoftrust.com/
https://positivepsychologyprogram.com/
https://www.learnmindpower.com/

ARTICLES

Find the Clifton StrengthsFinder here:
        https://www.gallupstrengthscenter.com/
https://www.psychologytoday.com/ca/blog/what
        -mentally-strong-people-dont-do/201504/7
        -scientifically-proven-benefits-gratitude
Take the Learned Optimism test based on Martin's Seligman's
        research here: https://web.stanford.edu/class/msande271
        /onlinetools/LearnedOpt.html

TED TALKS/VIDEOS

Shawn Achor's TED Talk on "The Happiness Advantage":
        https://www.ted.com/talks/shawn_achor_the_happy_secret
        _to_better_work?language=en
Robert Waldinger's TED Talk, "What Makes a Good Life? Lessons
        from the Longest Study on Happiness":
        https://news.harvard.edu/gazette/story/2017/04/over-nearly
        -80-years-harvard-study-has-been-showing-how-to-live
        -a-healthy-and-happy-life/
Amy Cuddy's power poses: https://www.ted.com/talks/amy_cuddy_
        your_body_language_shapes_who_you_are?language=en
Brendon Burchard on personal responsibility, success, and positivity:
        https://www.youtube.com/watch?v=kJVUPL_aAkw

https://www.youtube.com/watch?v=o5n919vsIFg

Brené Brown—"The Power of Vulnerability": https://www.ted.com/
talks/brene_brown_on_vulnerability

Marshall Goldsmith—"Six Questions to Increase Employee
Engagement" (5 minutes): https://www.youtube.com/
watch?v=k882gTkCCxY&list=PLCDJe_hdM2Jjzp
-gawhqJm9BAk4ngvzmJ&index=5

Chip Heath—"Why Change is So Hard" (5 minutes):
https://www.youtube.com/watch?v=RpiDWeRN4UA

Communication/ Interpersonal Relationships/ Emotional Intelligence

BOOKS

Thanks for the Feedback: The Science and Art of Receiving Feedback Well by Stone and Heen

Difficult Conversations: How to Discuss What Matters Most by Stone, Patton, and Heen

Fierce Conversations: Achieving Success at Work and in Life One Conversation at a Time by Susan Scott

Learning in Relationship: Foundation for Personal and Professional Success by Ron Short

The Five Dysfunctions of a Team: A Leadership Fable by Patrick Lencioni

Emotional Intelligence 2.0 by Travis Bradberry

The Speed of Trust: The One Thing that Changes Everything by Stephen M.R. Covey

Working with Emotional Intelligence by Daniel Goleman

TED TALKS/VIDEOS

How to have awkward feedback conversations: https://youtu.be/28N2p3smEsw

How to have a good conversation: https://www.ted.com/talks/ celeste_headlee_10_ways_to_have_a_better_conversation/ up-next?language=en

How to have difficult conversations: https://www.managetoengage .com/online-courses/

Patrick Lencioni—*The Five Dysfunctions of a Team* short video:
    https://www.youtube.com/watch?v=6dRKa700RaQ

WEB SITES FOR PODCASTS, ARTICLES, VIDEOS, AND BOOKS

https://stoneandheen.com/books
www.brenebrown.com
www.danielgoleman.info
www.travisbradberry.com
https://www.marshallgoldsmith.com/
Emotional Intelligence Assessment: http://www.talentsmart.com/test/
http://www.myspeedoftrust.com

Meditation and Mindfulness

BOOKS

Thich Nhat Hanh books: https://plumvillage.org/books/
Jack Kornfield books: https://jackkornfield.com/
     books-audio-programs/

ARTICLES

http://time.com/3479384/meditation-benefits/
https://www.sharonsalzberg.com/new-york-times-how-to-meditate-guide/
https://www.nytimes.com/guides/well/be-more-mindful-at-work
https://www.inc.com/marissa-levin/why-google-nike-and-apple
     -love-mindfulness-training-and-how-you-can-easily-love-.html

TEACHERS (WEB SITES INCLUDE VIDEOS, POD-CASTS, ARTICLES, AND DOWNLOADS)

https://www.mindfulnesscds.com/
https://www.sharonsalzberg.com/
https://www.ramdass.org/meditation-2/
https://www.mindfulnessinstitute.ca/neuroscience-labs
https://plumvillage.org/
https://www.dalailama.com/
https://www.tarabrach.com/
https://www.eckharttolle.com/
https://jackkornfield.com/books-audio-programs/

APPS

Calm
Headspace
Smiling Minds

ONLINE YOGA CLASSES WITH MY AMAZING YOGA TEACHER (FEATURED IN THE WORKING WELL VIDEO):

https://www.managetoengage.com/online-courses/

Changing Your Relationship with your Phone/E-mail

ARTICLES

http://sitn.hms.harvard.edu/flash/2018/
dopamine-smartphones-battle-time/
https://www.forbes.com/sites/daviddisalvo/2017/04/09/the-reasons
-why-we-cant-put-down-our-smartphones/#550c129c4970
https://www.nytimes.com/2017/11/20/opinion/how-evil-is-tech.html
https://www.inc.com/peter-gasca/improve-your-emails-today-with
-these-simple-20-tips.html

BOOKS

*Thrive: The Third Metric to Redefining Success and Creating A Life of
Wellbeing, Wisdom, and Wonder* by Arianna Huffington
*How to Break Up with your Phone: The 30-Day Plan to Take Back
Your Life* by Catherine Price

APPS

Moment

Managing Workplace Stress/ Increasing Productivity

BOOKS

Thrive by Arianna Huffington

The Happiness Advantage: The Seven Principles That Fuel Success and Performance at Work by Shawn Achor

Smarter Faster Better: The Transformative Power of Real Productivity by Charles Duhigg

The Power of Habit: Why We Do What We Do in Life and Business by Charles Duhigg

Your Brain at Work: Strategies for Overcoming Distraction, Regaining Focus, and Working Smarter All Day Long by David Rock

Your Best Year Ever: A 5-Step Plan for Achieving Your Most Important Goals by Michael Hyatt

The Way We're Working Isn't Working: The Four Forgotten Needs That Energize Great Performance by Tony Schwartz

High Performance Habits: How Extraordinary People Become That Way by Brendon Burchard

The 5 Choices: The Path to Extraordinary Productivity by Kory Kogon, Adam Merrill, and Leena Rine

Pick Three: You Can Have It All (Just Not Every Day) by Randi Zuckerberg

First Things First by Stephen Covey

The 7 Habits of Highly Effective People by Stephen Covey

ARTICLES

https://hbr.org/2019/03/what-makes-some-people-more-productive-than-others

https://hbr.org/2007/10/manage-your-energy-not-your-time

https://www.apa.org/helpcenter/work-stress
https://www.forbes.com/sites/forbescoachescouncil/2018/02/23/
　　　how-to-reduce-workplace-stress-levels-9-practical
　　　-tips/#5b37e07f7da4
https://cmha.ca/documents/stress
https://www.forbes.com/sites/lizryan/2018/02/17/ten-ways-to-be
　　　-more-productive-at-work/#33a21fa5126a
https://hbr.org/2017/01/the-stretch-goal-paradox
The Pomodoro Technique: "Do More and Have Fun with
　　　Time Management": https://francescocirillo.com/pages/
　　　pomodoro-technique

WEB SITES FOR PODCASTS, ARTICLES, VIDEOS, AND BOOKS

http://ariannahuffington.com/thrive
https://michaelhyatt.com/
http://www.shawnachor.com/the-books/
https://charlesduhigg.com/books/
https://davidrock.net/books/
https://theenergyproject.com/
www.brendonburchard.com
Take Tony Schwartz's energy audit here: https://theenergyproject
　　　.com/offering/energy-audit-individuals/

Bibliography

BOOKS

Achor, Shawn. *The Happiness Advantage: The Seven Principles That Fuel Success and Performance at Work.* London: Virgin, 2011.

Brown, Brené. *Braving the Wilderness: The Quest for True Belonging and the Courage to Stand Alone.* Farmington Hills, Michigan: Thorndike Press, 2017.

Brown, Brené. *The Gifts of Imperfection: Let Go of Who You Think You're Supposed to Be and Embrace Who You Are.* Center City, Minn.: Hazelden, 2010.

Buckingham, Marcus and Donald O. Clifton. *Now, Discover Your Strengths.* New York: Free Press, 2001.

Duhigg, Charles. *Smarter Faster Better: The Secrets of Being Productive in Life and Business.* New York: Random House, 2016.

Duhigg, Charles. *The Power of Habit: Why We Do What We Do in Life and Business.* New York: Random House, 2012.

Heen, Sheila and Douglas Stone. *Thanks for the Feedback: The Science and Art of Receiving Feedback Well.* London: Portfolio Penguin, 2015.

Hyatt, Michael. *Your Best Year Ever: A 5-step Plan for Achieving Your Most Important Goals.* Grand Rapids, Michigan: Baker Books, 2018.

Rock, David. *Your Brain at Work: Strategies for Overcoming Distraction, Regaining Focus, and Working Smarter All Day Long.* New York: Collins Business, 2009.

WEB: BLOGS

The website for Harvard Medical School; "Sour Mood Getting You Down? Get Back to Nature." *Harvard Health Publishing* (blog), July, 2018. https://www.health.harvard.edu/mind-and-mood/ sour-mood-getting-you-down-get-back-to-nature.

The website for The Mayo Clinic; "In-Depth" page; "Stress Symptoms: Effects on Your Body and Behavior." April 28, 2016. http://www .mayoclinic.org/healthy-lifestyle/stress-management/in-depth/ stress-symptoms/art-20050987?pg=1.

The website for the National Institute for Occupational Safety and Health; the "NIOSH-Issued Publications" page; "Stress at Work." last reviewed June 6, 2014. https://www.cdc.gov/niosh/ docs/99-101/.

The website for Tony Robbins; "Discover Your Peak State: Your Three Steps to a Breakthrough." *Tony Robbins* (blog). https://www.tonyrobbins.com/stories/unleash-the-power/ discover-your-peak-state/.

The website for Tony Robbins; "Change Your Words, Change Your Life: The Simplest Tool for Immediately Transforming the Quality of Your Life." *Tony Robbins* (blog). https://www.tonyrobbins.com/mind-meaning/ change-your-words-change-your-life/.

The website for Willis Towers Watson; the "Press" page; "Eighty-Five Percent of Canadian Employers Say Stress is the Number-One Workplace Issue." June 29, 2016. https://www.willistowerswatson .com/en-CA/press/2016/06/75-percent-of-us-employers-say -stress-is-top-health-concern.

WEB: ARTICLES

Bradberry, Travis. "How Emotionally Intelligent People Handle Toxic People." *TalentSmart* (blog). http://www.talentsmart.com/articles/article.php?title=How-Emotionally-Intelligent-People-Handle-Toxic-People&ID=1028629190.

Burkus, David. "You're NOT the Average of the Five People You Surround Yourself With." *The Mission Podcasts,* May 23, 2018. https://medium.com/the-mission/youre-not-the-average-of-the-five-people-you-surround-yourself-with-f21b817f6e69.

Burkus, David. "Work Friends Make Us More Productive (Except When They Stress Us Out)." *Harvard Business Review*, May 26, 2017. https://hbr.org/2017/05/work-friends-make-us-more-productive-except-when-they-stress-us-out.

Caprino, Kathy. "How Happiness Directly Impacts Your Success." *Forbes*, June 6, 2013. https://www.forbes.com/sites/kathycaprino/2013/06/06/how-happiness-directly-impacts-your-success/#19bd9f0a618b.

Chignell, Barry. "6 Reasons Why Taking Breaks Is Good For You AND Your Employer." *CIPHR*, April 21, 2015. https://www.ciphr.com/blog/taking-breaks/.

Clark, Dorie. "Actually, You Should Check Email First Thing in the Morning." *Harvard Business Review*, March 7, 2016. https://hbr.org/2016/03/actually-you-should-check-email-first-thing-in-the-morning.

Coleman, John. "Take Ownership of Your Actions by Taking Responsibility." *Harvard Business Review*, August 30, 2012. https://hbr.org/2012/08/take-ownership-of-your-actions.

Comaford, Christine. "Got Inner Peace? 5 Ways To Get It NOW." *Forbes*, April 4, 2012. https://www.forbes.com/sites/christinecomaford/2012/04/04/got-inner-peace-5-ways-to-get-it-now/#492908ff6672.

Elsesser, Kim. "Power Posing is Back: Amy Cuddy Successfully Refutes Criticism." *Forbes*, April 3, 2018. https://www.forbes.com/sites/kimelsesser/2018/04/03/power-posing-is-back-amy-cuddy-successfully-refutes-criticism/#4b2f2253b8ef.

Fink, George. "Stress: The Health Epidemic of the 21st Century." *SciTech Connect,* April 26, 2016. http://scitechconnect.elsevier .com/stress-health-epidemic-21st-century/.

Gillett, Rachel. "The Email Habits of Tim Cook, Bill Gates, and 16 Other Successful People." *Business Insider,* December 21, 2016. https://www.businessinsider.com/ how-successful-ceos-email-2016-12.

Groth, Aimee. "You're the Average of the Five People You Spend the Most Time With." *Business Insider,* July 24, 2012. https://www .businessinsider.com/jim-rohn-youre-the-average-of-the-five -people-you-spend-the-most-time-with-2012-7.

Fleming, Peter. "Do You Work More Than 39 Hours a Week? Your Job Could Be Killing You." *Guardian,* January 15, 2018. https://www.theguardian.com/lifeandstyle/2018/jan/15/ is-28-hours-ideal-working-week-for-healthy-life.

Goldsmith, Marshall. "6 Questions That Will Set You Up to Be Super Successful." *Marshall Goldsmith,* July 20, 2015. http://www .marshallgoldsmith.com/articles/6-questions-that-will-set -you-up-to-be-super-successful/.

Henry, Alan. "Productivity 101: A Primer to The Pomodoro Technique." *Lifehacker,* February 7, 2014. https://lifehacker .com/productivity-101-a-primer-to-the-pomodoro -technique-1598992730.

Howatt, Bill. "Workplace Stress a Main Cause of Mental Health Issues, Study Finds." *The Globe and Mail,* July 5, 2018. https:// www.theglobeandmail.com/business/careers/workplace-award/ article-workplace-stress-a-main-cause-of-mental-health-issues -study-finds/.

Hurlock, Heather. "Two Lessons on Blame from Brené Brown." *Mindful,* August 4, 2017. https://www.mindful.org/ two-lessons-on-blame-from-brene-brown/.

Lebowitz, Shana. "A Decades-Old Time-Management Strategy Can Help You Become More Productive and Less Stressed at Work." *Business Insider,* March 9, 2018. https://www.businessinsider.com/ how-to-use-stephen-coveys-time-management-matrix-2015-12.

Morin, Amy. "7 Scientifically Proven Benefits of Gratitude." *Psychology Today*, April 3, 2015. https://www.psychologytoday .com/ca/blog/what-mentally-strong-people-dont-do/201504/ 7-scientifically-proven-benefits-gratitude.

Popomaronis, Tom. "Science Says You Shouldn't Work More Than This Number of Hours a Week." *Inc.*, May 9, 2016. https://www .inc.com/tom-popomaronis/science-says-you-shouldnt-work- more-than-this-number-of-hours-a-day.html.

Raphael, Rina. "Here's Arianna Huffington's Recipe for a Great Night of Sleep." *Fast Company*, June 10, 2016. https://www.fastcompany.com/3060801/ heres-arianna-huffingtons-recipe-for-a-great-night-of-sleep.

Rock, David. "Beat Back Distractions: The Neuroscience of Getting Things Done." *HuffPost*, February 3, 2016. https://www .huffingtonpost.com/david-rock/beat-back-distractions -th_b_498120.html.

Rock, David and Jeffrey Schwartz, "The Neuroscience of Leadership." *strategy+business*, May 30, 2006. https://www.strategy-business .com/article/06207.

Saint, Nick. "Stop Yelling at Your Employees—It's Making Them Stupid." *Business Insider*, September 10, 2009. https://www .businessinsider.com/stop-yelling-at-your-employees-its -making-them-stupid-2009-9.

Sansone, Randy A. and Lori A. Sansone. "Gratitude and Well Being: The Benefits of Appreciation." *Psychiatry*, 7, no. 11 (Nov 2010): 18–22. https://www.ncbi.nlm.nih.gov/pmc/articles/ PMC3010965/.

Sohn, Emily. "More and More Research Shows Friends Are Good for Your Health." *Washington Post,* May 26, 2016. https://www .washingtonpost.com/national/health-science/more-and-more -research-shows-friends-are-good-for-your-health/2016/05/26/ f249e754-204d-11e6-9e7f-57890b612299_story.html?utm_ term=.da8eed4019d4.

Stillman, Jessica. "The 1 Type of Complaining That Will Make You Feel Better, According to Science." *Inc.*, June 30, 2016. https:// www.inc.com/jessica-stillman/science-this-is-the-only-type-of -complaining-that-s-good-for-you.html.

Stillman, Jessica. "This Is Exactly How You Win (and Lose) Trust," *Inc.*, December 10, 2015. https://www.inc.com/jessica-stillman/this-is-exactly-how-you-win-and-lose-trust.html.

Sullivan, Bob. "Memo to Work Martyrs: Long Hours Make You Less Productive." *CNBC*, January 26, 2015. https://www.cnbc.com/2015/01/26/working-more-than-50-hours-makes-you-less-productive.html.

SWNS. "Americans Check Their Phones 80 Times a Day: Study." *New York Post*, November 8, 2017. https://nypost.com/2017/11/08/americans-check-their-phones-80-times-a-day-study/.

Ubelacker, Sheryl. "Surgeons Study Benefits of Visualizing Procedures." *The Globe and Mail*, May 12, 2018. https://www.theglobeandmail.com/life/health-and-fitness/health/surgeons-study-benefits-of-visualizing-procedures/article22681531/.

Zak, Paul J. "The Neuroscience of Trust." *Harvard Business Review*, January 2017. https://hbr.org/2017/01/the-neuroscience-of-trust.

Notes

INTRODUCTION

1 "Workplace Stress," *American Institute of Stress*, https://www.stress.org/workplace-stress.
2 George Fink, "Stress: The Health Epidemic of the 21st Century," *SciTech Connect* (April 26, 2016), http://scitechconnect.elsevier.com/stress-health-epidemic-21st-century/.
3 Jennifer Breheny Wallace, "Even the small stresses of daily life can hurt your health, but attitude can make a difference," *Washington Post* (March 3, 2018), https://www.washingtonpost.com/national/health-science/even-the-small-stresses-of-daily-life-can-hurt-your-health-but-attitude-can-make-a-difference/2018/03/02/1ad9659a-eb32-11e7-9f92-10a2203f6c8d_story.html?utm_term=.6c11605e59f9.
4 Mohd. Razali Salleh, "Life Event, Stress and Illness," *The Malaysian Journal of Medical Science*, vol. 4, no. 9–18 (Oct, 2008), https://www.ncbi.nlm.nih.gov/pmc/articles/PMC3341916/.
5 Bill Howatt, "Workplace Stress a Main Cause of Mental Health Issues, Study Finds," *The Globe and Mail* (July 5, 2018), https://www.theglobeandmail.com/business/careers/workplace-award/article-workplace-stress-a-main-cause-of-mental-health-issues-study-finds/.
6 Fink, "Stress."
7 Gabor Maté, When the Body Says No: The Cost of Hidden Stress (Hoboken: John Wiley and Sons, 2011), 28.

CHAPTER TWO

1 Steadman, Andrew, "Neuroscience for Combat Leaders: A Brain-Based Approach to Leading on the Modern Battlefield," *Military Review* 91, no. 3 (June 2011), https://www.questia.com/library/journal/1G1-256457069/neuroscience-for-combat-leaders-a-brain-based-approach.

CHAPTER THREE

1   Sheila Heen and Douglas Stone, *Thanks for the Feedback: The Science and Art of Receiving Feedback Well* (London: Portfolio Penguin, 2015), 8.
2   Shawn Achor, *The Happiness Advantage* (London: Virgin, 2011), 61.
3   Kyle Benson, "The Magic Relationship Ratio, According to Science," the Gottman Relationship Blog (October 4, 2017), https://www.gottman .com/blog/the-magic-relationship-ratio-according-science/.
4   Shawn Achor, *The Happiness Advantage* (London: Virgin, 2011), 61.

CHAPTER FOUR

1   David Rock, *Your Brain at Work* (New York: Harper Collins, 2009), 61.
2   Arianna Huffington, *Thrive: The Third Metric to Redefining Success and Creating a Life of Well-Being, Wisdom, and Wonder* (New York: Random House, 2014), 14.
3   Brigid Schulte, "Making Time for Kids? Study Says Quality Trumps Quantity," *Washington Post* (March 28, 2015), https://www .washingtonpost.com/local/making-time-for-kids-study-says-quality -trumps-quantity/2015/03/28/10813192-d378-11e4-8fce-3941fc548f1c _story.html.
4   Schulte, "Making Time for Kids?".
5   Jennifer Breheny Wallace, "Even the Small Stresses of Daily Life Can Hurt Your Health, But Attitude Can Help," *Washington Post* (March 3, 2018), https://www.washingtonpost.com/national/health-science/even -the-small-stresses-of-daily-life-can-hurt-your-health-but-attitude-can -make-a-difference/2018/03/02/1ad9659a-eb32-11e7-9f92 -10a2203f6c8d_story.html?utm_term=.6c11605e59f9.
6   Nick Saint, "Stop Yelling at Your Employees—It's Making Them Stupid," *Business Insider* (September 10, 2009), https://www.businessinsider .com/stop-yelling-at-your-employees-its-making-them-stupid-2009-9.

CHAPTER FIVE

1   Achor, *The Happiness Advantage*, 41.
2   Kathy Caprino, "How Happiness Directly Impacts Your Success," *Forbes* (June 6, 2013), https://www.forbes.com/sites/kathycaprino/2013/06/06/ how-happiness-directly-impacts-your-success/#2fadb515618b.
3   Achor, *The Happiness Advantage*, 52.
4   Liz Mineo, *Harvard Gazette* (April 11, 2017) "Good Genes Are Nice, But Joy is Better," https://news.harvard.edu/gazette/story/2017/04/over -nearly-80-years-harvard-study-has-been-showing-how-to-live-a -healthy-and-happy-life/.

5   Alice G. Walton, "6 Ways Social Media Affects Our Mental Health,"
     Forbes (June 30, 2017), https://www.forbes.com/sites/
     alicegwalton/2017/06/30/a-run-down-of-social-medias-effects
     -on-our-mental-health/#c62113e2e5af.

6   Rina Raphael, "Here's Arianna Huffington's Recipe
     for a Great Night of Sleep," *Fast Company* (June
     10, 2016), https://www.fastcompany.com/3060801/
     heres-arianna-huffingtons-recipe-for-a-great-night-of-sleep.

7   Travis Bradberry, "How Emotionally Intelligent People Handle Toxic
     People," TalentSmart (blog), https://www.talentsmart.com/articles/
     How-Emotionally-Intelligent-People-Handle-Toxic-People
     -1028629190-p-1.html.

8   Tony Schwartz, *The Way We're Working Isn't Working*, 60.

9   This article was first printed in the Special Health Report
     "Understanding Depression" from Harvard Medical School. For more
     information, please go to www.health.harvard.edu/UD.

10   Jamie Ducharme, "Do This Kind of Exercise If You Want to Live Longer,
     Study Says," *Time* (September 4, 2018), http://time.com/5384491/
     best-exercise-for-longevity/.

11   Charles Duhigg, *The Power of Habit* (New York: Random House, 2012),
     108–109.

12   Bob Sullivan, "Memo to Work Martyrs: Long Hours Make You Less
     Productive," *CNBC* (January 26, 2015), https://www.cnbc
     .com/2015/01/26/working-more-than-50-hours-makes-you
     -less-productive.html.

13   Peter Fleming, "Do You Work More Than 39 Hours a Week?
     Your Job Could Be Killing You," *Guardian*, (January 15, 2018),
     https://www.theguardian.com/lifeandstyle/2018/jan/15/
     is-28-hours-ideal-working-week-for-healthy-life.

14   Haley Sweetland Edwards, "You're Addicted to Your Smartphone. This
     Company Thinks It Can Change That," *Time* (April 13, 2018), http://
     time.com/5237434/youre-addicted-to-your-smartphone-this-company
     -thinks-it-can-change-that/.

15   SWNS, "Americans Check Their Phones 80 Times a Day: Study,"
     New York Post (November 8, 2017): https://nypost.com/2017/11/08/
     americans-check-their-phones-80-times-a-day-study/.

16   David Brooks, "How Evil Is Tech?", *New York Times* (November 20,
     2017), https://www.nytimes.com/2017/11/20/opinion/how-evil-is-tech
     .html.

17   Trevor Haynes, "Dopamine, Smartphones and You: A Battle
     for Your Time," Science in the News (Harvard University web-
     site), (May 1, 2018), http://sitn.hms.harvard.edu/flash/2018/
     dopamine-smartphones-battle-time/.

18 Tony Schwartz, "Relax! You'll Be More Productive," The Energy Project (blog), (May 4, 2018), https://theenergyproject.com/relax-youll-be-more-productive-2/.

19 Barry Chignell, "6 Reasons Why Taking Breaks is Good for You and Your Employer," CIPHR (April 21, 2015), https://www.ciphr.com/advice/taking-breaks/.

CHAPTER SIX

1 Amy Morin, "7 Scientifically Proven Benefits of Gratitude," *Psychology Today* (April 3, 2015), https://www.psychologytoday.com/ca/blog/what-mentally-strong-people-dont-do/201504/7-scientifically-proven-benefits-gratitude.

2 Achor, *The Happiness Advantage*, 52.

3 Markham Heid, "You Asked: Is Meditation Really Worth It?", Time (October 8, 2014), http://time.com/3479384/meditation-benefits/.

4 Heid, "You Asked."

5 Rock, *Your Brain at Work*, 91.

6 David Gelles, "How to Be More Mindful at Work," *New York Times* (November 1, 2018), https://www.nytimes.com/guides/well/be-more-mindful-at-work.

CHAPTER SEVEN

1 Fernando Doménech-Betoret, Laura Abellán-Roselló, and Amparo Gómez-Artiga, "Self-Efficacy, Satisfaction, and Academic Achievement: The Mediator Role of Students' Expectancy-Value Beliefs," Frontiers in Psychology (July 18, 2017), https://doi.org/10.3389/fpsyg.2017.01193.

2 University of Melbourne, "Self-Confidence the Secret to Workplace Advancement," Science Daily (October 18, 2012), https://www.sciencedaily.com/releases/2012/10/121018103214.htm.

3 Jack Zenger, "The Confidence Gap in Men and Women: Why It Matters and How to Overcome It," *Forbes* (April 2018), https://www.forbes.com/sites/jackzenger/2018/04/08/the-confidence-gap-in-men-and-women-why-it-matters-and-how-to-overcome-it/#33d555883bfa.

4 Marshall Goldsmith, "6 Questions That Will Set You Up to Be Super Successful," MG Thinkers 50 Blog (July 20, 2015), https://www.marshallgoldsmith.com/articles/6-questions-that-will-set-you-up-to-be-super-successful/.

5 Charles Duhigg, *Smarter Faster Better*, 20.

6 Jessica Stillman, "Venting Just Makes You More Miserable, Science Shows," Inc. (April 5, 2017), https://www.inc.com/jessica-stillman/venting-just-makes-you-more-miserable-science-shows.html.

7   Stillman, "Venting Just Makes You More Miserable."

CHAPTER EIGHT

1   Rock, *Your Brain at Work*, 113–114.
2   Rock, 113–114.
3   Rock, 113–114.
4   Team Tony, "Discover Your Peak State: Your Three Steps to a Breakthrough," Tony Robbins (blog), https://www.tonyrobbins.com/stories/unleash-the-power/discover-your-peak-state/.
5   Kim Elsesser, "Power Posing is Back: Amy Cuddy Successfully Refutes Criticism," *Forbes* (April 3, 2018), https://www.forbes.com/sites/kimelsesser/2018/04/03/power-posing-is-back-amy-cuddy-successfully-refutes-criticism/#7e847a6f3b8e.
6   Achor, *The Happiness Advantage*, 100–101.
7   Aimee Groth, "You're the Average of the Five People You Spend the Most Time With," *Business Insider* (July 24, 2012), https://www.businessinsider.com/jim-rohn-youre-the-average-of-the-five-people-you-spend-the-most-time-with-2012-7.
8   David Burkus, "You're NOT the Average of the Five People You Surround Yourself With," *The Mission Podcast*, (May 23, 2018), https://medium.com/the-mission/youre-not-the-average-of-the-five-people-you-surround-yourself-with-f21b817f6e69.
9   University of Calgary, "Is Your Stress Changing My Brain?", *Science Daily* (March 8, 2018), https://www.sciencedaily.com/releases/2018/03/180308143212.htm.
10   Pamela Gerloff, "You're Not Laughing Enough, and That's No Joke," *Psychology Today* (June 21, 2011), https://www.psychologytoday.com/ca/blog/the-possibility-paradigm/201106/youre-not-laughing-enough-and-thats-no-joke.
11   Duhigg, *Smarter Faster Better*, 112.

CHAPTER NINE

1   David Burkus, "Work Friends Make Us More Productive (Except When They Stress Us Out)," *Harvard Business Review* (May 26, 2017), https://hbr.org/2017/05/work-friends-make-us-more-productive-except-when-they-stress-us-out.
2   Paul J. Zak, "The Neuroscience of Trust," *Harvard Business Review* (January 2017), https://hbr.org/2017/01/the-neuroscience-of-trust.
3   Zak, "The Neuroscience of Trust."
4   Zak, "The Neuroscience of Trust."

5   Stephen M.R. Covey, *The Speed of Trust*, https://www.franklincovey.com/
the-7-habits/habit-5.html.

6   Rock, *Your Brain at Work*, 190.

7   Rock, 162.

8   Christine Porath, "Give Your Team More Effective Positive Feedback,"
Harvard Business Review (October 2016), https://hbr.org/2016/10/
give-your-team-more-effective-positive-feedback.

9   Rock, *Your Brain at Work*, 193.

10   Rock, *Your Brain at Work*, 194.

11   Jessica Stillman, "This is Exactly How You Win (and Lose) Trust," *Inc.*
(December 10, 2015), https://www.inc.com/jessica-stillman/this-is
-exactly-how-you-win-and-lose-trust.html.

12   Covey, *The Speed of Trust*, https://archive.franklincovey.com/facilitator/
minisessions/handouts/13_behaviors_minsession_handout_PDF.

CHAPTER TEN

1   David Rock, "Beat Back Distractions: The Neuroscience of Getting
Things Done," *HuffPost* (May 15, 2010), https://www.huffpost.com/
entry/beat-back-distractions-th_n_498120.

2   Rock, *Your Brain at Work*, 21.

3   Rock, 36.

4   Rock, 35.

5   Rock, 36.

6   Rock, 12, 18.

7   Kermit Pattison, "Worker, Interrupted: The Cost of Task Switching,"
Fast Company (July 28, 2008), https://www.fastcompany.com/944128/
worker-interrupted-cost-task-switching.

8   Pattison, "Worker, Interrupted."

9   Pattison, "Worker, Interrupted."

10   Peter Gasca, "20 Ways to Improve Your Emails Today," *Inc.* (August 31,
2018), https://www.inc.com/peter-gasca/improve-your-emails-today
-with-these-simple-20-tips.html.

11   Rachel Gillett, "The Email Habits of Tim Cook, Bill Gates, and 16 Other
Successful People," *Business Insider* (December 21, 2016), https://www
.businessinsider.com/how-successful-ceos-email-2016-12.

12   Marcus Buckingham and Donald O. Clifton, *Now, Discover Your
Strengths* (New York: Free Press, 2001), 26.

13   CliftonStrengths (website), https://www.gallupstrengthscenter.com/.

CHAPTER ELEVEN

1   Stephen R. Covey, *The 7 Habits of Highly Effective People* (New York: Simon and Schuster, 1989).

2   Michael Hyatt, "The Surprising New Science of Achievement," *Lead to Win* (podcast transcript), (November 28, 2017), https://michaelhyatt .com/podcast-achievement-science/?transcript.

3   Sim B. Sitkin, C. Chet Miller, and Kelly E. See, *Harvard Business Review* (February 2017), https://hbr.org/2017/01/the-stretch-goal-paradox.

4   Cirillo Consulting GMBH, *The Pomodoro Technique: Do More and Have Fun with Time Management*, https://francescocirillo.com/pages/ pomodoro-technique.

5   Frederic Patenaude, "Boosting Brain Power With Classical and Baroque Music," Renegade Health Blog (March 3, 2014), www.renegadehealth .com/blog/baroque.

6   Robert C. Pozen and Kevin Downey, "What Makes Some People More Productive Than Others," *Harvard Business Review* (March 28, 2019), https://hbr.org/2019/03/ what-makes-some-people-more-productive-than-others.

7   Tony Schwartz, "Relax! You'll Be More Productive," The Energy Project (blog), (May 4, 2018), https://theenergyproject.com/ relax-youll-be-more-productive-2/.

8   Rock, *Your Brain at Work*, 77.

CHAPTER TWELVE

1   Duhigg, *The Power of Habit*, 19.

2   Charles Duhigg, "Habits: Why We Do What We Do," *HBR IdeaCast* (podcast transcript), (June 7, 2012), https://hbr.org/2012/06/ habits-why-we-do-what-we-do.

3   Duhigg, "Habits."

4   Duhigg, Charles, The Golden Rule of Habit Change, July 2018, https:// psychcentral.com/blog/the-golden-rule-of-habit-change/.

5   Christine Comaford, "Got Inner Peace? 5 Ways To Get It NOW," *Forbes* (April 4, 2012), https://www.forbes.com/sites/christinecomaford/ 2012/04/04/got-inner-peace-5-ways-to-get-it-now/#3e7039667275.

6   Duhigg, *The Power of Habit*, 108–109.

7   Duhigg, 85.

8   Duhigg, 85.

9   Duhigg, 85.

10 Duhigg, 89.

About the Author

Stephanie Berryman got her start as an annoying older sister dispensing unwanted advice to her three younger brothers. She's found the perfect fit as a leadership coach and consultant and runs her own company, Manage To Engage. Stephanie holds a master's in leadership and degrees in English literature and education. She's taught with leadership programs in universities and colleges and has worked with executives, middle managers, front line supervisors, and staff.

Stephanie's years of coaching clients in high pressure jobs inspired her passion for supporting people to reduce their stress, find a healthy life-work balance, and invest in themselves. She weaves together humor, research, and engaging stories in her teaching, coaching, and writing.

Stephanie is the author of Amazon best sellers *Nine Strategies for Dealing with the Difficult Stuff* and *Nine Strategies for Dealing with Stress.* She has been published in *Grain Magazine, The Ascent, Medium,* and on Thrive Global.

She is the embodiment of her recommendations for dealing with stress. She's worked high-pressure jobs while handling challenging family situations. One of her younger brothers died at the age of twenty-seven and her mother died of Alzheimer's at the age of fifty-nine. Based on her experiences, Stephanie is deeply committed to supporting people to live fulfilling lives in spite of the stressors and challenges they are experiencing.

A prairie girl who spent decades living on the west coast of Canada, she's currently living in Australia with her husband and two young children.

You can find out more about her and her work at
www.managetoengage.com.